THE
MICHELIN
GUIDE

SAN FRANCISCO

MICHELIN

THE MICHELIN GUIDE'S COMMITMENTS

Whether they are in Japan, the USA, China or Europe, our inspectors apply the same criteria to judge the quality of each and every establishment that they visit. The MICHELIN guide commands a **worldwide reputation** thanks to the commitments we make to our readers—and we reiterate these below:

Our inspectors make **anonymous visits** to restaurants to gauge the quality of cuisine offered to the everyday customer. They pay their own bill and make no indication of their presence. These visits are supplemented by comprehensive monitoring of information—our readers' comments are one valuable source, and are always taken into consideration.

Our choice of establishments is a completely **independent** one, made for the benefit of our readers alone. Decisions are discussed by the inspectors and editor, with the most important considered at the global level. Inclusion in the Guide is always free of charge.

The Guide offers a **selection** of the best restaurants in each category of comfort and price. A recommendation in the Guide is an honor in itself, and defines the establishment among the "best of the best."

All practical information, the classifications, and awards are revised and updated every year to ensure the most **reliable information** possible.

The standards and criteria for the classifications are the same in all countries covered by the MICHELIN guides. Our system is used worldwide and easy to apply when selecting a restaurant.

As part of Michelin's ongoing commitment to improving **travel and mobility**, we do everything possible to make vacations and eating out a pleasure.

THE MICHELIN GUIDE'S SYMBOLS

Michelin inspectors are experts at finding the best restaurants and invite you to explore the diversity of the gastronomic universe. As well as evaluating a restaurant's cooking, we also consider its décor, the service and the ambience - in other words, the all-round culinary experience.

Two keywords help you make your choice more quickly: red for the type of cuisine, gold for the atmosphere.

Italian • Elegant

FACILITIES & SERVICES

🐾	Notable wine list
🍸	Notable cocktail list
🍺	Notable beer list
🍶	Notable sake list
♿	Wheelchair accessible
🏠	Outdoor dining
🍽	Private dining room
🍳	Breakfast
🥐	Brunch
🥢	Dim sum
🚗	Valet parking
💵	Cash only

AVERAGE PRICES

🪙	Under $25
$$	$25 to $50
$$$	$50 to $75
$$$$	Over $75

STARS

Our famous one ❀, two ❀❀ and three ❀❀❀ stars
identify establishments serving the highest quality
cuisine – taking into account the quality of ingredients,
the mastery of techniques and flavors, the levels of
creativity and, of course, consistency.

❀❀❀ Exceptional cuisine, worth a special journey

❀❀ Excellent cuisine, worth a detour

❀ High quality cooking, worth a stop

BIB GOURMAND

Inspectors' favorites for good value.

MICHELIN PLATE

Good cooking.
Fresh ingredients, capably
prepared: simply a good meal.

DEAR READER,

It's been an exciting year for the entire team at the MICHELIN guides in North America, and it is with great pride that we present you with our 2019 edition to San Francisco. Over the past year our inspectors have extended their reach to include a variety of establishments and multiplied their anonymous visits to restaurants in our selection in order to accurately reflect the rich culinary diversity this great city has to offer.

As part of the Guide's highly confidential and meticulous evaluation process, our inspectors have methodically eaten their way through the entire city with a mission to marshal the finest in each category for your enjoyment. While they are expertly trained professionals in the food industry, the Guides remain consumer-driven and provide comprehensive choices to accommodate your every comfort, taste, and budget. By dining and drinking as "everyday" customers, they are able to experience and evaluate the same level of service and cuisine as any other guest. This past year has seen some unique advancements in San Francisco's dining scene. Some of these can be found in each neighborhood introduction, complete with photography depicting our favored choices.

Our company's founders, Édouard and André Michelin, published the first MICHELIN guide in 1900, to provide motorists with useful information about where they could service and repair their cars as well as find a good quality meal. In 1926, the star-rating system was introduced, whereby outstanding establishments are awarded for excellence in cuisine. Over the decades we have made many new enhancements to the Guide, and the local team here in San Francisco eagerly carries on these traditions.

As we take consumer feedback seriously, please feel free to contact us at: michelin.guides@michelin.com. You may also follow our Inspectors on Twitter (@MichelinGuideSF) and Instagram (@michelininspectors) as they chow their way around town. We thank you for your patronage and truly hope that the MICHELIN guide will remain your preferred reference to San Francisco's restaurants.

CONTENTS

■ INDEXES

SAN FRANCISCO

CASTRO & CIVIC CENTER

The Castro is punctuated by chic boutiques, hopping bars and handsomely restored Victorians. It's a perpetual party here and to feed its buzzing population, it teems with cool cafeterias. Start your day with mascarpone-stuffed, deep-fried French toast at **Kitchen Story**, then stop in at **Thorough Bread & Pastry** for the best almond croissant in town. Linger on the quaint patio at **Café Flore**, but for a quick lunch, the original **Rosamunde Sausage Grill** serves a variety of sandwiches. Afterwards, look no further than the kitschy kiosk **Hot Cookie** for a bit of sweet.

Reverie is a stroller-friendly spot for a snack, whereas the 1930s throwback **Ice Cream Bar** is mobbed by hipsters. Counter-culturalists have long sought haven in the hippiefied Haight-Ashbury where smoke shops and record stores still dominate the landscape. **Inovino** continues to thrive as a favored wine bar for its tasty Italian small plates and an interesting selection of—you guessed it—vino. The Valley's adoration for laid-back spots is evident in lines that snake out the door of Puerto Rican favorite, **Parada 22**

COLE VALLEY

Neighboring Cole Valley may be small in size, but flaunts a big personality. On Monday nights, dog lovers treat the whole family to dinner at **Zazie**. Equally fun is a visit to **Val de Cole**, a wine shop offering value table wines to go with a delish dinner. The back garden patio at quaint **Cafe**

for authentic pernil asado; or **Cha Cha Cha**, a groovy tapas bar flowing with fresh-fruit sangria. Nurse that hangover with greasy hash browns and hotcakes at **Pork Store Cafe**, or head to **Haight Street Market** for a ready-made gourmet feast. On game night, kick back with a pint and plate of wings at old-school **Kezar Pub**.

NOE VALLEY

Noe Valley is known for its specialty shops, and **Noe Valley Bakery** bakes the best bread around, after which a pour of coffee from **Castro Coffee Company** is a must. Imported chocolates are front and center at **Chocolate Covered**. **Swirl on Castro** is a sleek space that is big on boutique wines, or opt

for a soothing brew at **Spike's Coffees & Teas**.

CIVIC CENTER

On Wednesdays and Sundays, SF's oldest market, **Heart of the City**, erupts in full form on the vast promenade outside City Hall. This independent and farmer-operated arcade is a hit among locals thanks to an extensive offering of high-quality, locally sourced and attractively priced produce—not to mention rare Asian ingredients like young ginger and Buddha's hand. Neighboring Tenderloin is home to numerous Asian—particularly Vietnamese—communities and thereby boasts an incredible array of authentic ethnic eateries. Larkin Street (also known as **"Little Saigon"**) is crowded

13

with mom-and-pop shops like **Saigon Sandwich**—leading the way with spicy báhn mì. Nearby, **Turtle Tower** has amassed quite a patronage (celebrity chefs included) for fragrant pho ga. Reservations are a must at the swanky **Bourbon & Branch**, while local suits head over to **Elmira Rosticceria** for a range of Italian-inspired eats. **Tradition** is a hip cocktail venue in a vintage speakeasy setting.

West of the Civic Center, Hayes Valley is undeniably polished, with a coterie of designer boutiques set amid a medley of sleek retreats. **Chantal Guillon** spotlights exquisite macarons served in a French-style setting. Carnivores delight in **Fatted Calf Charcuterie** where fresh, smoked and cured meats abound in loaded display cases (the cheese selection is also solid). Slake your thirst at **True Sake**, a super-cool, all-sake business. Finish with sweet treats from the charming **Miette** or **Christopher Elbow Artisanal Chocolate**.

LOWER HAIGHT

The Lower Haight attracts hipster groups for sake-infused libations at **Noc Noc**, while some dress to impress at **Maven**, with its inventive cocktails, tasty bites and groovy tunes. Speaking of beats, the Fillmore Jazz District continues to seduce music lovers today, and the annual Fillmore Jazz Festival is a must-see celebration of musical magnificence.

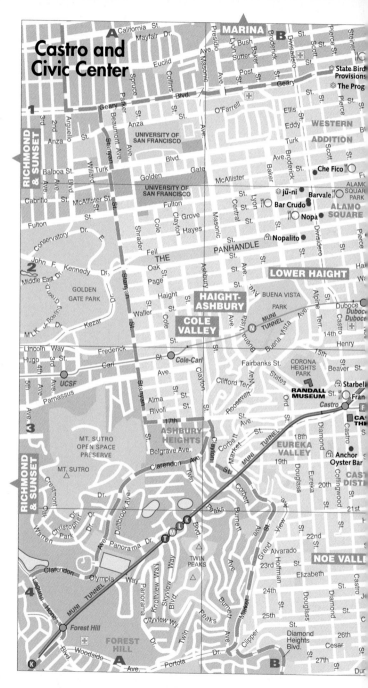

Castro and Civic Center

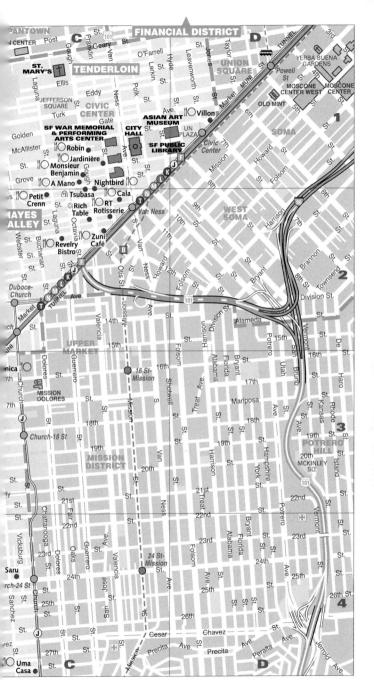

A MANO ¶⃝

Italian • *Contemporary décor*

&

"A mano" is Italian for "by hand," and that's exactly how your pasta will be made at this delicious Italian, where diners can frequently witness dough being rolled, cut and folded just minutes before arriving at the table. Options include vivid green pea and pesto tagliatelle and delicately shaped agnolotti dal plin. For those who'd rather eschew carbs, there are hearty mains like braised short ribs.

The crowd is diverse, with young professionals and families alike sharing Margherita pizzas and spicy chicken meatballs. Loud, funky music and floor-to-ceiling windows that open onto the bustle of Hayes Valley's main drag add to the lively vibe. Order up another cocktail or an affordable glass of Italian red to make the fun last a little longer.

◾ 450 Hayes St. (bet. Octavia & Gough Sts.)
℘ (415) 506-7401 — **WEB:** www.amanosf.com
◾ Lunch & dinner daily   PRICE: $$

ANCHOR OYSTER BAR ☻

Seafood • *Simple*

MAP: B3

Landlubbers seeking a taste of the sea can be found pulling up a stool at this Castro institution, where waves of waiting diners spill out the doors. This tiny, minimally adorned space filled with old-fashioned charm is better for twosomes than groups.

While the menu may be petite, it's full of fresh fare like a light and flavorful Dungeness crab "burger" on a sesame bun; Caesar salad combining sweet prawns and tangy anchovy dressing; or a cup of creamy Boston clam chowder loaded with clams and potatoes. As the name portends, raw oysters are a specialty—so briny that the accompanying mignonette may not be necessary. And of course, the cioppino is unmissable as this signature item turns sublime when paired with delicious and buttery garlic bread.

◾ 579 Castro St. (bet. 18th & 19th Sts.)
℘ (415) 431-3990 — **WEB:** www.anchoroysterbar.com
◾ Lunch Mon – Sat Dinner nightly   PRICE: $$

AVERY ❙⚬
Contemporary · *Minimalist*

Like many a restaurant success story these days, Avery began as a pop-up before taking up brick-and-mortar residence. Its ambitious menu pays homage to the chef's prior experiences at some of the city's more elite kitchens: elements of smoke, for instance, are a signature move as is the influence of Eastern Asian cuisines. Grilled oysters, served with seaweed, ramps, spring peas and Meyer lemon, are beloved by all, as is the A5 Wagyu fat topped with a sweet-smoky barbecue sauce, crème fraîche and Golden Osetra caviar.

The narrow ground floor offers the more impressive menu, while the mezzanine offers a concise tasting. Walls smeared with blue-and-white paint, oversized wooden tables and modern music give the space a youthful yet refined vibe.

■ 1552 Fillmore St. (bet. Ellis St. & Geary Blvd.)
✆ (415) 817-1187 — **WEB:** www.averysf.com
■ Dinner Wed – Sun
PRICE: $$$$

BAR CRUDO ❙⚬
Seafood · *Contemporary décor*

Visitors without reservations should be prepared to wait for a table at this Divisadero gem. In fact, they may even find people lined up on the sidewalk for a seat at the counter. As the name suggests, this seafood haven offers supreme crudos. Whether it's Arctic char with horseradish crème fraîche, wasabi tobiko and dill; or scallop with sweet corn purée, tarragon oil and popped sorghum, the combos are delicious. Shellfish platters are available, and there are a few hot dishes including a chowder chock-full of fish, shrimp, squid and bacon.

Inside, the space is often standing room-only, with just a few tables; most guests gather around the bar. Grab a glass of wine or beer, peek into the kitchen and be sure to check out the futuristic art on the walls.

■ 655 Divisadero St. (bet. Grove & Hayes Sts.)
✆ (415) 409-0679 — **WEB:** www.barcrudo.com
■ Dinner Tue – Sun
PRICE: $$

BARVALE 🍴
Spanish • Trendy

Move over, Mission District. Divisadero is quickly becoming this city's new dinner 'hood darling, and Barvale is the perfect place to start your tour. If you're worried about not having a reservation, don't. Once you see the lively scene flowing inside, you'll realize that this tapas house saves half their tables for walk-ins.

The menu toys with fun riffs on traditional Spanish tapas and bite-sized pintxos—all of them matched to terrific sangria and cocktails. Try the smoky chorizo and manchego before indulging in the petite but hugely delicious paella, laced with a creamy aïoli, charred lemon, prawns, mussels and clams. Service moves quickly but attentively, and weekend brunch offers a handful of egg dishes as well as—you guessed it—tapas.

661 Divisadero St. (at Grove St.)
📞 (415) 654-5211 — **WEB:** www.barvalesf.com
Lunch Sat – Sun Dinner nightly

PRICE: $$

CALA 🍴
Mexican • Contemporary décor

A Mexico City superstar with the seafood-centric Contramar, Gabriela Cámara has brought her magic touch to this Civic Center hottie, where she serves similar food. Nothing is lost in translation: filleted black cod with red chile adobo is silky and smoky after a wood grilling in collard leaves, while Cámara's famed tuna tostadas get a Bay Area sustainability update with ocean trout. And you won't want to miss the griddled black bean sopes, which seem simple but sing with flavor.

Cala's minimalist aesthetic matches that of Contramar, with vaulted, skylight-dotted ceilings, a planter box full of climbing vines and lots of light wood for a rustic-urban feel. Service can be spotty, but for a flavorful, unfussy meal, it's quickly become a hot ticket.

149 Fell St. (bet. Franklin St. & Van Ness Ave.)
📞 (415) 660-7701 — **WEB:** www.calarestaurant.com
Dinner nightly

PRICE: $$$

CHE FICO 🍴🍽

Italian • *Trendy*

MAP: B1

Che fico ("what a fig") is Italian slang for "How cool!" And the sharply dressed crowd at this good-looking spot is indeed very cool—but they give quite a fig about landing a highly coveted reservation. If you're not a celebrity or tech mogul with an inside line, expect to wait in one. The balanced and beautiful array of cocktails, like a gently spicy banana milk punch, will help bide the time nicely.

The vibe is chic, but this food is approachable with rotating pastas like the saffron spaghetti with 'nduja, quirky, compelling pizzas (try the pineapple, red onion and fermented chili number) and Roman-Jewish appetizers like the artistically plated grilled duck liver with matzo.

Desserts are an absolute must: the coffee-blueberry pavlova may sound odd, but it's divine.

838 Divisadero St. (bet. Fulton & McAllister Sts.)
📞 (415) 416-6959 — **WEB:** www.chefico.com
Dinner Tue – Sat

PRICE: $$$

FRANCES 🍴🍽

Californian • *Cozy*

MAP: B3

This tiny, intensely personal restaurant from Chef/owner Melissa Perello has been a local hit from the get-go. Chic and always packed, it's as perfect for a low-key date night as it is for dinner with the kids. And while reservations are a nigh-impossible score, the gracious staff saves ten counter seats for walk-ins—and serves every diner with equal aplomb.

Perello eschews trendy powders and foams for hearty, seasonal fare like charred baby octopus with homemade yogurt and olive tapenade. Honey-brined pork chop rests over creamed escarole and fennel slaw; and McGinnis Ranch carrots are roasted with sunchokes for an interesting blend of sweet and savory. Desserts like a black sesame pavolva with chicory root ice cream offer a fresh, light conclusion.

3870 17th St. (at Pond St.)
📞 (415) 621-3870 — **WEB:** www.frances-sf.com
Dinner Tue – Sun

PRICE: $$

JARDINIÈRE 🍴

Californian • Elegant

For a memorable night on the town, don your best dress, find a hand to hold and head to this longtime favorite—tinged with a sense of bygone romance. Stop off at the circular bar and join the well-heeled couples sipping cocktails pre- or post-opera. Prime seats on the upstairs balcony overlook the bustling lower level, and stunning arched windows show off views of the street. Approachable, seasonal dishes abound on Jardinière's menu, from tender tajarin pasta with morel mushrooms and butter to a Mediterranean-inspired duo of lamb belly and shoulder with fresh fava beans and smoked yogurt sauce.

Indecisive sweet tooths will thrill to the bonne bouche, an array of candies, cookies, small cakes and profiteroles that makes a striking conclusion.

▨ 300 Grove St. (at Franklin St.)
☎ (415) 861-5555 — **WEB:** www.jardiniere.com
▨ Dinner nightly

PRICE: $$$

MONSIEUR BENJAMIN 🍴

French • Bistro

Chef Corey Lee's take on timeless bistro cuisine is as sleek and striking as the space it's served in. Fit for the cover of a magazine, this black-and-white dining room's minimalist, yet intimate décor is trumped only by its pièce de résistance: an exhibition kitchen where you'll find the meticulous brigade of cooks hard at work, producing impressively authentic French food.

Begin with the pâté de campagne, enhanced with liver and shallots and presented with strong mustard, cornichons and country bread. The Arctic char amandine is excellent, dressed with fragrant beurre noisette and served over a bed of crispy haricot verts and sunchokes. For a sweet finish, purists will delight in the dessert menu's île flottante.

▨ 451 Gough St. (at Ivy St.)
☎ (415) 403-2233 — **WEB:** www.monsieurbenjamin.com
▨ Lunch Sat – Sun Dinner nightly

PRICE: $$$

JŪ-NI ❁

Japanese • Contemporary décor

MAP: B2

"Jū-ni" is Japanese for "twelve," which also happens to be the number of seats in this petite, omakase-only spot just off the busy Divisadero corridor. Its segmented, L-shaped sushi bar ensures personalized attention from the trio of chefs, often led by Chef/owner Geoffrey Lee. They're a young, lively crew and they've designed this space with a crowd of similarly young, moneyed professionals in mind. Note the spotlights above the counter, placed for perfect Instagram snaps of dishes, and the thoroughly curated sake menu.

A meal may begin with a tasting of seasonal vegetables—think tomatoes over edamame hummus—before proceeding to an array of nigiri, painstakingly sourced straight from Tokyo's own Tsukiji fish market and delicately draped over well-seasoned rice. Standouts include sakura masu with a salt-cured cherry blossom leaf, buttery Hokkaido scallop and the signature ikura—cured in soy, sake and honey and finished with a grating of velvety frozen monkfish liver.

Decadent supplements, like torched A5 Wagyu beef and luscious uni, can be added along the way. But the meal finishes with a surprisingly gentle send-off: sweet, tender mochi dabbed with adzuki bean paste.

■ 1335 Fulton St. (bet. Broderick & Divisadero Sts.)
℘ (415) 655-9924 — **WEB:** www.junisf.com
■ Dinner nightly

PRICE: $$$$

NIGHTBIRD ‖○

Californian • Elegant

MAP: C1

Located just behind a beautiful wooden door with a carved owl and in a prime Hayes Valley location, Nightbird invites you into its nest with a small and sleek dining room. If you arrive early, don't miss a delicious craft cocktail at their sibling spot next door, Linden Bar, as it's the perfect lead-up to Chef/owner Kim Alter's five-course tasting.

Though the menu changes often, Alter's presentations are consistently gorgeous. Witness a tender scallop "cooked" in yuzu juice, topped with uni, spring peas, radish, pea shoots and a truffle vinaigrette. Or go for a beautiful tableside presentation of white asparagus from the Loire Valley with paddlefish and salmon roe, a single leaf of nasturtium, as well as a drizzle of beurre blanc studded with escargot.

330 Gough St. (at Linden St.)
(415) 829-7565 — **WEB:** www.nightbirdrestaurant.com
Dinner Tue – Sat

PRICE: $$$$

NOMICA ‖○

Fusion • Contemporary décor

MAP: C3

Japanese and Western flavors collide at this hip Castro address, where "cassoulet" is actually a five-spice duck leg with soybeans and duck-fat rice; chicken wings come stuffed with gyoza filling; and chicken and waffles are done karaage-style with accents of shiso béarnaise and matcha salt. Even the cocktails incorporate unusual features like sea beans and shiitakes.

But despite the culinary culture clash, Nomica's food is playful and satisfying, and anxious foodies bend over backwards to score an advance order of its coveted whole chicken in brioche (which requires 24 hours' notice). With its vast selection of Japanese whisky and awamori, this a big draw for young professional types, who congregate at the bar for sips and quirky bites.

2223 Market St. (bet. 15th & 16th Sts.)
(415) 655-3280 — **WEB:** www.nomicasf.com
Dinner Mon – Sat

PRICE: $$$

NOPA ⫛○

Californian • Contemporary décor

🍸 ♿ 🛳️   **MAP:** B2

Before you're able to enjoy a single forkful at this Bay Area sensation, you'll have to secure a table—and that takes some serious effort. Reservations are snapped up at lightning speed, and hopeful walk-ins must line up prior to the start of service to add their name to the list.

The good news? Your efforts will be well rewarded. Inside, an open kitchen, soaring ceilings and hordes of ravenous sophisticates produce a cacophonous setting in which to relish Nopa's wonderful, organic, wood-fired cuisine. Dig into a bruschetta of grilled levain spread with smashed avocado, pickled jalapeños, lemon-dressed arugula and shaved mezzo secco, or go for the roasted king salmon fillet over creamed corn, smoky maitakes, crisp green beans and sweet tomato confit.

▧ 560 Divisadero St. (at Hayes St.)
✆ (415) 864-8643 — **WEB:** www.nopasf.com
▧ Lunch Sat – Sun Dinner nightly   **PRICE:** $$

NOPALITO 😃

Mexican • Trendy

♿ ⛱️   **MAP:** B2

Whether they're digging into a refreshing ensalada de nopales or sharing a platter of blue-corn tacos stuffed with spicy-smoky marinated fish, local couples and families adore this sustainable Mexican spot. Sister to Cal-cuisine icon Nopa, Nopalito is so beloved that an equally good and popular Inner Sunset location is also thriving.

The small, cheerful space with reclaimed wood and bright green accents doesn't take reservations; call ahead to get on the list, or try takeout. Once seated, friendly servers will guide the way with house-made horchata for the kids and an extensive tequila selection for grown-ups. Both groups will certainly agree on a sweet finish: the excellent vanilla bean flan topped with orange caramel and orange supremes is unbeatable.

▧ 306 Broderick St. (bet. Fell & Oak Sts.)
✆ (415) 437-0303 — **WEB:** www.nopalitosf.com
▧ Lunch & dinner daily   **PRICE:** $$

PETIT CRENN

French • Bistro

MAP: C2

In a homey corner of booming Hayes Valley, Chef Dominique Crenn serves a menu more approachable (in both technique and price) than her acclaimed Atelier Crenn. With its open kitchen, chalkboard menus and nautical feel inspired by Brittany, Petit Crenn is a hit among locals.

While the eats are rib-sticking—think wood-roasted trout with cider sabayon, or rustic bread slathered with espelette aïoli and earthy sautéed mushrooms—the execution of this kitchen is precise. Find evidence of this in the exquisite gem lettuce salad—which is so much more than its name suggests—or even the rolled omelet tucked with fragrant herbs. Whether you opt for the early evening à la carte seating or multi-course prix-fixe, expect to leave sated and smitten.

609 Hayes St. (bet. Buchanan & Laguna Sts.)
(415) 864-1744 — **WEB:** www.petitcrenn.com
Lunch Sat - Sun Dinner Tue - Sun **PRICE: $$$$**

REVELRY BISTRO

French • Bistro

MAP: C2

Though this colorful corner bistro boasts some fusion-forward items, diners in the know stick with the French classics. No quarter is given to tired menu standards like onion soup and boeuf bourguignon; instead, you'll find truly seasonal fare, like endive in a creamy, umami-rich gratin that nicely softens its bitterness. The rotating specials might include decadent tournedos Rossini—filet mignon topped with a seared lobe of foie gras.

Low-key vibes, excellent food and soft tunes make this a date-night bijou; and couples typically occupy the tightly packed tables. However, even if you're rolling solo, you might find yourself falling for the pristine profiteroles, stuffed with vanilla ice cream and drenched in a thick, rich chocolate sauce.

297 Page St. (at Laguna St.)
(415) 241-6833 — **WEB:** www.revelrybistro.com
Lunch Sat - Sun Dinner Tue - Sun **PRICE: $$$**

THE PROGRESS ✤

Californian • *Contemporary décor*

🍷 ♿ ⊡

MAP: B1

This is the rare restaurant that guarantees its diners will never be bored, thanks to the sophisticated energy that flows directly from a notably ambitious kitchen.

The gorgeous space has that Nordic look that California so loves, with plenty of bare wood, skylights and an affluent crowd appearing informal in their Patagonias. The hipster staff echoes the casual mood but performs attentive service.

The focus is on family-style dining, but go ahead and order a few smaller dishes to accompany their platter-sized plates. Perfectly crisp artichokes, for instance, are at the center of an exceptionally good combination of preserved lemon and coriander chermoula, garnished with fresh herbs and tender artichoke leaves. Liberty Farms barbecue duck is cooked to absolute delight and presented with garlic- and ginger-infused crisped rice as well as meat so tender that it is practically falling off the bone. When they hit their mark, creations like this transcend their ingredients and technique to result in something genius, including the properly executed île flottante. Be sure to match this with one of their refreshing cocktails, like the house martini, finished with a droplet of rosemary oil.

■ 1525 Fillmore St. (bet. Geary Blvd. & O'Farrell St.)
✆ (415) 673-1294 — **WEB:** www.theprogress-sf.com
■ Dinner nightly

PRICE: $$$

RICH TABLE ✿

Contemporary • Trendy

🍸

MAP: C2

A rustic-chic décor highlighting reclaimed and raw wood gives Rich Table a farmhouse feel, and the crowds that pack it are equally stylish. The young professionals and pre-theater diners know that reserving in advance is a must. If you're not lucky enough to secure a table, get in line 30 minutes before opening to snag one of the dozen coveted bar seats.

Why all the fuss? Because Chefs/owners Evan and Sarah Rich execute casual Californian fare with fine-dining precision, interweaving a bevy of global influences along the way. An Indian-influenced foie gras torchon is set over a pool of tangy mango lassi and toasted meringue, all to be heaped upon buttery brioche. The seared pierogies, stuffed with ricotta, morels and peas, are pristine enough to win a Polish grandmother's approval, and a char siu-style pork chop is beautifully smoky and charred.

The super-hip staff is thoroughly polished and happy to recommend a cocktail or wine. They'll push the duo of famous "snacks"—crispy sardine-threaded chips and umami-packed porcini doughnuts with raclette dipping sauce. But skip them in favor of a seasonal dessert, like the tart cherry ice with almond ice cream and shiso.

■ 199 Gough St. (at Oak St.)

✆ (415) 355-9085 — **WEB:** www.richtablesf.com

■ Dinner nightly

PRICE: $$$

ROBIN 🍴

Japanese • *Trendy*

 ♿

MAP: C1

Trust is the name of the game at Robin, a hip sushi-focused destination, where no menu is ever presented. Instead, guests happily submit themselves to the very capable skills of Chef Adam Tortosa (formerly of Akiko), and his modern take on omakase. This kitchen's decadent vision includes lots of elite ingredients like A5 Wagyu, foie gras and caviar, though the staff will kindly ask what your budget is (or if you have allergies). The upscale space is a mix of posh and street cool—think graffiti-esque bathrooms and hip-hop beats. Young sushi chefs are the focal point of the room, working fastidiously with tweezers, torches and gel in front of a bright backdrop.

A small, carefully curated list of beer, sake and wine pairs nicely with the food.

▨ 620 Gough St. (at Ash St.)
  📞 (415) 548-2429 — **WEB:** www.robinsanfrancisco.com
▨ Dinner nightly   **PRICE: $$$$**

RT ROTISSERIE 🍴

Californian • *Simple*

MAP: C2

Can't manage to snag a seat at Rich Table? You'll dine equally well at the restaurant's fast-casual sibling, just a block away. Though it resembles the mothership with its simple, wood-heavy décor and earthenware plates, RT's compact menu and counter service make it far more affordable—a bonus with the Hayes Valley crowds seeking a quick-but-quality lunch or pre-theater dinner.

The menu is centered on a few rotisserie items, including tender, juicy half-chicken with crisp, burnished skin. When accompanied by perfectly roasted cauliflower that shines in a pita sandwich, with beet hummus, cucumber salad, lemon and herbs, it's an utter delight. Add on a dipping sauce like chipotle yogurt or a side of charred corn with ricotta, and you're in business.

▨ 101 Oak St. (at Franklin St.)
  📞 (415) 829-7086 — **WEB:** www.rtrotisserie.com
▨ Lunch & dinner daily   **PRICE:** 🍜

SARU ⅏⚬

Japanese • Simple

MAP: C4

Hilly Noe Valley is the perfect setting for this jewel of a sushi restaurant, and lest you have an original idea, the line here will thwart you in your tracks. The menu is thoroughly Japanese with a few Californian touches—think grilled shishito peppers tossed with crunchy daikon in a ponzu dressing.

Be sure to start with the signature tempura-fried seaweed cracker topped with spicy tuna and avocado. Then, perfectly sized tasting spoons of seared ankimo with scallions, as well as halibut tartare with yuzu make for delightful quick bites. Though rolls are available, regulars opt for the nigiri, which might include kampachi, baby snapper and snow crab. If you'd like the chefs to choose, several omakase (including an all-salmon variation) are also on offer.

▢ 3856 24th St. (bet. Sanchez & Vicksburg Sts.)

✆ (415) 400-4510 — **WEB:** www.akaisarusf.com

▢ Lunch & dinner Tue – Sun

PRICE: $$

STARBELLY ☻

Californian • Rustic

🍺 ♿ 🚻 🛋

MAP: B3

The simplest things are often the best, as a meal at Starbelly deliciously proves. Whether you're twirling a forkful of spaghetti with garlicky tomato sauce, jalapeños and house-made bacon, or tucking into a juicy burger on a grilled sesame seed challah bun, you're sure to savor something beautifully made, seasonal and unfussy. Desserts are just as satisfying, like a salted caramel pot de crème served with rosemary shortbread cookies.

A nexus of the Castro social scene, this cheerful, wood-paneled space is always full of locals hopping from table to table to greet their friends, and the back patio (heated and sheltered when it's foggy) is an appealing refuge.

Be sure to make reservations: this is an area favorite, and for good reason.

▢ 3583 16th St. (at Market St.)

✆ (415) 252-7500 — **WEB:** www.starbellysf.com

▢ Lunch & dinner daily

PRICE: $$

STATE BIRD PROVISIONS ✿

American • *Trendy*

MAP: B1

Welcome to the evolution of fine dining, where streams of plates are passed between guests in dim sum-style, and the supremely seasonal Californian cooking is always very good, even vibrant and surprising. You may not understand all of what you ordered at first, but prices are reasonable so pile on a few extras and try everything that comes your way. No one leaves hungry here.

Servers circulate through the room carrying platters or push carts that are brimming with creative and utterly unique dishes. Highlights that will leave you begging for more include pan-seared dumplings—filled with tender, pulled guinea hen and earthy shiitake mushrooms—accompanied by a tableside pour of aromatic and umami-rich broth. Heartier but wow-inducing bites of fried black cod tail glazed in a delicious tamari-butter and garnished with toasted sesame seeds, followed by hot-pink rhubarb-and-passion fruit granita draped over an oat mousse make for a fine study in wonderfully unexpected flavors and textures.

Be forewarned: getting a reservation here is the ultimate challenge and walk-in spots require lining up around 4:30 P.M. Best to avoid nights when large parties are booked—this may negatively impact your experience.

▨ 1529 Fillmore St. (bet. Geary Blvd. & O'Farrell St.)

☏ (415) 795-1272 — **WEB:** www.statebirdsf.com

▨ Dinner nightly

PRICE: $$

TSUBASA 🈂️

Japanese • Simple

Amidst the pricey boutiques and top-dollar restaurants of Hayes Valley, a good deal can be hard to come by. However, Tsubasa is a delightful exception, offering well-made nigiri, sashimi and maki at a price point that belies the high quality of its fish.

The sleek dining room offers table seating, but the best seats in the house are at the sushi bar, where you'll be presented with generously portioned nigiri that range from cleanly flavored turbot to intense, vinegar-kissed saba (mackerel). There are also more elaborate maki, like a salmon and avocado roll topped with raw scallops and miso sauce. But the deepest pleasures are simple ones: excellent miso soup, a tuna roll with beautifully seasoned rice and rich, custardy tamago.

■ 429 Gough St. (bet. Hayes & Ivy Sts.)
📞 (415) 551-9688 — **WEB:** www.tsubasasf.com
■ Lunch Tue – Sat Dinner Tue – Sun   PRICE: $$

UMA CASA 🍴

Portuguese • Contemporary décor

♿

High ceilings and azulejo-adorned walls set the scene at this Noe Valley jewel, which succeeds longtime local spot Incanto. It's also one of the few high-end San Francisco restaurants spotlighting the cuisine of Portugal, and Chef Telmo Faria delivers a traditional seafood-centric menu. Read: grilled sardines, salt cod fritters, as well as garlic- and chili-inflected shrimp moçambique.

Most diners opt to share a flurry of small plates, commencing with potato chips and piri-piri sauce. The entrées are satisfying, too. Try the alcatra, red wine-braised short ribs; or pan-roasted sea bass with molho cru, the Portuguese take on chimichurri. Finally, sip on one of the bar's signature low alcohol cocktails, made with port, sherry and other fortified wines.

■ 1550 Church St. (at Duncan St.)
📞 (415) 829-2264 — **WEB:** www.umacasarestaurant.com
■ Dinner Tue – Sun   PRICE: $$

VILLON ║○

Contemporary · *Chic*

MAP: D1

This up-and-comer in the sleek Proper Hotel has style to spare—from its polished checkerboard floors all the way up to the floor-to-ceiling library shelves behind the stunning bar. No detail is too small here, especially those heavy etched glasses that hold complimentary sparkling water, and the smart shirts donned by the waitstaff. Even the gold flatware will catch your eye.

The good looks extend to the plate as well, where the chef and team offer clever riffs on everything from Hawaiian sweet rolls topped with "everything" seasoning and served with a trio of spreads, to Japanese okonomiyaki, which gets a Spanish twist with prawns and chorizo. Seek out the outstanding cocktail list as it boasts 49 options, one for each square mile of San Francisco.

▨ 1100 Market St. (at Charles J. Brenham Pl.)

✆ (628) 895-2040 — **WEB:** www.properhotel.com

▨ Lunch & dinner daily

PRICE: $$

ZUNI CAFÉ ║○

Mediterranean · *Bistro*

MAP: C2

Almost forty years young and still thriving as if it were newborn, locals and visitors remain drawn to this SF institution. Famous for its laid-back California vibe and great, locally sourced eats, this iconic space embraces its unique shape, and is styled with bold artwork-covered walls, a copper bar and wood-burning oven sending out delightful pizzas that fill the room with mouthwatering aromas.

Given its ace location, Zuni makes for a divine lunch destination—and proof is in the many business folk, trendy ladies-who-lunch, and tourists who fill its tables midday. Menu treasures include sliced persimmon scattered with shaved Jerusalem artichokes and baby arugula leaves, tailed by artisanal rigatoni clutching a fragrant lamb sugo.

▨ 1658 Market St. (bet. Franklin & Gough Sts.)

✆ (415) 552-2522 — **WEB:** www.zunicafe.com

▨ Lunch & dinner Tue – Sun

PRICE: $$

FINANCIAL DISTRICT

EMBARCADERO · UNION SQUARE

Booming with high-rises and large-scale companies, the Financial District is world-renowned. While the city itself is reputed for its easygoing vibe and cool 'tude, the financial sector is ever-bustling with the prominence of Fortune 500 companies, multi-national corporations, major banks and big law. Settled along the west of the waterfront, expect to see streetcars, pedestrians and wildly tattooed bicycle messengers on weekdays clogging the routes of the triangle bounded by Kearny, Jackson and Market streets. Come noon, lines snake out

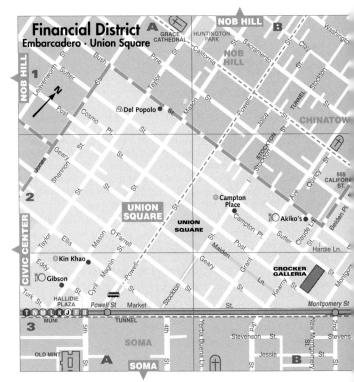

the doors of better grab-and-go sandwich shops and salad spots. Of course, there is always a steady stream of expense-account clients who continuously patronize this neighborhood's host of fine-dining establishments; whereas along Market Street, casual cafés and chain restaurants keep the focus on families, tourists and shoppers alike.

EMBARCARDERO

Despite all that this area has to offer, its greatest culinary treasures lies within the famed **Ferry Building**. This 1898 steel-reinforced sandstone structure is easily recognized by its 244-foot clock tower that rises up from Market Street and way above the waterfront promenade— **The Embarcadero**. It is among the few survivors of

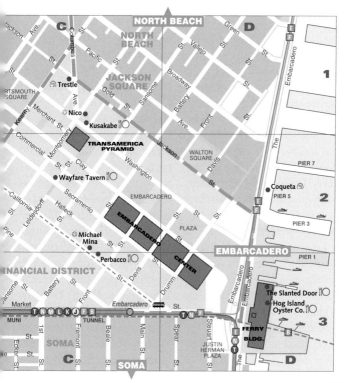

the 1906 earthquake and fire that destroyed most of this neighborhood. Thanks to a 2004 renovation, the soaring interior arcade makes a stunning showcase for regional products, artisanal foods, rare Chinese teas and everything in between. Popularly referred to as the **Ferry Building Marketplace**, every diligent foodie is destined here for the likes of Chef Amaryll Schwertner's breakfast specialties at the beloved **Boulettes Larder**, where guests literally sit in the kitchen as their spread is prepared—multigrain griddle cakes with ricotta and seasonal fruit are a favorite for good reason. This emporium also pays homage to the surrounding food community by highlighting small producers. Two of the most popular among them are **Cowgirl Creamery**'s farmstead cheeses, and Berkeley's **Acme Bread Company**, whose organic breads are a sight (and smell) to behold! Following this philosophy, find numerous organic and exotic mushrooms, medicinal herbs and themed products at **Far West Fungi**. Here, patient enthusiasts can even purchase logs on which to grow their own harvest. Legendary **Frog Hollow Farm** is also stationed nearby, offering pristine seasonal fruit alongside homemade chutneys, marmalade and fresh-baked pastries. Known for their Parisian-style chocolates and caramels, **Recchiuti Confections** has elevated their craft to an art form that can only be described as "sublime."

Completing this gourmet trend are gleaming bottles of **McEvoy Ranch Olive Oil** from their Petaluma ranch that also includes an impressive array of olive oil-based products. While such world-class food shopping may whet the appetite of many, more immediate cravings can be satisfied at the Building's more casual dining delights like **DELICA**, popular for beautifully prepared Japanese fusion food, from signature sushi rolls to savory croquettes. Join the corporate lunch rush seated at picnic tables in **Mijita** (run by Traci Des Jardins of **Jardinère** fame) to sample such treats as queso fundido or Baja-style fish tacos. Alternatively, claim a patio seat at **MarketBar** for market-inspired salads, flatbreads and American brasserie fare. On Tuesday, Thursday and Saturday mornings, high-minded chefs share laughs with the locals at **Ferry Plaza Farmer's Market**, which deals in everything from organic produce and baked goods to fresh pastas and tons more. On market days, open-air stands and tents line the picturesque sidewalk in front of the Ferry Building and rear plaza overlooking the bay.

Tourists and unwearied locals are sure to enjoy some visual stimulation at The Bay Lights—an undulating light installation by artist Leo Villareal—illuminating the west span of the Bay

Bridge. **The Embarcadero** boasts the best view of this beautiful piece. Meanwhile, corporate types know to head on over to the **Embarcadero Center** (spanning five blocks and boasting reduced parking rates on weekends) to get their midday shopping fix in the sprawling three-story indoor mall, or to grab a quick lunch at one of their many eateries ranging from mini-chains to noodle shops. A speck of sweet from **See's Candies** or caffeine from **Peet's** makes for an ideal finale.

UNION SQUARE

While upscale department stores like Barneys, Neiman Marcus and Saks Fifth Avenue preside over Union Square (where foodies gather for a gourmet experience and fashionistas flock to the parade of designer shops), regulars in the know as well as noodle lovers join the infamous queue outside **Katana-Ya** for their steaming bowls of slurp-worthy ramen and satisfying bowls of donburi.

AKIKO'S 🍴

Japanese • Cozy

🝆

Though Akiko's may look like an average neighborhood sushi joint from the outside (especially since it's often confused with a nearby spot of the same name), a meal here is a reminder that appearances can be deceiving. Those planning on dining in will want to make a reservation, as the small, industrial space is mighty popular—especially those coveted counter seats.

Second-generation Chef/owner Ray Lee does wonders with nigiri from around the globe, from silky New Zealand king salmon to full-flavored Cyprian sea bream. Cooked dishes like gently battered agedashi tofu, in a flavorful broth accented with "pearls" of ikura, are just as appealing. And be sure to sample the excellent applewood-aged soy sauce, which brings out the flavors of each dish.

▨ 431 Bush St. (bet. Grant & Kearny Sts.)
℘ (415) 397-3218 — **WEB:** www.akikosrestaurant.com
▨ Lunch Mon – Fri Dinner Mon – Sat   PRICE: $$$

COQUETA 😳

Spanish • Contemporary décor

♿

A tasty little morsel of a space serving up mouthwatering tapas, Michael Chiarello's Pier 5 destination offers shimmering views of the Bay from its rustic dining room, equipped with rough-hewn wooden tables, cowhide rugs and a big, theatrical open kitchen and bar. There's a bit more space on the tented outdoor patio, but if your heart is set on a table, book early.

Its name is Spanish for "flirt," and Coqueta's alluring menu has caused more than one enraptured diner to over-order. Some fine options: crunchy-creamy chicken and pea croquetas, mini sandwiches of smoked salmon with queso fresco and truffle honey and wood-grilled octopus with tender fingerling potatoes. Complete the experience with the Asturian apple pie with Cabrales blue cheese ice cream.

▨ Pier 5 (at The Embarcadero)
℘ (415) 704-8866 — **WEB:** www.coquetasf.com
▨ Lunch Tue – Sun Dinner nightly   PRICE: $$

CAMPTON PLACE ✿

Indian • Elegant

MAP: B2

As is to be expected from a luxury hotel restaurant, Campton Place is a tastefully decorated space serving the finest in local, seasonal cuisine. The twist? It's also an Indian restaurant, and a glamorous one at that. Chef Srijith Gopinathan offers two nightly menus—one for vegetarians and one for omnivores that emphasizes pungent spices, clever presentation and a staggering variety of tastes, textures and temperatures. In keeping with the cooking, the dining room is equal parts elegant and playful—its soothing palette contrasted against a striking central glass light fixture.

Each carte here begins with a range of exquisite canapés—imagine a warm ricotta-filled naan paired with avocado butter or potato raita garnished with a dollop of caviar. Vegetarians will thrill to a deceptively simple combination of puffed grains, grapes and yogurt "snow;" or meat-like pulled jackfruit in a complex curry. Carnivores may rest easy as this kitchen also flaunts a luxe riff on lamb biryani, with a juicy medallion set over basmati rice, as well as butter-poached lobster tail in a delicate gravy.

Thoughtful wine servers easily navigate these tricky pairings, suggesting a variety of ace local vintages.

340 Stockton St. (bet. Post & Sutter Sts.)
☎ (415) 955-5555 — **WEB:** www.camptonplacesf.com
Dinner nightly

PRICE: $$$$

DEL POPOLO 🐷

Pizza • Minimalist

  ♿

MAP: A1

If you've got eyes for pies, you'll want to make a beeline to this chic and simple Italian hot spot. The open space is centered around a big, blazing oven and crowds arrive early to score every last no-reservations seat.

Del Popolo may have gotten its start as a food truck, but one bite of their wood-fired pizzas and it's clear how it earned its address. Chewy, blistered and deliciously caramelized, the crusts arrive laden with toppings both traditional (mozzarella, crushed tomato and basil) and California cool (roasted winter squash, mascarpone, spring onions). Don't sleep on the antipasti, either since the starters are first-rate. The lightly charred carrots set atop house-made yogurt and garnished with crispy red quinoa are dizzyingly delicious.

▒ 855 Bush St. (bet. Mason & Taylor Sts.)
♨ (415) 589-7940 — **WEB:** www.delpopolosf.com
▒ Dinner Tue – Sun

PRICE: $$

GIBSON 🍴

Contemporary • Chic

🍹 ♿ ⎳

MAP: A3

This swanky spot in the Hotel Bijou is truly a tale of two cities—while the Tenderloin-bordering exterior is derelict, the shimmering interior is a Gatsby-worthy altar of Deco glamour. But look beyond the ornate ceilings and aquamarine banquettes, and you'll find a menu that revolves around two ancient techniques—live-fire cooking on an open hearth, and a robust fermentation program with jars lining the kitchen walls.

The results are impressive. Imagine fire-baked sourdough rolls with a delicate duck liver mousse, tailed by charred roast carrots served over an impressively rich sunflower seed "risotto." Portions are petite, so all the better to share them over cocktails or house-made sodas.

For a deeper dive, opt for the prix-fixe menu.

▒ 111 Mason St. (at Eddy St.)
♨ (415) 771-7709 — **WEB:** www.gibsonsf.com
▒ Dinner Mon – Sat

PRICE: $$$

HOG ISLAND OYSTER CO. 🍴

Seafood • *Trendy*

MAP: D3

Can't make the trip to Marin to shuck oysters on Hog Island's docks? They'll bring Tomales Bay's finest to you at this buzzing cityside outpost in the Ferry Building, which draws long lines of both tourists and locals for platters of some of the sweetest, freshest bivalves on the West Coast. You'll receive all the accompaniments—lemon, Tabasco, mignonette—but they're good enough to slurp solo.

Once you've had your fill, be sure to sample the other aquatic offerings: Peruvian-style crudo with silky sea bass; a hefty bowl of cioppino loaded with prawns, clams, mussels and squid; and the exceptional Manila clam chowder, a bestseller for good reason. Throw in the expansive Bay views from the patio and dining room, and those lines come as no surprise.

1 Ferry Building (at The Embarcadero)

☎ (415) 391-7117 — **WEB:** www.hogislandoysters.com

Lunch & dinner daily

PRICE: $$$

KUSAKABE 🍴

Japanese • *Minimalist*

MAP: C1

Serene with warm lighting and clean lines, distinctive creativity is the motto of this sushi-focused operation. Inside, a stunning counter crafted from a piece of live-edge elm, oyster-hued leather chairs and a ceiling of wood slats complete the Japanese-chic look.

While the preparation of their nightly omakase might seem like a production line, by employing myriad cooking techniques, the kitchen ensures that every bite is memorable. Begin with warm kelp tea, before embarking on a sashimi parade of bluefin slices served with a yuzu-onion-sesame sauce. A soup course may feature a soy foam-miso broth with rice dumplings and duck meatballs. And finally, a top rendition of sushi yields shima aji with daikon and ayu that is torched just enough to blister the skin.

584 Washington St. (bet. Montgomery & Sansome Sts.)

☎ (415) 757-0155 — **WEB:** www.kusakabe-sf.com

Dinner Mon – Sat

PRICE: $$$$

KIN KHAO ❀
Thai • Trendy

Tucked into an alcove of the unprepossessing Parc 55 hotel, this restaurant won't win any awards in the décor department—it's spare and casual, with tables set with chopstick canisters and bowls of chili oil. But when it comes to delivering authentically layered, fiery Thai flavor with a produce-driven northern California flair, it has no equal.

Kin Khao's menu conjures up dishes from across Thailand and is a virtual homage to local purveyors. Imagine a meaty and rich five-spice noodle soup infused with duck bones and stocked with bok choy and delightfully tender duck leg confit; or a deliciously fresh take on som tum, with julienned green papaya tossed with golden tomatoes, long beans, dried shrimp and crushed red chili. More traditional options may include classic pad kee mao showcasing wide, flat noodles stir-fried with a potent mixture of ground pork bits, bell pepper, onion and holy basil.

Needless to say, those avoiding spicy food or craving plain old pad Thai should look elsewhere. But, if you're in the mood for a vibrant and zesty meal, then strap in for a wild and enticing ride. Come dessert, try the black rice pudding served warm and with myriad toppings.

---

55 Cyril Magnin St. (entrance at Ellis & Mason Sts.)

(415) 362-7456 — **WEB:** www.kinkhao.com

Lunch & dinner daily

PRICE: $$

MICHAEL MINA ✿
Contemporary • Elegant

🕸 ♿ ⬚ ✋

MAP: C2

Power players can't seem to get enough of mega-popular Chef Michael Mina's San Francisco flagship, even though it sports a completely revamped menu. If the crisp, contemporary dining room was a favorite, don't fret, as the overall demeanor remains the same. It's still ground zero for fine dining and you're likely to see the same expense-account types, along with a handful of occasion-celebrating duos.

The approach now showcases Middle Eastern flavors and incorporates classic ingredients, like labneh, which appears in both sweet and savory dishes. Wild king salmon is accompanied by a coriander-green tomato sauce; the dry-aged strip loin with matbucha sauce is a prime example of the kitchen's novel direction. While you won't find the famed trios on this carte any longer, you'll relish the signature tuna tartare, mixed with quail egg, diced pear and ancho chili powder. A multi-course tasting allows you to select your own options, including the hand-cut tajarin and a properly rendered dark chocolate crèmeux with fresh strawberries.

Be sure to spend time with the wine list as well: though expensive, it offers an impressive roster of familiar labels and unusual varietals.

🔲 252 California St. (bet. Battery & Front Sts.)
📞 (415) 397-9222 — **WEB:** www.michaelmina.net
🔲 Lunch Mon – Fri Dinner nightly

PRICE: $$$$

NICO ✿

Contemporary • Bistro

&

After moving to the Financial District, Chef Nicolas Delaroque has succeeded in ensuring that this contemporary French bistro does not miss a beat. The new, petite dining room is polished and sophisticated but not stuffy, combining brown leather banquettes and exposed brick with a backlit white marble bar. Find the best seats towards the immaculate, white-tiled open kitchen located in the back.

The choice of four- or six-course dinner menus changes frequently, promising that each dish showcases peak-season ingredients. The three-course lunch menu is well priced and sure to attract business diners. No matter the time of day, this all translates into tremendous value for such expertly prepared cuisine. À la carte dining is offered only at the bar, serving simpler fare like oysters or a croque monsieur.

Everything is perfectly cooked and seasoned, beginning with lightly poached white asparagus with thin slices of chilled foie gras, trout roe and lemon. Freshly shelled peas with spring onion, clams and smoked cod custard combine acidity, creaminess and incredible flavors. Delectable desserts have included apricot confit on almond crumble with refreshing bay leaf-ice cream.

▨ 710 Montgomery St. (bet. Jackson & Washington Sts.)

℘ (415) 359-1000 — **WEB:** www.nicosf.com

▨ Lunch Tue – Fri Dinner Tue – Sat   PRICE: $$$

PERBACCO 🍴○

Italian • *Contemporary décor*

MAP: C3

Slick financial types flex their expense accounts at this longtime Northern Italian retreat. Its polished décor belies a comforting menu of house-made pastas and items like roast chicken and meatballs at lunch, with slightly more refined takes at dinner. Dishes are executed with care—from slow-roasted vitello tonnato and semolina-dusted petrale sole to handmade pastas.

The space is larger inside than it looks, with plenty of booths and seats at the gleaming marble bar up front to the buzzy tables in the back with a view of the open-plan kitchen. Well-versed servers will encourage saving room for the end of the meal—as the cheese display, an impressive selection of grappas and the inventive, delicious desserts are all highlights.

230 California St. (bet. Battery & Front Sts.)

(415) 955-0663 — **WEB:** www.perbaccosf.com

Lunch Mon – Fri Dinner Mon – Sat

PRICE: $$

THE SLANTED DOOR 🍴○

Vietnamese • *Contemporary décor*

MAP: D3

Reservations are a challenge at this modern stunner with a killer view of the Bay Bridge. The Slanted Door has managed to stay atop tourists' hit lists even as its Northern Californian spin on Vietnamese food has steadily become less inspired. It's an efficient and professional place, but with little warmth; the hospitality is hit-or-miss at best.

Instead of the cellophane noodles with crab or overpriced shaking beef, diners should stick to more solid offerings like gau choy gow, featuring pan-fried dumplings with Gulf shrimp and garlic chives accompanied by a zippy soy and fish-sauce dip. Take advantage of this kitchen's varied repertoire by sampling more than one of their vegetable sides, like the crisp and spicy broccoli with pressed tofu.

1 Ferry Building (at The Embarcadero)

(415) 861-8032 — **WEB:** www.slanteddoor.com

Lunch & dinner daily

PRICE: $$

TRESTLE 😊

American • *Cozy*

♿

MAP: C1

In SF's dizzyingly expensive dining landscape, this hot spot, which offers a three-course menu for under $40, is an incredible steal—provided you're willing to sacrifice freedom of choice. The two options for each course change daily based on what's freshest: your repast may feature wild mushroom risotto, fork-tender short ribs with charred onions and romesco, as well as a milk chocolate devil's food pudding cake with Mission figs.

As with any killer deal, there are caveats: reservations are necessary (and hard to score) and the noise level is through the roof. However, this historic brick space is lots of fun, with cool, contemporary art and a namesake central trestle table. The fact that the price is right only adds to the overall allure.

▣ 531 Jackson St. (at Columbus Ave.)

☎ (415) 772-0922 — **WEB:** www.trestlesf.com

▣ Dinner nightly

PRICE: $$

WAYFARE TAVERN 🍴

Gastropub • *Elegant*

♿ ▤ ✉

MAP: C2

Though it feels like it's been around for decades, celebrity chef Tyler Florence's FiDi favorite is actually a toddler—at least in tavern years. In fact, it's become a standby for business types doing deals or enjoying post-work cocktails. Complete with dark wood and leather furnishings, a private billiards room and bustling bar, Wayfare Tavern has the air of a gastropub-turned-private club.

Hearty Americana with seasonal accents defines the menu. Meals here usually begin with piping-hot popovers, and then proceed to buttermilk-brined fried chicken—both of which are the chef's signature dishes. Even fish specials, like pan-roasted salmon with wilted leeks, are pure comfort, as is the strawberry cheesecake finished with a graham cracker tuile.

▣ 558 Sacramento St. (bet. Montgomery & Sansome Sts.)

☎ (415) 772-9060 — **WEB:** www.wayfaretavern.com

▣ Lunch & dinner daily

PRICE: $$$

MARINA

Following the havoc wreaked by the 1906 earthquake, San Francisco began reconstructing this sandy marshland by selling it to private developers. They, in turn, transformed the Marina into one of the most charming residential bubbles in town. Picture young families, tech wealth and an affluent vibe straight out of a 21st-century edition of The Yuppie Handbook, and you're in the Marina! Pacific Heights is considered the area's upper echelon—known for older family money and members who couldn't care less about being edgy. Here, bronzed residents can be found jogging with their dogs at Crissy Field, or sipping hot chocolate from the **Warming Hut**. Parents can be seen pushing strollers in haute couture boutiques or vying for parking in luxe German-engineered SUVs.

Marina girls as well as Pac Heights socialites are always on the go, and quick-bite cafés are their calling card. Find these denizens gathering at **Jane** for pastries

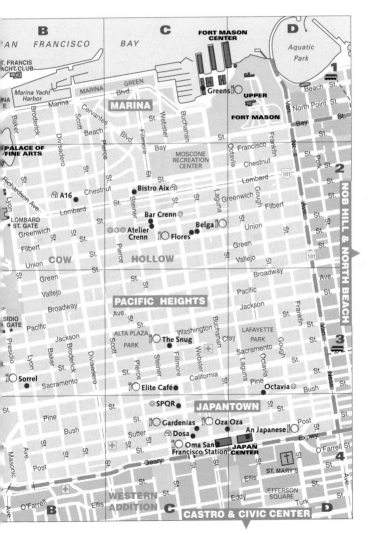

and paninis to nibble along with sips from a range of excellent teas, coffees and smoothies. **The Tipsy Pig** is a welcoming gastropub boasting an impressive bevy of bites and brews. True burger buffs in the Marina seem to have an insatiable appetite for locally founded **Roam Artisan Burgers**. Equally popular and sought-after are the contemporary, flavor-packed offerings at SoCal favorite, **Umami Burger**. In truth, quality cuisine has little to do with a Marina restaurant's success: the locals are unapologetically content to follow the buzz to the latest hot spot, where the clientele's beauty seems to be in direct proportion to its level of acclaim and popularity.

However, in the Presidio (home to Lucasfilm HQ) squads of tech geeks opt for convenience at nearby **Presidio Social Club**, cooking up tasty, regionally focused fare in a classic northern Californian setting. **Off the Grid-Fort Mason** is California's most coveted street food fair that gathers every spring through fall and features a fantastic collection of vendors and food trucks— from **Curry Up Now** and the **Lobsta Truck**, to **Johnny Doughnuts** and everything in between. Then again, food is mere sustenance to some, and simply a sponge for the champagne and chardonnay flowing at the district's numerous watering holes. The bar scene here is not only fun but also varied, with a playground for everyone. Oenophiles plan far in advance for the annual **ZAP Zinfandel Festival** in the winter; while preppy college kids swap European semester stories at sleek wine spots like **Nectar Wine Lounge**.

JAPANTOWN

Evident in the plethora of restaurants, shopping malls, banks and others businesses, the Asian community in the Marina is burgeoning. Thanks to the prominent Japanese population and abundant cultural events, **Japantown** is an exceptional and unique destination for tourists and locals alike. The Northern California Cherry Blossom Festival and **Nihonmachi Street Fair** bring to life every aspect of Asian-American heritage and living. Date night is always memorable at the **AMC Dine-In Kabuki 8** theater, which happens to be equipped with two full bars. For post-work snacks, prepared meals or even authentic imported ingredients, **Super Mira** is a market that offers a myriad of options. But for lunch on the run, grab excellent sushi, sashimi or bento boxes at nearby **Nijiya Market**. Visitors and laid-back locals sojourn to **Daikoku by Shiki** (in the Kintetsu Mall) if only to admire their assortment of beautiful Japanese ceramics, cast-iron teapots, sake sets and glazed bowls. Just a couple blocks from Japantown is perhaps the best spice shop in the country. Featuring walls lined with stacks of jars, **Spice Ace** boasts of extensively curated spices, extracts and salts that can all be sampled before purchase.

AN JAPANESE ⏸️🍴

Japanese • *Intimate*

MAP: D4

This tucked-away space in Japantown promises a great evening complete with specialized Japanese cuisine. At the helm of the kitchen is the talented chef, Kiyoshi Hayakawa, who along with his wife, the head server, plus a second sushi chef, provides a concise menu with a $30 à la carte minimum. Serious sushi lovers, however, can always go for the two nigiri-only menus or an all-out omakase with some hot appetizers.

The nigiri are excellent—their gently seasoned rice draped with exceptionally pristine fish. And for the finale—a buttery slice of seared Wagyu beef. Cooked dishes might include a vivid matsutake mushroom soup featuring an intense kelp broth.

Though the dress code is casual, the room is still small and very hushed, making for an intimate meal.

▨ 22 Peace Plaza, Ste. 510 (bet. Buchanan & Laguna Sts.)

✆ (415) 292-4886 — **WEB:** www.sushiansf.com

▨ Dinner Tue – Sat

PRICE: $$$

A16 😋

Italian • *Trendy*

❀ ♿

MAP: B2

An undying favorite of yuppies, families and tourists alike, A16 is known for rustic Italian cooking and a vast selection of delicious, unusual wines from all over the boot. Dinner reservations are indispensable, especially if you want one of the prime counter seats facing the open kitchen and wood-burning pizza oven.

The menu's pies, pastas and antipasti change with the season, so you could sample anything from a highly enjoyable zuppa di ceci verde flecked with green garbanzo beans and parsley, to perfectly al dente cavatelli tossed in a slow-cooked lamb sugo made extra hearty with the addition of plump borlotti beans. For dessert, look no further than the fig crostata with vanilla gelato, which tastes like the work of a particularly talented nonna.

▨ 2355 Chestnut St. (bet. Divisadero & Scott Sts.)

✆ (415) 771-2216 — **WEB:** www.a16sf.com

▨ Lunch Wed – Sun Dinner nightly

PRICE: $$

ATELIER CRENN ✿✿✿

Contemporary · Elegant

🐝 ♿ 🍴

At the hands of accomplished Chef Dominique Crenn, guests have rightly come to expect a thrilling meal at her singular atelier, replete with lustrous combinations, a keen understanding of flavors and an impeccable sense of grace. Another exclusory hallmark of dining here is the deeply hospitable and exemplary staff. They appear to virtually float in and out of the kitchen, which in turn prides itself on a sense of poetry expressed figuratively through dishes and quite literally via the actual poem composed by Chef Crenn to her father—it's even etched into marble and on full display.

Original is the name of this culinary game—one that is as thoughtful in serving brioche with cultured butter as it is with caviar crowned by turbot gelée and gold leaf. Poached sea bass with black truffles then happily wins over the most discerning of palates. It is indeed possible to dine here and not see any meat, but it's also never missed, thanks to the team's masterful hand with seafood.

The cheese course is stellar, but Pastry Chef/partner Juan Contreras' desserts make for a novel finale. A faux-coconut shell coated in dark chocolate and filled with pineapple as well as coconut foam takes home the gold.

🔲 3127 Fillmore St. (bet. Filbert & Pixley Sts.)
📞 (415) 440-0460 — **WEB:** www.ateliercrenn.com
🔲 Dinner Tue – Sat

PRICE: $$$$

BAR CRENN ✿

French • Chic

✿✿

MAP: C2

It may be located next to Chef Dominique Crenn's notable Atelier, but Bar Crenn is a destination in its own right. Designed with an eye on Paris during Les Années Folles with a splash of speakeasy, this room is a flea market-chic amalgam of cozy lounge furniture, glinting chandeliers and vintage accents. Fine silver, crystal, champagne and caviar complete the decadence. The wine list is presented as a gold-embossed book of wooden pages.

The classic French cooking strives to recreate many of the century's great dishes through recipes on loan from culinary masters, such as Alain Ducasse and Paul Bocuse. The concise menu evolves with the seasons as it offers traditional cooking alongside some of Bar Crenn's own creations. Start with the rendition of Chef Guy Savoy's huîtres en nage glacée, with two Washington State oysters on the half shell topped with oyster cream and a gelée made from its liquor. Chef Pierre Troisgros is honored with perfectly poached king salmon in a pool of beurre blanc with a few wilted leaves of lemony sorrel for tang. Finish with this kitchen's own take on an exquisite apple tart, stacking thin slices of apples that almost melt into one another beneath a rich caramel sauce.

▨ 3131 Fillmore St. (at Pixley St.)

☏ (415) 440-0460 — **WEB:** www.barcrenn.com

▨ Dinner Tue – Sat

PRICE: $$$

BELGA 🍴

Belgian · Brasserie

MAP: C2

Belgian brews and bites are the cornerstones of this buzzing brasserie. All the classics are accounted for: well-salted frites with garlic aïoli; bowls of mussels; and of course, house-made sausages—try the combo board, which comes with andouille, boudin noir, boudin blanc and currywurst, not to mention a generous bowl of spaetzle. From schnitzel to salads, there's something to satisfy all appetites (including a quinoa salad; that culinary siren song of the Lululemon-clad). Flatbreads and salads round things out.

The Euro-café vibe is fun with red banquettes, classic bistro chairs and marble floors to complement the big beer selection (both European and domestic) and cocktails. Happy hour, either at the bar or on the dog-friendly patio, is a madhouse.

■ 2000 Union St. (at Buchanan St.)
☏ (415) 872-7350 — **WEB:** www.belgasf.com
■ Lunch & dinner daily

PRICE: $$

BISTRO AIX 😊

Mediterranean · Bistro

MAP: C2

In the competitive Marina market, lovely Bistro Aix remains a charming and relatively affordable neighborhood option for thoughtfully made Southern French fare with a California touch. The dining room offers two distinct culinary experiences, beginning with seats in front at the convivial marble bar and small bistro tables. Beyond this, find the sunny bubble of the intimate back atrium, verdant with olive trees and flooded with natural light. A well-heeled crowd enlivens the space.

Dishes are simple and well executed, like roasted eggplant with toasted sesame seeds, gypsy peppers and a topping of creamy burrata; or the excellently grilled sea scallops with earthy chanterelles and silky beurre blanc. Thoughtfully chosen French wines complement each dish.

■ 3340 Steiner St. (bet. Chestnut & Lombard Sts.)
☏ (415) 202-0100 — **WEB:** www.bistroaix.com
■ Dinner Mon - Sat

PRICE: $$

DOSA 😊

Indian • Elegant

🍹 ♿ 🛋️   **MAP:** C4

Glamour infuses every inch of this stylish restaurant, whose soaring ceilings, colorful walls and swanky demeanor augment the bold and fragrantly spiced food. As the name suggests, dosas are indeed a highlight here. Warm servers will explain Cali-inspired takes on other South Indian dishes like almond ambur curry, which replaces traditional cashews with local almonds; or shake things up with idli fries, tailed by a Bengali gimlet with gin, curried nectar and lime. Desserts are every bit as exotic as the rest of the menu, and may reveal rasmalai—patties of fresh cheese in sweet cream flavored with cardamom and rosewater.

A second, smaller location on Valencia Street draws fans, while those in a hurry opt for fast casual at the East Bay sib, dosa by DOSA.

▨ 1700 Fillmore St. (at Post St.)
📞 (415) 441-3672 — **WEB:** www.dosasf.com
▨ Lunch Fri – Sun Dinner nightly   **PRICE:** $$

ELITE CAFÉ 🍴○

Southern • Contemporary décor

♿ 🛋️   **MAP:** C3

This Southern charmer might have you California dreaming with its array of seasonal salads and other lighter bites, but wise diners know to skip straight to the old-school goods: crunchy fried chicken (try the spicy "Nashville hot" version), buttery grits and tender, porky collard greens. Of course, you'll need to save room for pie. Thick and custardy chocolate pecan, to be exact.

Such an indulgent menu might not be expected from this cool, modern space set on a posh stretch of Fillmore Street, but Chef Chris Borges, a New Orleans native, ensures the authenticity of such faves as crawfish mac and cheese, blackened catfish and duck gumbo. Be sure to keep an eye out for daily specials, including half-priced fried chicken dinners on Tuesdays and wine bottles on Wednesdays.

▨ 2049 Fillmore St. (bet. California & Pine Sts.)
📞 (415) 346-8400 — **WEB:** www.theelitecafe.com
▨ Lunch Sat – Sun Dinner nightly   **PRICE:** $$

FLORES ⅋○

Mexican • *Colorful*

🍸 ♿ ⛱ 🎦 🛶   **MAP:** C2

It's always a fiesta at this lively spot on Cow Hollow's main drag, where you're as likely to find young families sharing a bowl of guac as you are Marina girls getting tipsy on mezcal margaritas. Patterned tiles, bright murals and chill beats create a modern vibe, and though you may have to wait (only limited reservations are available), the friendly staff will make it worth your while.

Flores is among the city's best upscale Mexican spots—with the bonuses of heftier portions and a lower price tag. You'll be able to taste the difference in the handmade corn tortillas that encase an oozy huitlacoche quesadilla, and the tender, citrusy carnitas. Save room for churros: the spicy "Mexican hot chocolate" dipping sauce is well worth the calories.

▨ 2030 Union St. (bet. Buchanan & Webster Sts.)

✆ (415) 796-2926 — **WEB:** www.floressf.com

▨ Lunch Sat – Sun Dinner nightly   **PRICE:** $$

GARDENIAS ⅋○

Californian • *Contemporary décor*

♿ ⛱   **MAP:** C4

Though it's moved across town from the Mission to the Fillmore, the former Woodward's Garden has maintained its tasteful, unpretentious vibe with a bolder, more current aspect. It now even has an actual garden, with a few outdoor tables for dining in the warmer months. Thoughtful service makes Gardenias an equally beloved destination among groups of millennials and leisurely couples on a dressy date night.

Owners Dana Tommasino and Margie Conard are local restaurant veterans. Their Californian cooking may not be cutting-edge, but it has a timeless appeal. Whether you're savoring fork-tender red wine-braised short ribs with celery root purée or a rustic plum and raspberry tart, it's the kind of seasonal, soul-warming food that never goes out of style.

▨ 1963 Sutter St. (bet. Fillmore & Webster Sts.)

✆ (415) 621-7122 — **WEB:** www.gardenias-sf.com

▨ Dinner nightly   **PRICE:** $$$

GREENS 🍴
Vegetarian · Rustic

♿ ♨

MAP: C1

Annie Somerville's pioneering vegetarian restaurant has been around since 1979. Still, fresh, energetic cuisine abounds, with a light touch and slight global inspiration. Brunch draws a big crowd, so be prepared to wait for those perfectly fried eggs over griddled potato cakes. Vegetarians and carnivores will rejoice after sampling the honest, colorful, down-to-earth seasonal entrées at dinner, followed by delightful desserts like a huckleberry upside down cake with a subtle kick from Meyer lemon.

Housed in historic Fort Mason, the warehouse-style space is rustic but refined, with sweeping views of the Golden Gate Bridge and sailboats on the Bay. It's pricey, but the pleasant ambience makes it worthwhile.

For a quick lunch, there's also a to-go counter.

▢ Building A, Fort Mason Center

☎ (415) 771-6222 — **WEB:** www.greensrestaurant.com

▢ Lunch Tue – Sun Dinner nightly   **PRICE: $$$**

HONG KONG LOUNGE II 👻
Chinese · Family

♿ 🍽

MAP: A4

If the bland peach exterior of this restaurant doesn't entice you, trust that a juicy treasure lies within: some of the Bay's best dim sum offered at lunch. Skipping the carts for a made-to-order approach, the sizable menu groans with winners, including flaky, buttery baked pork buns, sautéed pea shoots delectably flavored with garlic and one of the best egg custard tarts you're ever likely to taste—even if you've visited Hong Kong.

Throw in above-average tea options and a sizable vegetarian menu, and it's no wonder that this tiny gem draws legendary waits on weekend mornings. Just don't turn tail and head for the other Hong Kong Lounge further down Geary—despite their names, the two aren't affiliated, and the food isn't quite the same.

▢ 3300 Geary Blvd. (at Parker Ave.)

☎ (415) 668-8802 — **WEB:** www.hongkonglounge2.com

▢ Lunch & dinner Wed – Mon   **PRICE: $$**

OCTAVIA ✿

Californian • *Chic*

MAP: D3

Chef/owner Melissa Perello may already be a local culinary personality at Frances, but her sequel, Octavia, shines even brighter from its home in the tony lower Pacific Heights. Packed with a dynamic and diverse group of diners, the airy, open space feels minimalist and bistro-chic, from the white-tiled kitchen to those raw-wood benches lined with woolen pillows. Service is polite and efficient.

Chef Perello has a gift for elevating straightforward dishes through the use of superb ingredients and beautifully executed technique, beginning with a smoked trout fillet on a bed of cream cheese with green mustard seeds and steamed potatoes. Kale salad is deliciously crunchy and nicely matched with diced fennel, creamy avocado, salty aged parmesan and breadcrumbs in a light vinaigrette. A petite filet of beef arrives tender and perfectly cooked to order, atop potatoes mashed with olive oil, grilled broccolini and cabbage dressed in rapini pesto. Desserts are imaginative and masterful, so save room for their completely new take on profiteroles, soft and fresh, filled with poppy seed-ice cream that is accented with tart rhubarb and kumquat.

Tables fill early, so be sure to reserve well in advance.

▨ 1701 Octavia St. (at Bush St.)
✆ (415) 408-7507 — **WEB:** www.octavia-sf.com
▨ Dinner nightly

PRICE: $$$

OMA SAN FRANCISCO STATION 🍴

Japanese • *Simple*

&

MAP: C4

This simple wood counter serves some of the area's better nigiri, right from the corner of a mall in Japantown. Blink and you'll miss it—Oma is about the size of a kiosk near the Webster Street exit.

Behind the counter, find Chef Wilson Chan deftly slicing each morsel before your eyes, artfully placing it before every guest, piece by piece. Choose from five- eight- or twelve-piece prix-fixe menus to match your appetite and budget, though prices are reasonable for such quality. Clean flavors and rich, silky fish are the hallmarks of dining here. Highlights include a lightly torched wild star butterfish that melts in the mouth, and a delicious handroll combining chopped bluefin tuna balanced with pickled yellow daikon wrapped in crisp nori.

▨ 1737 Post St. #337 (in Japan Center West)
✆ N/A — **WEB:** www.omasfstation.com
▨ Lunch & dinner daily
PRICE: $$$

OZA OZA 🍴

Japanese • *Intimate*

MAP: C4

This hidden gem in Japantown offers authentic kaiseki cuisine in a second-floor room seating just nine. Kyoto native, Tetsuro Ozawa, oversees the kitchen, while his wife (Gana) infuses this austere space with genuine hospitality. Expect a set menu of around eight courses, each with superb cyclical ingredients and thoughtful garnishes—imagine freshly shaved wasabi and house-made kombu pickles to fresh flowers.

Depending on the month, you might sup on deep-fried, seaweed-wrapped smelt and sea urchin with kabocha squash; or even red snapper rice in a gingery dashi broth. While an array of pristine sashimi is a perpetual highlight, regardless of the season, expect to begin with creamy, delicate tofu and conclude over sweet, chewy mochi with plum wine gelée.

▨ 1700 Post St. Ste. K (bet. Buchanan St. & Webster Sts.)
✆ (415) 674-4400 — **WEB:** www.ozaoza.net
▨ Dinner Tue – Sat
PRICE: $$$$

THE SNUG 🍴

Gastropub • *Contemporary décor*

🍸 🍺 ♿ 🖨 🍃   **MAP:** C3

In keeping with its location on boutique-y Fillmore Street, The Snug reimagines the neighborhood bar in a very au courant context. Dark wood is subbed for sun-drenched white walls, big windows are lined with an array of house-made tinctures and visitors might even spot that rarest of SF species—children—alongside the laptop-bound techies wrapping up the day with a 4 P.M. craft beer.

Upscale but unpretentious, The Snug's menu is serious for a bar, spanning both snacks (think green garlic fritters rolled in an umami-rich wasabi pea powder) and more substantial plates like charred octopus with smoked avocado purée, ramps and melon. They meld nicely with the refreshing draft cocktails, like the nitrogenated, mezcal-spiked take on a Last Word.

◻ 2301 Fillmore St. (at Clay St.)
℘ (415) 562-5092 — **WEB:** www.thesnugssf.com
◻ Lunch Sat – Sun Dinner Tue – Sun   **PRICE:** $$

SOCIALE 😊

Italian • *Romantic*

🏠 🖨   **MAP:** A4

Italian in name but Californian in spirit, Sociale is a go-to for comfort fare that blends the best of both worlds. Chef/owner Tia Harrison crafts wonders; creamy burrata over pumpkin purée and melt-in-your-mouth braised pork belly are just two winners. Dessert is a must; you'll be hard-pressed to find a table that can resist ordering the signature chocolate oblivion cake, a sinfully rich ganache enhanced with olive oil, sea salt and amaretti cookie crumble.

Located at the end of an alley with a heated patio, the vibe here is bistro-chic, with a hint of European flair accented by the warm, accommodating staff and the Italian and French chanteuses on the playlist. It's the kind of neighborhood gem that everyone wishes they had on their block.

◻ 3665 Sacramento St. (bet. Locust & Spruce Sts.)
℘ (415) 921-3200 — **WEB:** www.sfsociale.com
◻ Dinner Mon - Sat   **PRICE:** $$

SORREL 🍴○

Californian • *Contemporary décor*

 ♿ ⛲

Presidio Heights residents are already obsessed with this Cal-Ital joint, which got its start as a pop-up before carving out this cool and classy niche in the city's ground zero for low-key millionaires. With its deep navy banquettes and swirling marble bar, it's an of-the-moment retreat for the moneyed, emphasizing impressive plating that's photo-perfect.

Handmade pastas star on the menu, like perfectly textured orecchiette and broccoli di cicco bathed in a chili-spiked pork sugo. Other dishes are more ambitious, most notably a brûléed foie gras torchon artfully strewn with pickled rhubarb and lavender. Wrap things up with a soft and delicate brown butter vanilla mousse, accented by sourdough ice cream and caramelized milk jam.

▨ 3228 Sacramento St. (bet. Lyon St. & Presidio Ave.)

✆ (415) 525-3765 — **WEB:** www.sorrelrestaurant.com

▨ Dinner Tue – Sat

PRICE: $$$

Look for our symbol 🍸
spotlighting restaurants
with a serious cocktail list.

SPQR ✿

Italian • *Contemporary décor*

✿ &

Pleasant and homey with excellent modern Italian cooking, there is little wonder why this destination is always bustling. Book in advance and assume that the dining counter reserved for walk-ins is already overflowing for the night. The space itself is narrow with tightly packed wood tables and furnishings; it would seem cramped were it not for the soaring ceiling, skylights and open kitchen to brighten the mood. No matter where you look, the passion and enthusiasm for Italian specialties are palpable here—even contagious.

From antipasti to dolci, celebrated Chef Matthew Accarrino's extensive menu evolves with the seasons, yet remains as satisfying as it is impressive. Memorable and very creative pastas include the supremely rich linguine Alfredo with abalone liver, grated bottarga and the faintest hint of Meyer lemon. A degustazione of suckling pig arrives as six unique preparations, including medallions of succulent loin, slices of crisp-edged porchetta and a cool terrine with pops of mustard seed.

Desserts feature the wonderfully sweet and tart flavors of thick and creamy maple panna cotta topped with wine-poached apple, a cloud of whipped cream and cookie crumble.

▧ 1911 Fillmore St. (bet. Bush & Pine Sts.)

℘ (415) 771-7779 — **WEB:** www.spqrsf.com

▧ Lunch Sat - Sun Dinner nightly

PRICE: $$$

SPRUCE ✿
Californian • Chic

Set in one of San Francisco's snazziest neighborhoods, Spruce draws a regular following of wealthy retirees and corporate types by day. Evenings bring couples out for date night. The dining room, with its cathedral-style ceilings and skylight, is masculine yet modern—think studded leather chairs and splashes of charcoal and chocolate. A small front café serves coffee and pastries, while the marble bar lures happy-hour crowds for a cocktail or glass of wine from the extensive list.

Micro-seasonal and thoroughly Californian, Spruce spotlights cooking that's both simple and undeniably elegant. Rustic and homey starters may include hand-shaped ravioli filled with fresh ricotta and bathed in a broth of tart whey with fava leaf purée. A roulade of guinea hen stuffed with pork and duck sausage is exquisitely moist, juicy and accompanied by thick fingers of nutty-sweet brown ale toast that is perfect for sopping up every last drop.

For dessert, a dense and decadent crème fraîche cheesecake is thick and creamy, with sweet vanilla flavor and a classic graham-cracker crust. Juicy citrus segments and a quenelle of brilliantly tart Makrut lime ice cream add a delicious bit of zing.

▦ 3640 Sacramento St. (bet. Locust & Spruce Sts.)
☎ (415) 931-5100 — **WEB:** www.sprucesf.com
▦ Lunch & dinner daily

PRICE: $$$

MISSION

It's like the sun never goes down in the Mission—a bohemian paradise dotted with palm trees and doted on by scores of artists, activists, as well as a thriving Hispanic community. Here, urban life is illustrated through graffiti murals decorating the walls of funky galleries, thrift shops and independent bookstores. Sidewalk stands burst with fresh plantains, nopales and the juiciest limes this side of the border. Mission markets are known to be among the best in town and include **La Palma Mexicatessen** teeming with homemade papusas, chips and fresh cheeses. **Lucca Ravioli** is loved for its legion of imported Italian goods; and the petite grocer, **Bi-Rite**, is big on prepared foods and flowers. Across the street, **Bi-Rite Creamery** is a cult favorite for ice cream. Moving on from markets to hip coffee haunts, **Ritual Coffee Roasters** is one of the leaders of the pack. Join their fan base in single file outside the door, order a special roast from the barista and find yourself in awe of this pleasing, very potent berry. Coffee connoisseurs also pay their respects at the original **Philz Coffee** for brews that cannot be beat, while green tea addicts join in on the fun at **Stonemill Matcha**, proffering Japanese-inspired bites, as well as vibrant matcha drinks.

CLASSIC MEETS CUTTING-EDGE

The Mission is home to many contemporary hangouts, although those bargain mercados and dollar stores might suggest otherwise. **Dynamo Donut + Coffee** over on 24th Street is a dreamy retreat for these fried and sugary parcels of dough, complete with delectable flavors such as lemon-buttermilk and chocolate-star anise. **Walzwerk** charms with East German kitsch and is the go-to spot for traditional delights; while carb fiends know to stop by **The Sandwich Place** for freshly baked bread loaded with flavorful fillings. Here in the Mission, pizza reigns supreme and thin-crust lovers are happy to wait in line at **Pizzeria Delfina** for a wickedly good slice with crisped edges. A

destination in its own right, **Tartine Bakery's** exceptional breads, pastries and pressed sandwiches are arguably unmissable. However, to best experience this region's range of culinary talents, forgo the table and chairs and pull up at a curb on Linda Street, where a vigilant street food scene is brimming with a wealth of international eats.

DAYTIME DELIGHTS

The city's hottest neighborhood also offers a cool range of sweets. For instance, a banana split is downright retro-licious when served at the Formica counter of 90-year-old **St. Francis Fountain**. If that's not enough, the sundaes here are made with Mitchell's Ice Cream, famous since 1953. Modish flavors like grasshopper pie and Kahlua mocha cream are in regular rotation at the newer **Humphry Slocombe**; while **Mission Pie** is another local gem that tempts with a spectrum of goodies—both sweet and savory. For more bold plates, **Plow** in Potrero Hill is a top breakfast and brunch hit. The space is small but massively popular, so

expect to wait a while before your first bite of lemon-ricotta pancake—there's even a menu for the little "plowers" who arrive by stroller. At lunch head to Peru by way of abuela-approved **Cholo Soy** for authentic, homemade and always-affordable fare, but when it comes to tacos, it's a toss up on whether **El Gallo Giro** or **El Tonayense** takes the title for best truck in town.

NIGHT BITES

The **Monk's Kettle** brags a beer list beyond par, with around 200 rotating craft brews on their carte. But, if heady cocktails are what you crave, then dash over to **Trick Dog** for tantalizing concoctions and creative small plates that go a long way in sating a late-night appetite. Then dance the night away (as well as these indulgences) at **El Rio** on Salsa Sunday—the dive bar with a bustling back patio. Growling stomachs also seem game to brave the harsh lighting at the many taquerias around, including **Taqueria Cancún** for a veggie burrito or **El Farolito** for mind-blowing meats.

Mission
Bernal Heights
Potrero Hill

C

Casey's Pizza

China Basin

MISSION BAY COMMONS PARK

MISSION BAY

UCSF Mission Bay

UCSF-MISSION BAY KORET QUAD

MISSION BAY CONFERENCE CTR.

South St.

16th St.

Mariposa

17th JACKSON PLGD. Mariposa

Papito

18th

19th

POTRERO HILL

20th

20th St

DOGPATCH

'aina

22nd

CALTRAIN 22ND ST. STATION

Piccino

POTRERO HILL RECR. CENTER

Serpentine

CENTRAL WATERFRONT

23rd St

23rd

24th

25th

25th

26th

Cesar

Chavez

Marin

Marin

Islais

Creek

Channel

Amador St.

Davidson

Evans

Cargo

Evans

Hudson

Innes

Newhall

Evans

INDIA BASIN

Hudson/Innes

Kirkwood/La Salle

Phelps

Newcombe

Oakdale

La Salle

Mendell

Middle Point Rd.

Hunters

SILVER TERRACE

Oakdale/Palou

Newhall

Palou

Lane

Hudson

HILLTOP PARK

Innes Ave.

C

D

D **Mission**

1

SAN

FRANCISCO

BAY

PIER 54

Central Basin

Francois

Illinois

2

PIER 94

3

PIER 96

Jennings

Point Blvd.

4

73

'ĀINA ⏦

Hawaiian • *Trendy*

♿ ⛲ 🛏

MAP: C2

Catch some aloha vibes at this Hawaiian pop-up gone permanent in the Dogpatch, which imports many of its ingredients directly from the islands. The brunch menu riffs on all the classics, from house-made "Spam" musubi in lettuce wraps to warm, fluffy malasada doughnuts stuffed with guava custard and rolled in palm sugar. Binchotan-charred octopus over kalo coconut cream is a must order, while ti leaf-steamed trout with smoked mushrooms and crispy trout skin chips is perfect for sharing. The space isn't glamorous, but it's relaxed and comfortable, with beautiful wood tables, greenery and floods of light.

Once the weekend arrives, the six-seat chef's counter plays host to a tasting menu of experimental dishes. There are just two seatings, so plan ahead.

◼ 900 22nd St. (at Minnesota St.)
📞 (415) 814-3815 — **WEB:** www.ainasf.com
◼ Lunch & dinner Wed – Sun

PRICE: $$

CASEY'S PIZZA ⏦

Pizza • *Contemporary décor*

♿

MAP: C1

After making its name as a food truck, Casey Crynes' pizza party has come indoors in fast-developing Mission Bay, where it's caught on hard with the condo-dwelling millennials who've swept into the neighborhood. This industrial space has all the of-the-moment markers, including cement walls, subway tiles, pendant lights and a roaring clientele.

The menu is simple and appealing, starring a handful of pizzas, seasonal salads and plenty of craft beers. Spice things up with the "Hot Pie," a combo of sizzling pepperoni, hot cherry peppers and feta; or go full Californian with a kale pie composed with bacon and red onion. At the end, opt for a hot fudge sundae, made adult-friendly with the addition of dark fudge sauce, sea salt and Luxardo cherries.

◼ 1170 4th St. (bet. Channel & Long Bridge Sts.)
📞 (415) 814-2482 — **WEB:** www.caseyspizzas.com
◼ Dinner Tue – Sat

PRICE: $$

AL'S PLACE ❀

Californian • *Contemporary décor*

♿ ☂

MAP: A3

Vegetables are the star of the menu at this bright blue oasis on busy Valencia Street, even though it adheres to a mostly pescatarian philosophy, with meat options also available on the side. Chef/owner Aaron London (a.k.a. AL) is wildly adept with the seasons' bounty, making a dish of blistered squash with pickled kohlrabi, hummus and creamy burrata feel as complex and luxurious as the offerings at a steakhouse.

London's menu is chockablock with creativity, from the brine-pickled French fries and flavorful ras el hanout olives that kick off each meal, to the silky grits topped with tangy goat's milk curds, Brussels sprouts, chanterelles and yuzu. At times, the combinations can read like a five-car pile-up—cured trout, mashed turnips and bagna cauda? But the crew always manages to smoothly navigate the layers of flavor, blazing new trails in diners' imaginations.

Like the menu, Al's space is bright, open and cheerful, with plenty of natural light, bold colors and a casual but engaging staff. Embrace this energy, perhaps with a glass of French wine or a craft beer, and let the boisterous, creative spirit of the restaurant win you over.

▪ 1499 Valencia St. (at 26th St.)

℘ (415) 416-6136 — **WEB:** www.alsplacesf.com

▪ Dinner Wed - Sun

PRICE: $$

ASTER ✿

Californian • *Contemporary décor*

&

The idea of a fine-dining space that features mainstream music, spare décor and young clientele in jeans may seem overdone, but Aster makes everything appear new and inventive, never forced. Set in a quiet residential neighborhood, its tawny banquettes, wood tables and strands of lights fashion a studied yet casual vibe that doesn't feel like it is trying too hard. The staff is attentive yet friendly, and eager to please.

The kitchen heightens every element of healthy, light Californian cuisine made from only the best organic ingredients around.

Like the space, the food has no sense of excessive complication; everything is cooked, seasoned and paired perfectly. Here, a simple garden salad is a graceful blend of tangerines, turnips and flowers tossed with pumpkin seeds over a bed of mashed avocado. This might be followed by a generous trout fillet, seared to crisp-skin perfection and set atop snap pea purée. Lighter main courses leave room for enjoying their excellent desserts, such as a sweet poached pear stuffed with vanilla ice cream and set beneath a crunchy pistachio scone and pear coulis. The fixed-price menu is reasonable for the trendsetting combination of cuisine and space.

▨ 1001 Guerrero St. (at 22nd St.)

✆ (415) 875-9810 — **WEB:** www.astersf.com

▨ Dinner nightly

PRICE: $$$

CALIFORNIOS ✿✿

Mexican • Chic

MAP: B2

Set in a bohemian area known for its street tacos and bare bones eateries, Californios aims to elevate the Mission district's south-of-the-border fare to contemporary Mexican cuisine and it more than succeeds. A complex, layered mole here isn't just likely to please—it's bound to turn your entire understanding of this nation's cuisine on its head.

The luxurious space only ups the appeal. Caramel-hued banquettes pop against dark-lacquered walls, while chandeliers and shelves of cookbooks further punctuate the upscale mien of the intimate room. You'll feel as though you're dining in Chef Val M. Cantu's very own atelier, made extra personal by the deeply knowledgeable staff, who seem to pride themselves on knowing every detail about the dishes coming out of the open kitchen.

One lengthy tasting menu is served nightly. It changes often, but expect inventive items like squid-ink tostadas heaped with guacamole, Monterey squid and truffles. A wonderfully spicy flauta is filled with duck barbacoa; while butter-poached lobster is tucked into blue corn tortillas and topped with fennel and aji amarillo. Sorbet made from local guavas, nestled in a spread of pistachio butter is an astounding send-off.

▮ 3115 22nd St. (bet. Capp St. & Van Ness Ave.)

℘ (415) 757-0994 — **WEB:** www.californiossf.com

▮ Dinner Tue – Sat   **PRICE:** $$$$

CENTRAL KITCHEN ⚭

Californian • *Contemporary décor*

    ♿ 🚻

MAP: B2

A chic and sleek crowd of area foodies gathers at this trendy restaurant, nestled in a complex and right beside sister shop/deli Salumeria (by night it transforms for private parties), cocktail bar Trick Dog and coffee shop Sightglass. Wend your way to the central courtyard, with a trickling fountain and glass doors leading into the main space, where a vast open kitchen with a wood-burning hearth faces the simple wood tables.

Along the way, you might taste a mound of burrata surrounded by melon cubes, cucumber slices and purslane tossed in a chili-herb vinaigrette. Gamey pork trotter agnolotti is balanced by lemon verbena; while smoked short ribs dotted with harissa and served with charred eggplant purée and mint sauce are fork-tender and flavor-packed.

◻ 3000 20th St. (at Florida St.)

📞 (415) 826-7004 — **WEB:** www.centralkitchensf.com

◻ Dinner nightly

PRICE: $$$

DELFINA 👓

Italian • *Trattoria*

    ♿

MAP: A2

One of the city of San Francisco's greats for rustic Italian meals, Delfina is nestled on a block of gems for food lovers, including Bi-Rite (and its creamery), Tartine Bakery and sister spot, Pizzeria Delfina. But even with this rarefied competition, Delfina continues to book well in advance and draws long lines for its few walk-in seats.

The simple, yet lively dining room is attended to by a warm cadre of servers, and the bill of fare shifts with the seasons. Soul-satisfying dishes might include house-made francobolli with prosciutto and mascarpone, as well as perfectly roasted chicken with silky olive oil-mashed potatoes. Seasonal desserts, like a warm pear Charlotte with salted caramel and brandy crème anglaise, are notably delightful.

◻ 3621 18th St. (bet. Dolores & Guerrero Sts.)

📞 (415) 552-4055 — **WEB:** www.delfinasf.com

◻ Dinner nightly

PRICE: $$

COMMONWEALTH ✿
Contemporary · Simple

&

The cool kids of the Mission flock to this upscale spot, all sleek vibe and warm welcome. Set on one of the neighborhood's grittiest stretches, the one-story brick building wears its history in the form of an old painted doughnut ad. And though frosted windows keep the environs at bay, Commonwealth cares for its own by donating a portion of profits from each night's seven-course tasting menu to charity.

Everything here is offered à la carte, but most opt for the aforementioned option, for which the cheerful servers are happy to mix and match dishes. The results are as creative and ambitious as the techie-hipster clientele, with breathtakingly beautiful, Asian-influenced bites: think sea urchin under a canopy of seaweed brioche topped with tomato and watermelon pearls, or seared diver scallop in a corn-and-white miso emulsion with tarragon and fennel.

Along the way, expect surprises utilizing the best seasonal produce, like tangy sudachi sorbet in a pool of sake soda, or pressed cantaloupe infused with honey and togarashi. All of this pairs nicely with an intriguing, terroir-driven wine list—or if you're feeling adventurous, a nightly frozen cocktail chilled with liquid nitrogen.

◾ 2224 Mission St. (bet. 18th & 19th Sts.)

✆ (415) 355-1500 — **WEB:** www.commonwealthsf.com

◾ Dinner nightly

PRICE: $$

FARMHOUSE KITCHEN THAI 😋

Thai • *Colorful*

  ♿

MAP: B2

For authentic Thai flavors, this lively gem is hard to beat—boasting a dedicated following among the young techies and families who reside in this area's industrial lofts. The space is eclectic with art installations and flower arrangements that spin to the seasons. It's the kind of affordable spot designed for repeat business.

The menu is vast but mostly unchanging, with dishes that display careful attention to detail, bold flavors and top ingredients—think marinated flank steak rolled around cucumber or coconut- and turmeric-marinated barbecue chicken with sticky rice. The herbal rice salad tossing green mango and dried shrimp is a signature and deservedly so.

An equally dazzling meal is assured at the newly minted sib in Jack London Square.

  ▦ 710 Florida St. (bet. 19th & 20th Sts.)
  ✆ (415) 814-2920 — **WEB:** www.farmhousesf.com
  ▦ Lunch & dinner daily

PRICE: $$

FLOUR + WATER 🍴

Italian • *Trendy*

  ♿   🖲

MAP: B2

As the name implies, two ingredients create a world of possibilities at this always-packed Mission hot spot. Neapolitan pizzas and handmade pastas (like al dente garganelli with whole-grain mustard and braised pork) will have you sighing after each bite, and a selection of more traditional mains (such as seared duck breast with chanterelles and pecorino-dusted charred Brussels sprouts) score every bit as big as the noodles and pies.

Laid-back service, up-to-the-moment music and a buzzy, effervescent vibe make flour + water the epitome of California cool.

Throw in a glass of their refined Italian wine, along with an alluring dessert like the salted caramel apple tart, and you can see why getting a table here is well worth the challenge.

  ▦ 2401 Harrison St. (at 20th St.)
  ✆ (415) 826-7000 — **WEB:** www.flourandwater.com
  ▦ Dinner nightly

PRICE: $$

FOXSISTER ††○
Korean • Colorful

MAP: B3

It's always a party at this boisterous 24th Street spot, where the wild décor (think: mirrored walls, a purple bar and disco-ball bathroom) is almost as blaring as the old-school hip-hop soundtrack. But it's not all about flash at Foxsister—while the young and hip gravitate here, Chef/owner Brandon Kirksey's Korean menu is serious enough to draw gourmands, regulars and visitors.

You'll see why once you sample his perfectly marinated kalbi, which arrives on a sizzling platter with all the trappings for lettuce wraps. Fried chicken is crispy, sticky and finger-licking good, while the vermicelli noodles with sweet, meaty Dungeness crab is a swoon-worthy treat. Pair it with a frosty Korean lager or fruity soju slushie for a playful finish.

■ 3161 24th St. (bet. S. Van Ness Ave. & Shotwell St.)
℘ (415) 829-7814 — **WEB:** www.foxsistersf.com
■ Dinner nightly

PRICE: $$

GRACIAS MADRE ††○
Vegetarian • Rustic

&

MAP: A2

Less mamacita and more Mother Earth, Gracias Madre is definitely not just another laid-back Mexican cantina. This is thanks largely due to its strict sourcing standards (tortillas are made from scratch with heirloom corn) and wholesome plant-based food. Large portions showcase plenty of local produce, but that nacho cheese drizzled all over your butternut squash- and caramelized onion-filled tortilla is crafted from—nuts, of course. These colorful, vegan items explode with flavor, as seen in the enchiladas con mole packed with potato, zucchini and peas, then topped with tomatillo salsa, crema and avocado. The surprises keep coming throughout the meal.

Take note of the flan, which created sans eggs still manages to have that trademark wobble.

■ 2211 Mission St. (bet. 18th & 19th Sts.)
℘ (415) 683-1346 — **WEB:** www.gracias-madre.com
■ Lunch & dinner daily

PRICE: $$

IZAKAYA RINTARO 😊

Japanese • *Minimalist*

                                              MAP: B1

Delicate izakaya cuisine with a produce-centric NorCal sensibility awaits at this Japanese sanctum, which transforms even the most humble dishes into works of art. Freshly made soft tofu is infused with fragrant bergamot peel, while meaty king trumpet mushrooms join classic chicken thighs and tender tsukune on the menu of smoky, caramelized charcoal-grilled skewers. The blancmange, infused with white sesame and topped with sweet black soybeans, is particularly unmissable.

Housed in the former Chez Spencer, which was destroyed in a fire, Rintaro has kept its predecessor's gorgeous (and charred) arched ceiling beams, but added a delicate, wood-framed bar and booths. The result is a serene environment perfect for sharing and sampling the exquisite food.

▨ 82 14th St. (bet. Folsom & Trainor Sts.)

✆ (415) 589-7022 — **WEB:** www.izakayarintaro.com

▨ Lunch Fri – Sun Dinner nightly   **PRICE: $$**

KHAMSA 🍴

Moroccan • *Contemporary décor*

                                              MAP: B1

Set in a luxury condo building amidst a row of auto body shops, this relaxed urban oasis brings the charm of Morocco to an otherwise divey stretch of the Mission. Inside, you'll find a cheerful turquoise dining room bedecked with colorful tiles, a small courtyard for outdoor dining and a diverse clientele—ranging from young techies to women dressed in traditional garb.

The pricey food boasts a few Californian accents, like Moroccan-inspired salads featuring seasonal produce, but most dishes are designed to please purists. The basteeya pie with shredded chicken and almonds in a phyllo crust is nothing less than flaky precision; while chicken tagine with preserved lemon followed by pistachio baklava and a pot of mint tea is all sweetness and appeal.

▨ 1503 15th St. (bet. Capp St. & Van Ness Ave.)

✆ (628) 233-1503 — **WEB:** www.khamsasf.com

▨ Dinner nightly   **PRICE: $$**

LA CICCIA ¶⃝

Italian • *Mediterranean décor*

MAP: A4

Sardinian cuisine takes the spotlight at this family-run charmer, which draws a loyal crowd of Noe Valley regulars—particularly parents on a well-earned date night. The intimate, dark green dining room is always full, and nestled right up against the kitchen, from which the chef regularly pops out to greet guests with welcoming banter.

Start with the house-made bread and the home-cured salumi of the day (think citron-studded mortadella). The pasta lunga with cured tuna heart slivers twirls fresh, delicious linguini with sea urchin and tomato, while an entrée of stewed goat is gamey but tender, served alongside braised cabbage, black olives and fried capers. For a pleasant conclusion, cap it all off with the fluffy and airy ricotta-saffron cake.

■ 291 30th St. (at Church St.)
✆ (415) 550-8114 — **WEB:** www.laciccia.com
■ Dinner Tue – Sat

PRICE: $$$

LA TAQUERIA ¶⃝

Mexican • *Simple*

MAP: B3

This local favorite always has a queue because everyone loves it—from tech bros in hoodies to families out for Sunday lunch. The jovial Miguel Jara runs this show—you may find him working the register or handing out roses to customers. Counter service makes it feel no-frills, but this is the kind of place that relishes in its simplicity.

Everything here is supremely fresh, as exhibited in the open kitchen with its mountains of char-grilled steak alongside vibrant tomato, cilantro and onion. The carne asada super burrito is everything you dream it should be. It may not be on the menu, but order your taco "Dorado-style," which begins as a corn tortilla crisped on the plancha, layered with cheese and another tortilla before getting loaded with toppings.

■ 2889 Mission St. (bet. 24th & 25th Sts.)
✆ (415) 285-7117 — **WEB:** N/A
■ Lunch Wed – Sun Dinner Wed – Sun

PRICE: ⊜

LAZY BEAR ❀ ❀
Contemporary · Chic

MAP: A2

Communal eating is at the heart of this fine-dining dinner party. Lazy Bear may have its origins as an underground phenom, but today anyone can try to score a seat. That is, after jumping through a few virtual hoops: buy a ticket in advance and wait for an e-mail listing house rules to be followed in earnest. Rest assured this is all worth the effort.

The nightly tasting menu is dished out in a cool, bi-level warehouse and starts upstairs in the loft with aperitifs and snacks, like tempura beer-battered maitake mushrooms with a sour cream and onion dip or pig's head cheese with black truffle shavings. Then move downstairs to a dining room boasting two giant tree slabs as communal tables, each lined with 20 chairs. Diners are given a pencil and pamphlet informing them of the menu (with space for note-taking underneath) and are invited to enter the kitchen to chat with the talented cooks themselves. This leaves the young crowd dreamy-eyed with chef worship.

Highlights include smoked trout on a blanket of trout roe, sorrel and brown rice, or dry-aged Sonoma County duck with a wonderful sweet and bitter yin and yang, courtesy of fermented kumquat and partially scorched broccolini.

▨ 3416 19th St. (bet. Mission & San Carlos Sts.)
℘ (415) 874-9921 — **WEB:** www.lazybearsf.com
▨ Dinner Tue – Sat

PRICE: $$$$

LOCANDA 🍴

Italian • *Osteria*

MAP: A1

This chic Roman-style osteria packs in the hipsters with a lively scene, killer cocktails and inspired pastas, like radiatore tossed in tomato-lamb ragù with pecorino and hints of fresh mint. Hearty main courses might include smoky and tender pancetta-wrapped chicken served over nutty farro verde. None of this is surprising, considering Locanda is from the team behind Mission favorite, Delfina.

Reservations here are a tough ticket, but the attire and vibe are casual and welcoming (if noisy). Can't get a table? Seats at the bar, where the full menu is served, are a solid backup.

Locanda's ultra-central address makes parking a challenge, so plan on using the valet or allotting extra time.

557 Valencia St. (bet. 16th & 17th Sts.)
(415) 863-6800 — **WEB:** www.locandasf.com
Lunch Sat – Sun Dinner Wed – Sun

PRICE: $$

THE MORRIS 🍴

Contemporary • *Neighborhood*

MAP: B2

After working at a number of SF's top restaurants, veteran sommelier Paul Einbund has settled down at this neighborhood charmer in the Mission, named for his father. Unsurprisingly, The Morris boasts a selection of wine (displayed in a handsome glass cellar), along with top-notch cocktails and a sophisticated yet highly craveable comfort-food menu.

Quell your hunger with slices of Tartine country loaf—baked just down the street—as you peruse the menu, which offers appealing bites both small (pork cracklins with honey and Aleppo pepper) and large (charred broccolini with succulent grilled squid in chili-lime dressing). Be sure to also sample their signature smoked duck. Brined for two days and aged for four, it is a smoky, tender and meaty marvel.

2501 Mariposa St. (at Hampshire St.)
(415) 612-8480 — **WEB:** www.themorris-sf.com
Lunch Mon – Fri Dinner Mon – Sat

PRICE: $$$

PAPITO ⟨icon⟩

Mexican • *Cozy*

⟨icons⟩

It might be French-owned (neighboring bistro Chez Maman is a sibling), but Papito is appealingly Mexican, as your first bite of the outstanding shrimp tacos, piled with spicy adobo and sweet mango salsa, will attest. An ear of caramelized, grilled corn slathered in spicy mayo, lime juice and cotija cheese will transport you to the streets of D.F., while the smoky coloradito sauce that bathes tender chicken enchiladas will have you scraping your plate for more. Papito's flavors are big, but its space is no more than a shoebox, so be prepared to wait or take your order to-go. If you dine in, the vibrant look matches the energetic food, with bright walls and a bustling side bar.

Note: Hayes Valley's Papito, once a satellite, now has different owners.

▨ 317 Connecticut St. (at 18th St.)
℘ (415) 695-0147 — **WEB:** www.papitosf.com
▨ Lunch & dinner daily

PRICE: ⟨icon⟩

PICCINO ⟨icon⟩

Italian • *Family*

⟨icons⟩

A progenitor of the increasingly hot Dogpatch restaurant scene, Piccino embodies this neighborhood's many flavors, drawing families with kids in tow, young tech types, gregarious retirees and more. Its memorable yellow exterior houses a relaxed, artsy-urban interior with lots of wood and natural light—a perfect venue for unwinding with friends.

Everyone comes here for deliciously blistered pizzas like the funghi, with roasted mushroom duxelles, sautéed wild mushrooms, stracchino and slivers of garlic. Though pizza is a focus, Piccino excels in appetizers like tender, skillfully prepared polpette in tomato sauce, and must-order desserts such as a delectable hazelnut-cocoa nib cake. Their adjacent coffee bar is an area favorite.

▨ 1001 Minnesota St. (at 22nd St.)
℘ (415) 824-4224 — **WEB:** www.piccino.com
▨ Lunch & dinner daily

PRICE: $$

RITU INDIAN SOUL FOOD 🍴○

Indian • *Colorful*

&

Formerly known as Dum, this hip Indian eatery has rebranded with a fresh menu of seasonal Californian produce ("Ritu" is Hindi for "seasons"). CIA-trained Chef/owner Rupam Bhagat remains at the helm, and longtime fans will recognize some of the kitchen's faves, including a light and frothy mango lassi that pairs delightfully with a reimagined version of the fried tandoori chicken featuring mustard-and curry-leaves.

Veterans of this cuisine shouldn't sleep on such seasonal gems either, like asparagus chaat with pickled carrots and spiced yogurt; or crisp artichoke pakoras. Even bog-standard butter chicken takes on new life here, with a tomato-rich gravy. Arrive on the later side to enjoy flaky naan and fluffy biryani along with the cool Mission crowds.

▪ 3111 24th St. (bet. Folsom & Shotwell Sts.)
✆ (415) 874-9045 — **WEB:** www.ritusf.com
▪ Lunch Fri – Sun Dinner Tue – Sun

PRICE: $$

SASAKI 🍴○

Japanese • *Minimalist*

&

Masaki Sasaki is well known among Bay Area sushi enthusiasts, having worked at a number of the area's top spots. Now, he's finally launched his own restaurant, housed on the ground floor of a quaint Mission Victorian. With only 12 seats at the counter, reservations are a must, but each guest is rewarded with personal attention from Masa-san.

As with many high-end temples of sushi, only one omakase-style menu is offered. But Sasaki throws out the rulebook on proceeding from light to heavy fish. Commence with silky maguro, rich mackerel and creamy monkfish liver, before veering back to a lighter crab and pickled cucumber dish. A parade of nigiri is equally deft, with specially seasoned rice that is individually chosen for each type of fish.

▪ 2400 Harrison St. (at 20th St.)
✆ (415) 828-1912 — **WEB:** www.sasakisf.com
▪ Dinner Tue – Sat

PRICE: $$$$

SERPENTINE 🍴○

American • Contemporary décor

🍸 ♿ 🛶

MAP: C2

This warehouse-chic spot was one of the first to plant its flag in the once-sleepy Dogpatch, where it quickly made a name for its «honest» American food and top-notch cocktails. After hitting the decade mark, it's now in the hands of Chef/owner Tommy Halvorson, who's recharged the space with stainless steel tables, black banquettes and dim Edison lights that accentuate the high ceilings.

The menu also received an update, though it hasn't strayed too far from its comfort food roots. There's something for everyone here, including burgers, salads and entrées like slow-cooked short ribs in a rich demi-glace. Lighter bites like steamed mussels in a smoky and spicy white wine-broth tease those taste buds, not unlike the cocktails, which must not be missed.

🔲 2495 3rd St. (at 22nd St.)

✆ (415) 252-2000 — **WEB:** www.serpentinesf.com

🔲 Lunch daily Dinner Mon – Sat

PRICE: $$

SHIZEN 🍴○

Vegan • Minimalist

♿

MAP: A1

At first glance, this stylish izakaya and sushi bar could be another in a line of similar places that dot the San Francisco landscape, were it not for a major twist: everything on the menu is vegan. Purists and die-hard carnivores may scoff, but the food is exceptional, skillfully manipulating vegetables and starches to recreate seafood-centric Japanese favorites.

Spicy tuna gets a run for its money from the impressive tofuna rolls, with chili-inflected minced tofu and cucumber, crowned with creamy avocado and dusted in chili "tobiko." A yuba salad with miso dressing and tempura-battered shiitake mushrooms stuffed with faux-crab is equally compelling. Throw in a sleek, contemporary setting, and Shizen is a winner for eaters of all stripes.

🔲 370 14th St. (at Stevenson St.)

✆ (415) 678-5767 — **WEB:** N/A

🔲 Dinner daily

PRICE: $$

TARTINE MANUFACTORY ¶O

Californian • *Contemporary décor*

MAP: B2

Like its much-loved loaves, Tartine Bakery's spinoff turns rusticity into an art form. Sharing a massive industrial space with the Heath Ceramics factory, it boasts large windows, floods of natural light and a crowd of millennial worker bees seeking morning ham-and-cheese danishes, as well as afternoon pick-me-ups of house-roasted coffee with cherry-almond bostocks. Also on the menu: beer, wine, soft-serve ice cream and perfectly tangy house-made shrub sodas.

In the evening, the bread ovens shut down to create a more intimate space for dinner, with entrées like roast chicken and little gem salad. Still, the best time to visit is while the sun is up and the scent of bread is wafting through the air, despite the notably casual self-service.

595 Alabama St. (at 18th St.)
(415) 757-0007 — **WEB:** www.tartinemanufactory.com
Lunch & dinner daily

PRICE: $$

TRUE LAUREL ¶O

Contemporary • *Design*

MAP: B2

Hipster-friendly and Mission-approved, this is an instant hit for everyone from early happy hour drinkers through late-night snackers. Sidle up to the custom bay laurel bar for delicious (if pricey) cocktails made with unique liquors like gooseberry brandy. The menu focuses on small plates of refined comfort food, as well as creative presentations like tender sweetbreads tucked into grilled cabbage with broccoli spigarello and Caesar dressing. You may even taste an amuse-bouche from sibling restaurant Lazy Bear, such as crisp hen of the woods mushrooms with allium dip.

Desserts seem straightforward but are beautifully crafted, especially the sweet, savory and even bitter combination of bay leaf-ice cream drizzled with new olive oil and citrus confit.

753 Alabama St. (bet. 19th & 20th Sts.)
(415) 341-0020 — **WEB:** www.truelaurelsf.com
Dinner nightly

PRICE: $$$

YUZUKI 😀

Japanese • *Simple*

MAP: A2

Formerly an izakaya, this Japanese restaurant offers delicate Washoku-style food (read: no sushi). It feels very much like dining in the home of a friend and the exquisite array of plates, not to mention outstanding organic sake and nutty buckwheat tea, is immediately transporting—provided you can snag a tough-to-get reservation.

Homemade tofu made from organic soybeans tastes of comfort, while Wagyu tataki marinated in fermented shio-koji has an amazing umami flavor. But, without a doubt, the dish to order is the salmon ikura. Starring Koshihikari rice (which requires 30 minutes to cook), salmon and salmon roe, it arrives in its lidded earthen pot and is then stirred tableside for a flourish that feels every bit like an inviting, albeit tasty, present.

▨ 598 Guerrero St. (at 18th St.)
✆ (415) 556-9898 — **WEB:** www.yuzukisf.com
▨ Dinner Wed – Sun

PRICE: $$

Your opinions are important to us.
Please write to us directly at:
michelin.guides@us.michelin.com

NOB HILL & NORTH BEACH

Nob Hill is San Francisco's most privileged neighborhood. Despite the large-scale devastation following the 1906 earthquake, this iconic part of town bordering the gorgeous Golden Gate Bridge and Alamo Square's "Painted Ladies" was able to retain its wealthy reputation thanks to an upswell of swanky hotels, door-manned buildings and opulent dining rooms. Wealthy families can be seen making the rounds at **Big 4**, cradled within The Huntington Hotel. Named after the 1800s railroad titans, this stately hermitage is known for its antique memorabilia and nostalgic chicken potpie. Stop at **Swan Oyster Depot** for fine seafood that impresses out-of-towners, but be prepared to wait up to several hours for one of their coveted few seats. The extravagant **Top of the Mark** restaurant boasts a sleek, lounge-like vibe and panoramic vistas of the sun setting over the cityscape. Moving from day to night, a handful of food-centric saloons fortuitously sate the tastes of young professionals with pennies to spare. At the top is **Cheese Plus**, showcasing over 300 international varieties, artisan charcuterie and of course,

chocolate for added decadence. Just steps away, **The Jug Shop** is an old-time favorite where locals lap up micro-brew beers and global wines. For a total departure, kick back with a mai tai (purportedly invented at Oakland's Trader Vic's in 1944) at **Tonga Room & Hurricane Bar**—a tiki spot in the très chic Fairmont Hotel, decked out with an indoor swimming pool that also functions as a floating stage.

RUSSIAN HILL

Chockablock with cute boutiques, dive bars and casual eateries, Russian Hill's staircase-like streets are scattered with predominantly un-Russian groups and singles that seem more than willing to mingle. Good, affordable fare abounds here at popular haunt **Caffè Sapore**, serving breakfast specials, sandwiches, soups and salads; or **Street** for fine, seasonal American cuisine. Tacky taqueria-turned-nighttime disco, **Nick's Crispy Tacos**, is a perennial favorite. The downright sinful chocolate earthquake from **Swensen's Ice Cream**'s flagship parlor (in business since 1948) is undoubtedly the town's most treasured dessert. **Bacchus Wine Bar** is an elegant Italian-style spot lauded for its beautiful interiors and exceptional wine, beer and sake selections.

CHINATOWN

Nob Hill's scene begins to change as you venture east to the country's oldest **Chinatown**. Amid these steep streets find some of the city's most addictive and crave-worthy barbecue pork buns at old and almost antique dim sum houses where jam-packed dining is the name of the game. Even gastronomes flock here to scour the shelves at family-owned and operated **Wok Shop**, bursting with unique cookware, linens, tools and all things Asian. Others take home juicy dumplings, buns and sweets from **Good Mong Kok Bakery**. Sample creamy, oven-fresh custard tarts at **Golden Gate Bakery** or prophetic little treats at **Golden Gate Fortune Cookie Factory**. Don't bother ordering from the menu at **House of Nanking** where the owner will usually take over the ordering, but nobody is complaining. Finally, the **Mid-Autumn Moon Festival** brings friends and families together over mooncakes—a traditional pastry stuffed with egg yolk and lotus seed paste—and to reflect upon summer's bounty.

NORTH BEACH

Steps from the docks and nestled between bustling **Fisherman's Wharf** as well as the steep slopes of Russian and Telegraph Hills, this neighborhood owes its vibrant nature to the Italian immigrants who passed through these shores in the late 1800s. Many were fishermen from the Ligurian coast, and the seafood stew (cioppino) that was perfected on their boats is a San Francisco trademark. Though Italian-Americans may no longer be in the majority here, classic ristorantes, pizzerias and coffee shops attest to their idea of the good life. At the annual **North Beach Festival** held in mid-June, a celebrity pizza toss, Assisi Animal Blessings and Arte di Gesso also pay homage to this region's Italian roots. Foodies can rest assured that dining here isn't all about red-sauce joints. Brave the crowd

to a ragtag array of beret-wearing poets; bohemian spirits still linger here at such landmarks as the City Lights bookstore or next door at **Vesuvio**, the quintessential boho bar.

FEASTING IN FISHERMAN'S WHARF

Fisherman's Wharf teems with souvenir shops, street performers and noisy rides, but you should stop by to feast on a sourdough bread bowl crammed with clam chowder, or fresh crabs cooked in huge steamers right on the street. Then, sample a bite of culinary history at **Boudin Bakery**. While it is now complete with a museum and bakery tour, it stays true to its roots by crafting crusty sourdough every day, using the same mother (dough) first cultivated here in 1849. **Ghirardelli Square** preserves yet another taste of old San Francisco. This venerable chocolate company, founded by Domenico "Domingo" Ghirardelli in 1852, flaunts a host of delectable wares at the **Original Ghirardelli Ice Cream & Chocolate Shop at Ghirardelli Square**, where you can glimpse their manufacturing equipment while enjoying a hot fudge sundae.

for some of the most fantastic fish and chips this side of the pond or fish tacos this side of the border at **The Codmother Fish and Chips**. Cutting its angle through North Beach, Columbus Avenue is home to the most notable restaurants, bars and lounges. Thanks to **Molinari's**, whose homemade salami has garnered a commendable following since 1896, whimsical, old-world Italian delicatessens are a regular fixture along these blocks. Preparing wood-fired pizzas featuring classic combinations since 1935, **Tommaso's Ristorante Italiano** is another citywide institution. **Bix**, a bi-level arena with a balconied dining room, classic cocktails and jazz club-ambience, makes for a divine date night. This neighborhood was also home

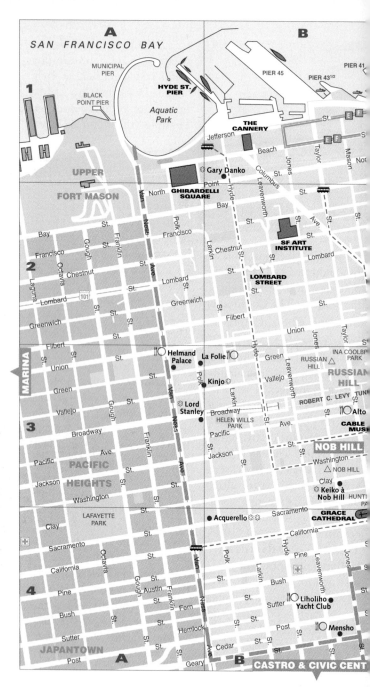

SAN FRANCISCO BAY

MUNICIPAL PIER

BLACK POINT PIER

HYDE ST. PIER

Aquatic Park

PIER 45

PIER 43½

PIER 41

Jefferson

THE CANNERY

Beach

Taylor

Mason

Nor

UPPER FORT MASON

Gary Danko

North Point

GHIRARDELLI SQUARE

Columbus

Leavenworth

Bay

Hyde

Francisco

Polk

Larkin

Chestnut

SF ART INSTITUTE

Lombard

LOMBARD STREET

Greenwich

Filbert

Union

Jones

Taylor

MARINA

Filbert

Helmand Palace

La Folie

INA COOLBRITH PARK

RUSSIAN HILL

Union

Kinjo

Vallejo

Green

Lord Stanley

Broadway

ROBERT C. LEVY TUN

Alto

Vallejo

HELEN WILLS PARK

CABLE MUS

Pacific

Jackson

NOB HILL

Washington

△ NOB HILL

PACIFIC HEIGHTS

Clay

Keiko à Nob Hill

HUNTI PA

LAFAYETTE PARK

Acquerello

Sacramento

GRACE CATHEDRAL

California

Clay

Sacramento

Hyde

Pine

California

Polk

Larkin

Pine

Leavenworth

Jones

Pine

Octavia

Bush

Austin

Bush

Sutter

Liholiho Yacht Club

Fern

Hemlock

Post

Mensho

Cedar

JAPANTOWN

Post

Geary

A

B

CASTRO & CIVIC CENT

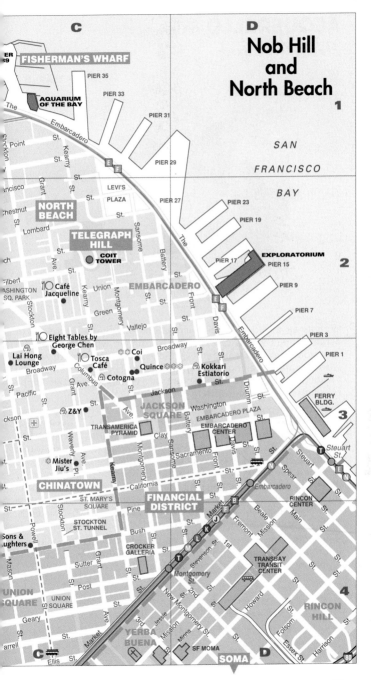

C

FISHERMAN'S WHARF

PIER 35

AQUARIUM OF THE BAY

PIER 33

PIER 31

PIER 29

The Embarcadero

Stockton Point St.

Kearny St.

ancisco

Grant St.

Chestnut

Lombard

LEVI'S PLAZA

St.

NORTH BEACH

St.

Sansome

TELEGRAPH HILL

COIT TOWER

PIER 27

PIER 23

PIER 19

D

Nob Hill and North Beach

1

SAN

FRANCISCO

BAY

EXPLORATORIUM

PIER 17

PIER 15

PIER 9

ch

Ave.

Filbert St.

WASHINGTON SQ. PARK

Café Jacqueline

Union St.

Battery St.

Montgomery

Green St.

Vallejo

EMBARCADERO

Front St.

St.

Davis

PIER 7

PIER 3

PIER 1

2

Eight Tables by George Chen

Lai Hong Lounge

Broadway

Tosca Café

Columbus Ave.

Cotogna

Coi

Quince

Broadway

Kokkari Estiatorio

St.

Drumm St.

FERRY BLDG.

Pacific

Grant

Ave.

St.

Z&Y

St.

Jackson

JACKSON SQUARE

Washington

St.

ckson

St.

Waverly

Mister Jiu's

Ave.

Pl.

TRANSAMERICA PYRAMID

Montgomery

Clay

Montgomery

EMBARCADERO PLAZA

EMBARCADERO CENTER

Sacramento St.

Sansome

Battery

Davis

St.

Front St.

St.

Steuart

St.

Steuart St.

3

CHINATOWN

California

St.

Stockton

ST. MARY'S SQUARE

FINANCIAL DISTRICT

Pine St.

Market

St.

Embarcadero

RINCON CENTER

Powell

Sons & ughters

STOCKTON ST. TUNNEL

Bush St.

CROCKER GALLERIA

Beale

Mission

Main St.

Mason

Grant

St.

Sutter

St.

Fremont

St.

St.

TRANSBAY TRANSIT CENTER

UNION SQUARE

UNION SQUARE

Post

Stevenson St.

Montgomery

St.

1st

St.

Howard

RINCON HILL

4

Geary

St.

New Montgomery St.

2nd

St.

Folsom

Essex St.

St.

Harrison

arrell

3rd

Jessie

Mima

St.

Mission

YERBA BUENA

SF MOMA

80

Ellis

St.

Market

C

D

SOMA

ACQUERELLO ✿✿

Italian · Elegant

With its air of old-world sophistication, Acquerello is the kind of establishment where one dresses for dinner, which is always an occasion. The room feels embellished yet comfortable, with vaulted wood-beamed ceilings, warm orange walls and contemporary paintings. It seems to draw celebrants of a certain age who are happy to splurge on a white truffle-tasting menu.

Each prix-fixe promises expertise and finesse, with a carefully curated wine list to match. Count yourself lucky if your meal begins with their famed parmesan budino surrounded by black truffle "caviar." Pasta must not be missed, such as the very fine and vibrant tajarin with a tableside shaving of impossibly earthy truffles. Venison medallions wrapped in crisped pancetta are served with beautiful simplicity alongside pear slices, onion jam, chanterelles and butternut squash purée. Refreshing desserts include delicate almond milk-panna cotta covered with vin santo jelly and crowned by buttery crushed almonds, quince and tufts of dehydrated balsamic vinegar.

Save room for one of the best mignardises carts you will ever encounter, stocked with superlative house-made chocolates, macarons, pâtes de fruits and caramels.

▦ 1722 Sacramento St. (bet. Polk St. & Van Ness Ave.)

𝒫 (415) 567-5432 — **WEB:** www.acquerello.com

▦ Dinner Tue – Sat

PRICE: $$$$

ALTO VINO ⅋○
Italian • Bistro

 ♿ ☔

This restaurant is divided into two equally lively spaces: a bar packed with millennials drinking Italian vino while nibbling crostini; and a dressier dining room where a sophisticated crowd settles in to a multi-course meal. Others may choose to venture into the heated outdoor patio to sip rosé and watch the cable cars go by.

Much of the menu seems ideal for sharing, particularly snacks like fried olives stuffed with oxtail, giardiniera and grissini. Don't miss the chicken liver pâté crostini with apple, mint and flower petals. You may want to keep the house-made pasta all to yourself, with offerings like two large ravioli doppio—one packed with ricotta and spinach, the other with wine-braised veal—in a lovely jus with Meyer lemon, English peas and fava.

◾ 1358 Mason St. (at Pacific Ave.)
℘ (415) 834-5766 — **WEB:** www.altovinosf.com
◾ Dinner Tue – Sun

PRICE: $$

CAFÉ JACQUELINE ⅋○
French • Romantic

MAP: C2

You'll float away on a cloud at the first taste of Jacqueline Margulis' signature soufflés, light and fluffy masterworks that have kept her tables full for over 35 years. Since the chef makes each of her creations by hand, expect to spend three or so hours at the table— it's the perfect romantic escape for couples lingering over a bottle of wine.

To sate your appetite while you wait, a bowl of light carrot soup or a delicate cucumber salad in champagne vinaigrette will do the trick. But the soufflés are the real draw, and keen diners plan on both a savory and a sweet course. For the former, a combination of flaky salmon, tender asparagus and caramelized Gruyère is a delight. And the utterly perfect lemon soufflé will haunt any dessert lover's dreams.

◾ 1454 Grant Ave. (bet. Green & Union Sts.)
℘ (415) 981-5565 — **WEB:** www.cafejacqueline.com
◾ Dinner Wed – Sun

PRICE: $$$$

COI ✿ ✿

Contemporary · Elegant

& ⊡

Warm, neutral tones and a soft, diffused glow from rice-paper panels welcome diners to this jewel. Over in the kitchen, Chef Erik Anderson is kicking things up with his very own culinary style. He has steered away from seafood, and as a result one is more likely to find a panoply of game birds on the menu now. Changes aside, meals remain a well-executed show.

Settle in to this admired retreat for an intimate parade of elegantly prepared and thoughtfully composed dishes. Topped with oxalis and matchsticks of radish, the citrus-infused "marshmallow" accompanied by curd is delicate and impressive. Thin slices of geoduck with tremulous clam-juice jelly is luscious, while Dungeness crab kissed by crab mayo and lemongrass-panna cotta is on point. Then relish a delicious tourte of duck, sweetbreads and foie gras, enriched by Aramagnac prunes and black truffles. It's hit after haute hit, where even the humble blood orange sorbet dances on the tongue and seals the deal.

The experience doesn't end there. Flip to the last page of the leather-bound wine list to discover a unique tea pairing, as well as a sweet-and-savory souvenir to enjoy tomorrow—if indeed you can wait that long.

▨ 373 Broadway (bet. Montgomery & Sansome Sts.)

✆ (415) 393-9000 — **WEB:** www.coirestaurant.com

▨ Dinner Tue – Sat

PRICE: $$$$

COTOGNA 😋

Italian · Rustic

♿ 🏠 🍴 🖐️

MAP: C3

Though rustic compared to high-end sibling Quince just next door, Michael and Lindsay Tusk's casual Italian offshoot would be elegant by any other standard. Exposed brick, a shiny copper chef's counter and bar, wooden tables...it's Italian to a T, and a hot-ticket reservation.

The space centers around an exhibition kitchen, from which crisp pizzas and hearty roasted meats emerge. The absolutely delicious menu highlights Chef Tusk's pristine pastas, like agnolotti del plin, stuffed with tender rabbit, veal and pork. Seasonal starters are equally pleasing, like kale and radicchio salad in a tangy vinaigrette with hard-boiled farm egg and pecorino. The rustic plum and ginger torta is moist and delicious, but those ever-so-sweet, ripe plums steal the show.

🔲 490 Pacific Ave. (at Montgomery St.)
📞 (415) 775-8508 — **WEB:** www.cotognasf.com
🔲 Lunch Mon – Sat Dinner nightly

PRICE: $$

EIGHT TABLES BY GEORGE CHEN 🍴

Chinese · Elegant

🍇 🍸 ♿

MAP: C3

The jewel of Chinatown's stylish China Live complex actually has nine tables, but it's still one of the most intimate spots in town (and priced accordingly). Patterned after the "private chateau" restaurants that are all the rage in the Far East, this one has good looks to spare—from its midcentury-meets-Chinese décor to the marvelous cocktails that are turned out by the hugely talented bartenders.

The nine-course tasting menu repurposes luxe Western ingredients in classic dishes, from crisp, lacy dumplings stuffed with foie gras, to char siu made with Ibérico pork. The notable "nine tastes of China" starter offers the greatest of pleasures, including poached chicken stuffed with cured egg yolk and beef tendon with those tingling Sichuan peppercorns.

🔲 8 Kenneth Roxroth Pl. (at Vallejo St.)
📞 (415) 788-8788 — **WEB:** www.eighttables.com
🔲 Dinner Tue – Sat

PRICE: $$$$

GARY DANKO ✽

Contemporary • Elegant

The elite meet to eat at this throwback favorite, which has been hosting the crème de la crème of the city (and its visitors) since the 90s. Set near Ghirardelli Square in Fisherman's Wharf, it features two lovely wood-paneled dining rooms and a small, bustling bar, all of them regularly full of hobnobbing business types and couples celebrating big occasions. With bursting flower arrangements, attentive servers and well-dressed diners everywhere you look, it's hard not to be captivated.

The menu focuses on classic cuisine with some global twists; diners can create their own three- four- or five-course prix-fixe, or hand over the reins to the chef's tasting menu. Luxurious dishes include a luscious rock shrimp and Dungeness crab risotto, accented with butternut squash; branzino with fennel purée, olives and a saffron-orange emulsion; as well as a perfectly cooked herb-crusted lamb loin, draped over date-studded farro and rainbow carrots.

While Danko may not be on the cutting-edge of fine dining, its top-notch wine list and outstanding service epitomize old-school luxury. Like the chocolate soufflé with vanilla bean crème anglaise that caps the meal, this is a classic for a reason.

---

800 North Point St. (at Hyde St.)

✆ (415) 749-2060 — **WEB:** www.garydanko.com

Dinner nightly

PRICE: $$$$

HELMAND PALACE ⵏⓞ

Afghan • Family

 ♿

MAP: A3

A drab exterior and an awkward Van Ness address haven't always worked in Helmand Palace's favor, but the food-savvy know it's one of the Bay Area's best for Afghan cuisine. The well-appointed interior is worlds away from the busy thoroughfare's steady stream of traffic, with linen-draped tables, big blue-cushioned armchairs and warm, inviting service.

Every meal here kicks off with a basket of fluffy flatbread, served with three irresistible dipping sauces. The kaddo, caramelized baby pumpkin and ground beef in a garlic-yogurt sauce, is a perennial favorite, as is the chapendaz, marinated beef tenderloin over a tomato-pepper purée, rice and lentils. Vegetarians will find numerous dishes to enjoy, all of them just as flavorful as the carnivorous feast.

▪ 2424 Van Ness Ave. (bet. Green & Union Sts.)
℘ (415) 345-0072 — **WEB:** www.helmandpalacesf.com
▪ Dinner nightly

PRICE: $$

KOKKARI ESTIATORIO 😋

Greek • Chic

 ♿ ⛶

MAP: D3

Zeus himself would be satisfied after a soul-warming meal at this Greek favorite, which serves up San Francisco-chic with a side of old-world taverna hospitality. Translation? Once you're seated at the bar or settled near one of the roaring fireplaces, the thoughtful staff will cater to your every need. Kokkari's sophisticated menu leans heavily on the wood grill and rotisserie, which produce smoky souvlaki with warm pita and tangy chickpea salad, as well as roasted head-on prawns in garlic butter. Braised lamb shank with orzo is a feast, but resist the urge to conquer their Olympus-sized portions: you'll want to sample the galaktoboureko, crispy phyllo rolls filled with creamy custard and topped with honey, figs and crème fraîche ice cream.

▪ 200 Jackson St. (at Front St.)
℘ (415) 981-0983 — **WEB:** www.kokkari.com
▪ Lunch Mon – Fri Dinner nightly

PRICE: $$

KEIKO À NOB HILL ✿

Fusion • Elegant

Elegant, discreet and romantic, Keiko à Nob Hill blends unique culinary style with traditional appeal. Cushioned banquettes wrap the square dining room, outfitted with subdued lighting, fabric-covered walls and heavy brown trim, resulting in a space that is lovely (if of a certain age).

It is always best to be prompt: the formal service team is gracious but handles each night's single seating with precision, serving all guests at once. Such punctuality is crucial as this kitchen takes its work and its mission rather earnestly.

Chef Keiko Takahashi's nightly tasting menu is a progression of French culinary technique with subtle hints of Japanese flavors. Her success is undeniable from the first taste of spiny lobster presented in a martini glass with lobster-tomato water foam and a chilled layer of fruity bell pepper mousse. Moist, fragrant and remarkably delicious Cornish hen then arrives tucked with razor-thin shavings of black truffle beneath its skin, complemented with parmesan foam, Ibérico ham-cream sauce and asparagus. A simple parfait is an extraordinary finale that includes coffee pâte de fruit, marron glacé and bits of crunchy meringue atop whipped cream with grilled pears.

1250 Jones St. (at Clay St.)

☎ (415) 829-7141 — **WEB:** www.keikoanobhill.com

Dinner Tue – Sun

PRICE: $$$$

KINJO ✿

Japanese • Minimalist

&

When it rains, it pours. Or, in Kinjo's case, it floods. This white-hot Edomae-style sushi spot may have not needed a rebirth per se, but thanks to a burst pipe it has been reincarnated. Chef/co-owner Billy Kong took full advantage of the restaurant's closure by heading to Japan to brush-up on his skills, and bringing back Chef Fujii Tahahiro for a menu reboot.

Decked out in neutral tones and pale wood, it is as zen as it ever was, but this kitchen is large and action-packed; the eight-seat counter remains the place to be. Plunk down your plastic where $135 will grant you a kaiseki-inspired omakase extravaganza that includes a striking hassun course. By way of Kinjo, each small dish will transport you to Kyoto—imagine water shield spiked with vinegar or a tender tiger prawn poached in dashi. Continue to wend your way through cooked items like creamy chawanmushi with sea bass and shiso flowers, before arriving at a procession that may reveal the likes of kanpachi from Kyushu or anago from Nagasaki.

Each menu also includes a dessert, so even though you may be tempted to order more nigiri, save room for such sweet treats as mochi topped with an addictive brown sugar syrup.

▨ 2206 Polk St. (at Vallejo St.)

☏ (415) 921-2222 — **WEB:** www.kinjosf.com

▨ Dinner Tue – Sun

PRICE: $$$$

LA FOLIE ⑪○

French • Elegant

MAP: A3

Few grandes dames of high-end French cuisine remain in the city, but this long-running elder from Chef/owner Roland Passot has held strong. With two formal dining rooms featuring starched tablecloths, polished servers and a tall art deco wine case, it's a favorite among occasion-celebrating couples and the luxury-loving tourist crowd.

Diners can build their own three- to five-course prix-fixe, with classic dishes like a double bone-in lamb chop or a tower of crispy goat cheese, eggplant and portobello mushroom. Thicker wallets can splurge on the chef's-choice tasting menu or the array of sumptuous supplements, like foie gras and butter-poached lobster. For dessert, chocolate lovers should be sure not to miss out on the velvety Valrhona mousse.

2316 Polk St. (bet. Green & Union Sts.)

✆ (415) 776-5577 — **WEB:** www.lafolie.com

Dinner Tue – Sat

PRICE: $$$$

LAI HONG LOUNGE ⊛

Chinese • Family

MAP: C3

This windowless dim sum lounge looks small from the outside, but there's room for over 100 diners inside its cherry-red dining room—with dozens more hopefuls lined up on the street outside. The largely Chinese crowd attests to the authenticity of the food, which ranges from steamed pork buns and taro dumplings to chicken feet with peanuts and Peking duck—if you're hoping to skip out on the wait, go at dinner instead of lunch, or call for takeout.

Favorites include rice noodle rolls stuffed with ground beef and aromatic herbs and crispy, golden pan-fried tofu with a silky interior. Shanghai pork soup dumplings arrive in a steam basket in individual metal cups. Served with black vinegar for dipping, they're achingly fragile but terrifically tasty.

1416 Powell St. (bet. Broadway & Vallejo St.)

✆ (415) 397-2290 — **WEB:** www.lhklounge.com

Lunch & dinner daily

PRICE: $$

LIHOLIHO YACHT CLUB 🍴

Hawaiian • *Trendy*

🍸 ♿

MAP: B4

There are no yachts to be found on the urban Tenderloin/Nob Hill border, but hordes of enthusiasts remain quite eager to book passage on Liholiho's love boat. Fusing Californian technique with the flavors of Chef/owner Ravi Kapur's native Hawaii, this sleek and sunny Instagrammer's paradise is known for strong cocktails, shareable plates and near-impossible reservations. Two bars are available for walk-ins, but those tend to fill up quickly.

Watched over by a big 70s-era snapshot of Kapur's mom, the dining room hums with groups savoring beef tongue bao, luscious coconut-clam curry and nori crackers heaped with tuna poke. If you turn your nose up at Spam, a Hawaiian staple, try the house-made (and off-menu) version. It just might convert you.

▨ 871 Sutter St. (bet. Jones & Leavenworth Sts.)
☎ (415) 440-5446 — **WEB:** www.liholiyoyachtclub.com
▨ Dinner Mon – Sat

PRICE: $$$

MENSHO 🍴

Japanese • *Trendy*

MAP: B4

This little ramen shop is the first in the U.S. from the chef behind the highly popular Tokyo outposts, and its wait times are nothing short of epic—even in queue-crazed San Francisco. No matter how early you arrive, snagging one of the 28 communal seats is at least a 30-minute affair that can easily run up to two hours. And the dicey Tendernob address means the line is often beset by aggressive panhandlers.

Only true aficionados can say if the ramen is worth it, but the tori paitan is one undeniably spectacular bowl, packed with springy, chewy noodles and outstanding duck chashu in a luxuriously creamy and umami-rich broth. Just know you'll be asked to slurp it down quickly: the hungry, huddled masses outside are anxious to take your seat.

▨ 672 Geary St. (bet. Jones & Leavenworth Sts.)
☎ (415) 800-8345 — **WEB:** www.mensho.tokyo
▨ Dinner Tue – Sun

PRICE: 🍜

LORD STANLEY ❀
Californian · *Contemporary décor*

&

Like the husband-and-wife team who own it, Lord Stanley is half European and half Californian. Superlative ingredients and a sun-filled space lend it an undeniable West Coast vibe, while house-made breads, confections and an intriguing wine list of European vintages make it clear that these chefs were trained across the pond.

Yet this is a charming little establishment right at home in its central Polk Street location, filled with a casual crowd of locals streaming in—imagine windows which offer a stellar, sweeping view of the neighborhood. Inside, the dining room is furnished with small bistro tables, while a larger communal table on the balcony welcomes groups. Bare wood tabletops set with hand-crafted cutlery and warmed by candlelight set a simple and cozy atmosphere for enjoying meals that highlight artisanal and organic ingredients. Not unlike the space, the cooking here is approachable yet refined. A Berkshire pork chop is meltingly tender, balanced with just the right blend of sweet and sour flavors. Come dessert, a deconstructed dark chocolate pudding with sesame crisp is unmissable.

Be sure to quiz the attentive staff on the dishes—they'll happily explain each intricate layer.

▨ 2065 Polk St. (at Broadway)

☏ (415) 872-5512 — **WEB:** www.lordstanleysf.com

▨ Dinner Tue – Sat

PRICE: $$$

MISTER JIU'S ✿

Chinese • Contemporary décor

😋 🍸 ♿

Chef/owner Brandon Jew has brought some of the sparkle back to Chinatown with this contemporary treasure, which puts a modern Californian spin on the Cantonese classics that once made this neighborhood a national dining destination. Impressively, the chef also makes all his Chinese pantry staples in-house, like the oyster sauce that coats a stir-fry of smoked tofu with long beans, tripe and tendon; or lap cheong (Chinese sausage), which comes stuffed into roasted quail with sticky rice and jujube.

The menu is full of these clever touches, from the tomalley that adds depth to a rich Dungeness crab egg custard to the "tentacles" of fried fennel that echo the texture of salt-and-pepper squid.

Set in a longtime banquet hall, Mister Jiu's is bright and airy, with dramatic brass lotus chandeliers overhead. Food is served family style, making it ideal for groups. But solo diners will also enjoy the sophisticated front bar that serves up thoughtful, complex cocktails with Asian inflections—like lemongrass milk and green tea.

Desserts are excellent, equally skillful and may incorporate black sesame, red bean and osmanthus cream into preparations that will satisfy any sweet tooth.

▨ 28 Waverly Pl. (bet. Clay & Sacramento Sts.)

✆ (415) 857-9688 — **WEB:** www.misterjius.com

▨ Dinner Tue – Sat

PRICE: $$$

QUINCE ✿ ✿ ✿
Contemporary • Elegant

An air of refinement touches this dining room—note the massive Murano chandelier, the stylish guests and everything in between. No wonder this is where affluent tourists and locals alike come to celebrate their special occasions. From the moment the champagne cart arrives at your table to the last bite of the guéridon's mignardises, the service is perfectly timed and attentive. Following suit, the room is as lovely as ever, allowing more space for private parties.

There was a time when Quince was home to traditional cooking, but Chef Michael Tusk's menu is increasingly contemporary. Thin strands of zucchini "noodles" are intertwined with strips of cool and tender squid in a refreshing composition, while a "lasagne" arrives as a square of squab liver layered with greens, accompanied by a piece of medium-rare breast meat and a morel mushroom stuffed with perfect squab mousse. Milk-fed lamb, prepared as a seared chop, braised shoulder and crisped belly, makes for a particularly delightful trio.

That mignardise cart is a sight to behold with its dazzling array of diminutive treats, such as the kouign amann, filled with huckleberry jam, as well as macarons, chocolates and nougats.

▪ 470 Pacific Ave. (bet. Montgomery & Sansome Sts.)

℘ (415) 775-8500 — **WEB:** www.quincerestaurant.com

▪ Dinner Mon – Sat

PRICE: $$$$

SONS & DAUGHTERS ✿
Contemporary • Cozy

MAP: C4

Everyone at this inviting space is warmly professional, including the eager, well-paced staff. Add in the mature, stylish crowd, architecturally detailed dining room—a hybrid between your grandmother's home and an art gallery with its black-and-cream palette, leather seating and vintage chandeliers—and you'll be counting down the days until your next visit.

Small but mighty, this kitchen under the guidance of Chef Teague Moriarty turns out a seasonal prix-fixe menu that consistently pleases. A meal here might begin with an unctuous butternut squash soup garnished with fried salsify; or crunchy asparagus accompanied by gently pickled mushrooms and topped with shaved cured egg yolk. Then a block of exquisitely smooth foie gras is crowned with strawberry purée and fried almonds for a delicious and nutty bite, while crisp bits of lamb are incorporated with minted peas to form a clever counterpoint of sweet and savory flavors.

Deep red and juicy cherry-ice cream is a sublime dessert. But it is the combination with intensely moist pistachio cake, tart verjus granité, juniper foam and fresh cherries that showcase the technical prowess of this gifted kitchen.

■ 708 Bush St. (bet. Mason & Powell Sts.)
✆ (415) 391-8311 — **WEB:** www.sonsanddaughterssf.com
■ Dinner Wed – Sun   PRICE: $$$$

TOSCA CAFÉ ⅋◯

Italian · Historic

🍸

MAP: C3

This historic bar has been expertly revived under NYC chef, April Bloomfield, who spent millions to add a kitchen and make its old-school charm seem untouched. White-coated bartenders shake and stir behind the glorious carved wood bar, while diners feast in the cushy red leather booths. Tables are few, so expect a wait if you don't have a reservation.

The food is Italian-American with Bloomfield's signature meaty influences, like flavorful, gamey grilled lamb ribs that nearly fall off the bone. Pastas are strong, from creamy gemelli cacio e pepe to rich, spicy bucatini all'Amatriciana. But don't neglect their vegetables: a dish of tender cauliflower and potatoes in a rich Taleggio sauce with crunchy breadcrumbs is a showstopper.

▨ 242 Columbus Ave. (bet. Broadway & Pacific Ave.)
✆ (415) 986-9651 — **WEB:** www.toscacafesf.com
▨ Dinner nightly

PRICE: $$$

Z & Y 😶

Chinese · Family

MAP: C3

Some like it hot, and here they are in heaven. Be forewarned: timid palates should steer clear of the super-spicy Sichuan dishes that have made Z & Y a Chinatown smash hit. Nearly every dish is crowned with chilies, from the huge mound of dried peppers that rests atop tender, garlicky bites of fried chicken to the flaming chili oil anointing tender, flaky fish fillets in a star anise-tinged broth with Sichuan peppercorns aplenty.

The well-worn dining room may seem unremarkable and the service perfunctory, but the crowds are undeterred. Plan to wait among eager fans for a seat; then settle in for delicate pork-and-ginger wontons swimming in spicy peanut sauce and more chili oil. Allot time to navigate the challenging parking situation.

▨ 655 Jackson St. (bet. Grant Ave. & Kearny St.)
✆ (415) 981-8988 — **WEB:** www.zandyrestaurant.com
▨ Lunch & dinner daily

PRICE: $$

RICHMOND & SUNSET

Named after an Australian art dealer and his home (The Richmond House), quiet yet urban Richmond is hailed for the surf that washes right up to its historic Cliff House and Sutro Baths. Springtime adds to the area's beauty with Golden Gate Park's blushing cherry blossoms and whimsical topiaries—never mind those bordering pastel rowhouses in desperate need of a lick of paint. More than anywhere else in the city, this sequestered northwest enclave is ruled by a sense of zen, and residents seem deeply impacted by it—from that incredibly stealthy sushi chef to über-cool Sunset surfer dudes. Given its multi-cultural immigrant community, Richmond's authentic cuisine options are both delicious and varied. Begin with an array of European specialty items at **Seakor Polish Delicatessen and Sausage Factory**, proffering an outstanding selection of smoked and cured meats, sausages, pickles, sauerkraut and more.

NEW CHINATOWN

While Richmond does cradle some western spots, it is mostly renowned for steaming bowls of piping-hot pho, as thick as the marine layer itself. This area has earned the nickname "New Chinatown" for good reason; and plates of deliciously moist and juicy siu mai are meant to be devoured at **Good Luck Dim Sum**. Speaking to this neighborhood's relatively new nickname, **Wing Lee Bakery** is famed for its comprehensive selection of dim sum—both sweet and savory. And while you're at it, don't miss out on Frisco's finest roast duck, on display at **Wing Lee BBQ** next door. Those looking to replicate this Asian extravaganza at home should start with a perfect wok, stockpot, noodle bowl and rice cooker among other stellar housewares and kitchen supplies available at **Kamei**. If that doesn't make you feel like a kid in a candy store, Hong Kong–style delights (on offer even late at night) at **Kowloon Tong Dessert Café** will do a bang-up job. Clement Street, also an inviting exposition for the adventurous home cook and curious chef, features poky sidewalk markets where clusters of bananas sway from awnings and the spices and produce on display are as vibrant as the nearby Japanese Tea Garden in bloom. While the Bay Area mantra "eat local" may not be entirely pertinent here, a medley of global goodies abound and everything from tamarind and eel, to live fish and pork

Richmond & Sunset

A   **B**   **C**

Washingto

THE PRESI

1

South   *Bay*

CHINA
BEACH

LAND'S END

PACIFIC
OCEAN

COASTAL
TRAIL

LINCOLN

SEA CLIFF

Lincoln Blvd.

THE LEGION
OF HONOR

PARK

Lake   St.   27th 25th   23rd   21st   19th   17th

California   St.   Pizzetta   Pearl
211

Lokma

Clemer

SUTRO
BATHS
RUINS

Clement   St.   Fiorella   Violet's
Tavern

Seal Rock Dr.

Point Lobos   Ave.

CLIFF
HOUSE

Sichua
Home

Geary   Blvd.

SUTRO
HEIGHTS
PARK

48th   47th   45th   43rd   41st   39th   37th

Anza   St.

RICHMOND

Balboa   Ave.

Balboa   St.

2

OCEAN
BEACH

La Playa

Ave.   Ave.   Ave.   St.

RICHMOND

Cabrillo   Ave.

Cabrillo

Fulton   St.

Park Presidio E

Spreckels
Lake

Chain of   John   F.   Kennedy   Dr.

Stow
Lake

GOLDEN   GATE   PARK

John   F.   Kennedy   Dr.

West   Dr.

Lincoln

Martin   Luther   King   Jr.   Dr.

Middle   Martin   Luther   King   Jr.   Dr.

Way

Lincoln   29th 27th 25th   23rd   21st   19th   7th

Irving

La Playa   48th   45th   43rd   41st   37th   35th

Ocean
Beach

Irving
St.

Judah   St.

Judah-Sunset

Judah

Judah
19 Av

Kirkha

Outerlands

Kirkham

Ave.

Ave.

Ave.   22nd

St.

3

Lawton   Ave.

Lawton

Moraga   St.

Moraga

OCEAN
BEACH

Noriega   St.

Noriega

36th

St.

SUNSET

Ortega   St.

Ortega

*Sunset
Reservoir*

Ave.   24th

1

Great   48th   43rd   37th

Pacheco   St.

Pacheco

Highway

Quintara   St.

Quintara

PACIFIC

47th   45th   41st   39th   35th   33rd   31st   29th   27th   25th   21st   19th

Rivera   St.

Rivera

OCEAN

Ave.   Ave.   Santiago   St.

Santiago

Taraval-
Sunset

Taraval-
22 Av

Tara

4

Ave.   Taraval   St.

PARKSIDE

23rd   19th

Ulloa   Ave.

Ulloa   Ave.

GOLDEN GATE
NATIONAL
RECREATION
AREA

Vicente   St.

Vicente

Ave.

SF Zoo

Wawona   St.

Wawona

Sloat

Yorba

PINE   LAKE   PARK

Crestlake   Dr.

Sloat   Blvd.

A   **B**   **C**

buns is available for less than a buck. There is a mom-and-pop joint for every corner and culture. In fact, this is *the* place to source that 100-year-old egg or homemade kimchi by the pound. The décor in these divey shops is far from remarkable and at times downright seedy, but really, you're here for the food, which is undeniably authentic. Buses of Korean tourists routinely pull up to **Han Il Kwan** for a taste of home. The space may be congested and service can be a disaster, but the kitchen's nostalgic cooking keeps the homesick hordes coming back for more. Native-born aficionados can be found combing the wares at **First Korean Market**, poised on Geary Boulevard and packed with every prepared food and snack under the sun. Meanwhile, culture vultures gather for an intense Burmese feast at **B Star Bar**, after which a refreshing sip at **Aroma Tea Shop** is nothing if not obligatory. Their owners even encourage free tastings of exclusive custom blends of individually sourced teas from around the world.

SUNSET

A dash more updated than bordering Richmond, Sunset—once a heap of sand dunes—retains a small-town vibe that's refined but still rough around the edges. Here, locals start their day with fresh-baked pastries at **Arizmendi Bakery** and then stroll around the corner for some much-needed caffeine at the **Beanery**. Asian appetites routinely frequent **Ebisu**—a Japanese restaurant —for their sashimi and creative sushi. Over on Noriega Street, the line lengthens out the door and down the sidewalk at **Cheung Hing**. If that isn't a sign that something special is going on here, sample the kitchen's Chinese barbecue including whole roast duck, or take slices of tender-charred pork to-go. In fact, those leaving with bags of roasted meat can be assured of envious glares from the crowds waiting around.

As the sun sets in the Sunset, savor dinner at **Pisces** **California Cuisine**, which flaunts dishes composed of local, seasonal and nutritional ingredients. Reflecting the same philosophy, **Thanh Long** on Judah Street has gained a substantial local fan-base who seem unperturbed at the thought of waiting endlessly for their famous garlic noodles and whole-roasted Dungeness crab. Outer Sunset residents who are at the mercy of time may rest assured as **Noriega Produce Market** resides just around the corner, and is as immaculate as any farmer's market for sustainable, organic produce. Finally, no repast can be termed "regal" without a bit of sweet at **Holy Gelato!**—a quirky shop serving coffees, teas and creamy gelatos in a wide range of flavors—including crème brûlée, goat cheese and honey-lavender. Top off this sugar high at age-old, Asian kitsch fave, **Polly Ann Ice Cream**, which boasts of such inventive flavors as durian, jasmine tea or taro—and know that nothing but happy dreams can follow.

BURMA SUPERSTAR 🍴

Burmese • Trendy

&

MAP: D1

Like any celebrity, it's easy to recognize this unusual dark wood superstar from the eager crowds swarming like paparazzi. Everyone endures their no-reservations policy to Instagram their favorite Burmese dishes. See the iPhones poised over the famed rainbow and tea leaf salads or samusa soup (also available as a lunchtime combo). Regulars stick to traditional items, marked by asterisks on the menu. Palate-tingling options include rice noodles with pickled daikon and tofu in a spicy tomato-garlic sauce, or pork and kabocha squash stewed in a gingery broth with coconut sticky rice. A creamy Thai iced tea is the perfect counterbalance to the spicy, boldly flavored fare.

Hipper digs, a cooler crowd and updated favorites can be found at sib, Burma Love.

▦ 309 Clement St. (bet. 4th & 5th Aves.)
☎ (415) 387-2147 — **WEB:** www.burmasuperstar.com
▦ Lunch & dinner daily

PRICE: $$

CHAPEAU! 😊

French • Bistro

&

MAP: D1

For an oh-so-French experience on Asian food-centric Clement, denizens head to Philippe Gardelle's authentic bistro, where tightly spaced tables and paintings of the titular hats create a convivial atmosphere. Packed with regulars receiving bisous from the chef, Chapeau! is warm and generous, a vibe that's aided by its strong Gallic wine list.

Dishes are traditional with a bit of Californian flair, like fingerling potato chips in a friseé and duck confit salad or salted-caramel ice cream that tops the pain perdu. The cassoulet, wholesome with braised lamb, rich with smoky sausage and earthy with white beans, is perfect for a foggy night in the Avenues. Come before 6:00 P.M. on certain nights for a $40 early bird prix fixe, or create your own from their many set menus.

▦ 126 Clement St. (bet. 2nd & 3rd Aves.)
☎ (415) 750-9787 — **WEB:** www.chapeausf.com
▦ Dinner Wed – Sun

PRICE: $$$

FIORELLA ⅃○

Italian · *Osteria*

In the foggy Outer Richmond, this casual neighborhood pizzeria has quickly become as hot as its wood-fired oven. Local families come in droves to share a pie or a plate of pasta in the vintage-chic dining room, where laid-back servers chat with patrons beneath funky wallpaper depicting a bevy of Bay Area landmarks and legendary locals.

The chewy, blistered crusts churned out of the kitchen are loaded with flavor, whether in a classic Margherita or salami pie with provolone and red chili. Throw in a seasonal salad, a pile of chicken wings tossed in a Calabrian chili-honey glaze and a glass of Italian wine from the compact list. Be sure to save room though for the warm almond- and Meyer lemon-ricotta cake, which gets toasted alongside the pies in the oven.

▢ 2339 Clement St. (bet. 24th & 25th Aves.)
℘ (415) 340-3049 — **WEB:** www.fiorella-sf.com
▢ Lunch Fri – Sun Dinner nightly   **PRICE:** $$

LOKMA ⅃○

Mediterranean · *Neighborhood*

This cozy neighborhood recruit has a quaint, laid-back vibe that seems a perfect match to its quiet corner location. The owner is a constant presence, welcoming young families (with tots in tow) and hustling to set up tables. Don't be dismayed by the regular crowds—those weekend lines move quickly and the food is absolutely worth it.

Traditional brunch dishes are served as lunch here, with such hearty favorites as a Turkish breakfast of fried eggs, crumbled feta, sliced sausages, pastyrma (cured beef) and much, much more. Come dinner, try a lemony grilled branzino or skewers of chicken with basmati rice. Every item flaunts a Mediterranean twist—think savory carrot hummus or sweet bal-kaymak (clotted cream with honey) and homemade pitas for scooping.

▢ 1801 Clement St. (at 19th St.)
℘ (415) 702-6219 — **WEB:** www.lokmasf.com
▢ Lunch Tue – Sun Dinner Tue – Sun   **PRICE:** $$

OUTERLANDS ¶◉

American • *Trendy*

ᵰ ᴸ   **MAP:** A3

For the residents of this Outer Sunset beachside community, this sweet spot is an ideal hangout. The salvaged wood-dominated décor is perfectly cozy, and all-day hours ensure that crowds flock here for breakfast and Bloody Marys to start their day. A friendly staff, good, locally roasted coffee and a nicely stocked bar with a fine listing of beers on tap encourages further lingering.

Stop in for fresh-baked pastries like coffee cake, scones and glazed doughnuts; or dig into heartier fare like an open-faced sandwich topped with black-eye pea purée, green tomato and griddled ham slices. Once the sun sets over Ocean Beach, expect more ambitious cooking from the dinner menu, like smoked chicken with tomato panzanella and charred gem lettuce.

▨ 4001 Judah St. (at 45th Ave.)
✆ (415) 661-6140 — **WEB:** www.outerlandssf.com
▨ Lunch & dinner daily   **PRICE:** $$

PEARL ¶◉

American • *Contemporary décor*

🍸 ♿ ᴸ ᴸ   **MAP:** C1

This recruit in a retro drugstore is already the toast of town, with crowds young and old packing in—not unlike neighboring sister, Pizzetta 211. The big and airy space is designed for all-day dining — whether that may be coffee and wood-fired bagels during the day, or a substantial dinner (and cocktail) later.

Co-chefs Mel Lopez and Joyce Conway turn out a Cal-Mediterranean menu heavy on seafood and pastas, like rustic handkerchiefs in a velvety white Bolognese sauce. Carnivores can get down on a grilled bone-in pork chop, accompanied by gently charred broccolini and nectarines. And that San Francisco must—brunch—is brilliantly executed here, with enticing eggs in purgatory or Dutch baby pancakes with fresh fruit and whipped crème fraîche.

▨ 6101 California St. (at 23rd Ave.)
✆ (415) 592-9777 — **WEB:** www.pearl-sf.com
▨ Lunch Sat– Sun Dinner Tue – Sun   **PRICE:** $$

PIZZETTA 211 ○|○

Pizza • Cozy

MAP: C1

This shoebox-sized pizzeria may reside in the far reaches of the Outer Richmond, but it's easily identifiable by the crowds hovering on the sidewalk to score a table. Once inside, you'll be greeted by pizzaiolos throwing pies in the tiny exhibition kitchen—ask for a counter seat to get a better view.

The thin, chewy, blistered pizzettas each serve one, making it easy to share several varieties. Weekly specials utilize ingredients like seasonal produce, house-made sausage and fresh farm eggs, while standbys include a pie topped with wild arugula, creamy mascarpone and San Marzano tomato sauce. Whatever you do, arrive early: once the kitchen's out of dough they close for the day, and the omnipresent lines mean the goods never last too long.

▢ 211 23rd Ave. (at California St.)
℘ (415) 379-9880 — **WEB:** www.pizzetta211.com
▢ Lunch & dinner Wed - Mon

PRICE: $$

SICHUAN HOME ☺

Chinese • Simple

MAP: C2

One of the brightest offerings on Geary Boulevard, Sichuan Home lures diners far and wide. Its spotless dining room is a vision of varnished wood panels and mirrors, with plexiglass-topped tables for easy chili oil clean-up and menus that feature tempting photos of each item.

A sampling of the wide-ranging Sichuan cuisine should include tender, bone-in rabbit with scallions, peanuts and a perfect dab of scorching hot peppercorns. Fish with pickled cabbage gets a delightfully restorative hit of bold flavors from mustard greens and fresh green chilies, while red chilies star in aromatic dry-fried string beans with minced pork. For dessert, rich and velvety mango pudding, topped with grapefruit sorbet and fresh pineapple, is a tropical treat.

▢ 5037 Geary Blvd. (bet. 14th & 15th Aves.)
℘ (415) 221-3288 — **WEB:** www.sichuanhomesf.com
▢ Lunch & dinner daily

PRICE: $$

VIOLET'S TAVERN ⅖○

American • *Tavern*

MAP: C1

Edgy restaurants are finally arriving to meet the needs of the Richmond's increasingly young and moneyed population, and Violet's is the first among equals, serving an enticing menu of cocktails, raw-bar favorites and hearty entrées. Done up in hues of blue and green and outfitted with a wraparound walnut bar, it has the same intimate and lively vibe as nearby sib—Fiorella—ideal for date night.

Don't miss the fresh, tender and chilled lobster, accompanied by Meyer lemon-mayonnaise, or the highly Instagrammable sipper Violet Skies, infused with strawberry brandy, mezcal and crème de violette. A grilled half-chicken with bread salad tailed by a tangy key lime tart is pure comfort, while the late-night $20 burger and cocktail combo is worth staying up for.

　■ 2301 Clement St. (at 24th Ave.)
　☏ (415) 682-4861 — **WEB:** www.violets-sf.com
　■ Dinner nightly

PRICE: $$

The ✿ symbol indicates
a private dining room option.

WAKO ✿

Japanese • *Contemporary décor*

&

Wako blends right in with the sea of Asian restaurants on Clement Street, but don't let its nondescript exterior fool you. Once inside, you will find a serene and spare dining room that is composed with beautiful, multi-hued wood surfaces and attended to by an exceedingly polite service staff. Fresh flowers add a bit of flourish and fun.

It's the kind of pristine culinary experience that connoisseurs and foodies crave. And since this kitchen boasts some of the best sushi in town, be sure to make reservations. The omakase (with a choice of two menus of varying length) may be the only option on offer, but rest assured as it's available throughout the restaurant. Nevertheless, a seat at the ubiquitous counter is likely to deliver a happier outcome.

From the non-sushi items, diners may be presented with poached monkfish liver, a creamy potato croquette dolloped with salmon roe or a salad of shaved apple and mizuna. The real knockouts though arrive on rice: squid with a touch of shiso and Meyer lemon zest; silky salmon with house-made yuzu kosho; custardy uni imported from Japan, wrapped in roasted seaweed; and to finish, a melt-in-your-mouth slice of gently seared A5 Wagyu beef.

▨ 211 Clement St. (bet. 3rd & 4th Aves.)

✆ (415) 682-4875 — **WEB:** www.sushiwakosf.com

▨ Dinner Tue – Sat

PRICE: $$$$

SOMA

Once the city's locus of industry, sprawling SoMa (short for South of Market) has entered a post-industrial era that's as diverse and energetic as San Francisco itself. From its sleek office towers and museums near Market, to the spare converted warehouses that house the city's hottest start-ups, SoMa teems with vitality, offering memorable experiences around every turn. Tourists may skip it for its lack of Victorians, but SoMa's culinary riches and cultural cachet are of a different, authentically urban kind—this is the neighborhood equivalent of a treasured fleamarket.

FINE ARTS & EATS

Most visitors to this neighborhood tend to cluster in the artsy northeast corridor (bordering downtown) for trips to the Museum of Modern Art, Yerba Buena Center for the Arts, Contemporary Jewish Museum, as well as a profusion of other galleries and studios. For a pit stop,

join the tech workers snagging a caffeinated "Gibraltar" from local coffee phenomenon, **Blue Bottle**, nestled in the back of Mint Plaza (there is also a rotating schedule of food trucks that visit Mint Plaza). For a more serene setting, gaze into Yerba Buena Gardens with a cup of rare green tea and some spa cuisine at **Samovar Tea Lounge**.

In a city where everyone loves to eat, even the **Westfield San Francisco Centre** mall is a surprisingly strong dining destination, offering cream puffs, a chocolatier, tea shop or even bibimbap in its downstairs food court.

And local chain **Buckhorn Grill**, in the Metreon Mall, is a sparkling delight for deliciously marinated, wood-fired tri-tip. A hard day's shopping done, hit happy hour on Yerba Buena Lane with the yupsters fresh from their offices, indulging in a strong margarita at festive Mexican cantina, **Tropisueño**. But for a more sedate sip, make way to chic **Press Club**, which focuses on Californian wine and beer. In the midst of it all, the Moscone Center may draw conventioneers to overpriced hotel restaurants and clumsy chains, however, the savvier ones beeline to **ThirstyBear Organic Brewery**, where classic Spanish tapas and organic brews come without the crowds or crazy prices. Then stroll over to the Rincon Center for a unique meal at **Amawele's South African Kitchen**—an establishment that has won the hearts of local office workers with such classic eats as bunny chow (a curry-filled bread bowl).

PLAY BALL

SoMa's southeast quarter has undergone a revival in the last decade, with baseball fans flooding AT&T Park to watch the Giants—perennial World Series contenders. The park's food options are equally luring and include craft beer, sushi and

Ghirardelli sundaes. Crabcake sandwiches at **Crazy Crab'z** have a fan club nearly as sizable as the team itself. Off the field, this corridor is dominated by the tech scene, which has transformed the area's former factories and warehouses into humming open-plan offices. An oasis of green amid these corporate environs, South Park is a lovely retreat, particularly with a burrito in hand from the vibrant taqueria, **Mexico au Parc**. Just outside the park, legions of young

engineers in their matching company hoodies form long lines every lunchtime outside **HRD Coffee Shop**. It may look like a greasy spoon but serves inventive Korean-influenced dishes like spicy pork and kimchi burritos. Hip graphic designers can be seen speeding their fixed-gear bikes towards Market to pick up desktop fuel from **The Sentinel**, where former Canteen chef, Dennis Leary, offers house-roasted coffee in the mornings and excellent corned-beef sandwiches for lunch.

For a casual lunch, **21st Amendment** (a brewpub with hearty food and popular beers like Back in Black) is beloved; whereas Farmerbrown's **Little Skillet** might just have some of *the* best fried chicken and waffles in town. Silicon Valley commuters begin pouring out of the Caltrain station at 5:00 P.M., giving the area's nightlife an extra shot in the arm. For those in need of a more understated retreat, the 700-label selection at ripped-out-of-France wine bar, **Terroir**, will enchant natural wine junkies.

SAN FRANCISCO ▶ SOMA

BEST OF THE WEST

SoMa's western half may appear grittier, but it is still a must for those in search of good food. After a brief closure and remodel, Vietnamese standby **Tú Lan** is once again drawing lines of customers for its killer imperial rolls, despite the drug-addled environs of its Sixth Street digs. Crowds also cluster regularly at neighboring **Popsons**, where an impressive selection of juicy burgers and thick ice cream shakes are definitely worth the wait—and extra calories! Indeed, very little is same old-same old on this side of the city—whether it's the tattooed skateboarders practicing their moves, the omnipresent cranes constructing condo towers or the drag performers who can be found entertaining and regaling bachelorette parties over Asian-fusion food at hopping nightspot, **AsiaSF**. Amidst these edgy bars, kitschy boutiques and design start-ups of Folsom delicious Ethiopian stews served alongside piles of spongy injera fuel a booming takeout business at **Moya**. From there, travel east to feast on flavorful Thai curries, noodles and larb at **Basil Canteen**—located in the original Jackson Brewery building. Finally, hit those 11th Street bars for some serious drinking and dancing before sealing the deal over a rich and heartwarming Nutella-banana triangle from late-night perma-cart, **Crêpes a Go Go**.

SoMa

CHINATOWN

NOB HILL

UNION SQUARE

UNION SQUARE

TENDERLOIN

M.Y. China

The Cavalier

Hashiri

OLD MINT

Lu

Birdsong

CIVIC CENTER

ASIAN ART MUSEUM

CITY HALL

SF PUBLIC LIBRARY

UN PLAZA

Civic Center

SF WAR MEMORIAL & PERFORMING ARTS CENTER

WEST SOMA

Van Ness

1601 Bar & Kitchen

Bellot

Bran

TRANSAMERICA
PYRAMID
C

EMBARCADERO
CENTER

FINANCIAL
DISTRICT

San Francisco Bay
SAN FRANCISCO BAY
D

FERRY BLDG.

SAN FRANCISCO-
OAKLAND BAY
BRIDGE

1

Steuart St
Boulevard ||◯

RINCON
CENTER

RINCON
PARK

Yank Sing

Folsom &
Embarcadero

Prospect ||◯

International
Smoke

TRANSBAY
TRANSIT
CENTER

PIER 26

PIER 28

Mourad ✿

SF MOMA

In Situ ✿

Benu ✿✿✿

YERBA
BUENA

A BUENA
GARDENS

MOSCONE
CENTER

SOMA

RINCON
HILL

PIER 30

PIER 32

Brannan &
Embarcadero

PIER 36

SOUTH
BEACH

PIER 38

Zero Zero ◯

SOUTH
PARK

Rooh ||◯

Saison ✿✿✿

PIER 40

Second St-
King St

Cockscomb

24Willie Mays Plaza

AT&T
PARK

Basin

CHINA BASIN
PARK

PIER 48

CALTRAIN
STATION

4th St-
King St

Caltrain
Station

China

PIER 50

Khai

Omakase ✿

ne ◯

MISSION

Mission
Rock

MISSION
BAY

China
Basin

Mission
Bay Blvd.

Mission
Bay Blvd.

Nelson Rising Ln.

UCSF-
MISSION BAY

UCSF
Mission Bay

PIER 54

2

3

4

BELLOTA ❙❙○

Spanish • Chic

MAP: B4

Iberian flavors and Cali-cool join forces at this Spanish stunner, where legs of the namesake jamón ibérico de bellota hang in a central glass case. They're flanked by a sumptuous exhibition kitchen framed in bronze and hand-painted tiles, as well as a glamorous U-shaped bar. Chic professionals (some of them from the neighboring offices of Airbnb) have already staked their claim for date night.

The menu adds seasonal touches to traditional Spanish tapas: picture yogurt-braised chicken albóndigas drizzled with pomegranate agridulce; or a fluffy tortilla Española with rainbow chard and chorizo crumbles. Paellas sized for 2-4 people are another popular option—try the Pluma, with Ibérico pork shoulder, summer squash and slivered squash blossoms.

888 Brannan St. (bet. 7th & 8th Sts.)
☏ (415) 430-6580 — **WEB:** www.bellotasf.com
Lunch Mon – Fri Dinner Mon – Sat

PRICE: $$$

BOULEVARD ❙❙○

Californian • Historic

MAP: D1

Housed in one of the city's most historic buildings, this Belle Époque stunner is still breathtaking after more than 20 years, with glamorous mosaic floors, colorful glass and polished bronze at every turn. The Embarcadero-adjacent location offers lovely views of the Bay Bridge and the water, and business lunchers as well as evening romance-seekers adore its transporting vibe—there's not a bad seat in this restaurant.

Chef/owner Nancy Oakes is known as a pioneer of Californian cooking, with comforting takes on standards like silky-smooth lobster bisque and a tweaked Cobb salad that eschews chicken for roasted white prawns and comes tossed with crispy bacon bits, feta cubes, cucumbers and tomato slices in different, visually appealing shapes.

1 Mission St. (at Steuart St.)
☏ (415) 543-6084 — **WEB:** www.boulevardrestaurant.com
Lunch Mon – Fri Dinner nightly

PRICE: $$$

BENU ✿✿✿

Asian • Design

✿ ♿ ⊡ 🖐

Benu is an oasis in the heart of the city. The mandatory stroll through the serene courtyard not only sets the mood, but also offers insight into the meal to come. Peruse the earthenware pots with fermenting ingredients you'll later find on your plate and glimpse the kitchen hard at work. The interior is awash in earthy colors and sleek banquettes, and the slate-gray dining room is serene, with clean lines drawing the eye across the meticulous design. Given the restaurant's high caliber, the staff is impressively warm and relaxed.

A series of highly technical small bites kicks off the meal. These delicacies alone rival some of the country's most ambitious tasting menus, but wait, there's more. Faux shark's fin and soup dumplings remain a constant, while Chef Corey Lee continues to reimagine and redefine his nightly tasting menu. Dishes like Beluga caviar and sweet sea urchin or Cantonese-style pork belly served alongside blood sausage crepinette reflect a unique marriage of contemporary Asian influences.

Patience seems to define this kitchen in its relentless pursuit of excellence, whether perfecting technique or waiting for just the right moment to serve an ingredient at its peak.

◻ 22 Hawthorne St. (bet. Folsom & Howard Sts.)

☎ (415) 685-4860 — **WEB:** www.benusf.com

◻ Dinner Tue – Sat

PRICE: $$$$

BIRDSONG ✿

American • *Contemporary décor*

MAP: B3

The front windows are stacked with logs, dried fish hangs from the rafters and the dining room is gently scented with wood smoke, but lofty ceilings and a contemporary aura make Birdsong feel lumberjack-chic. While Chef Christopher Bleidorn prides himself on live-fire cooking and using every part of the animal, he's still attuned to creature comforts, including a restful color scheme, gorgeous earthenware, elegant stemware and a staff that's as sharp as a well-made axe. The funky 80s rock music in the background certainly helps preserve a laid-back vibe.

His tasting menu underlines the cuisine of the Pacific Northwest, with a deeper emphasis on the intense flavors of wood fire. Perfectly grilled lamb-stuffed mushrooms are standouts, accompanied by the likes of custardy blue-corn bread matched with charcoal butter. The chef also flaunts immense skill with dehydrated and cured ingredients, transforming humble carrots into a tender, "meaty" marvel, or wrapping a cylinder of crisp pork belly around luscious caviar and chives for an enticing blast of flavor.

Even desserts get their turn in the embers: brioche soaked in jasmine custard is rich and moist, with deliciously caramelized edges.

1085 Mission St. (bet. 6th & 7th Sts.)
℘ (415) 685-4860 — **WEB:** www.birdsongsf.com
Dinner Tue – Sat

PRICE: $$$$

THE CAVALIER ⅠO
Gastropub • Brasserie

MAP: B2

One of the city's high-profile hangouts, this is the third effort from the team behind Marlowe and Park Tavern. Everything here has a British bent, echoed in the hunting-lodge-gone-sophisticated décor with red-and-blue walls accented by taxidermied trophies and tufted banquettes. Across-the-pond classics have Californian twists like a deep-fried Scotch duck egg wrapped in truffled duck rillettes. The restaurant has quickly become a see-and-be-seen haunt of the tech oligarchy (complete with a private club). However, the food is spot-on and homey, as seen in the corned beef-and-potato hash topped with a gently poached egg.

Though reservations are a must, its location in the Hotel Zetta means service runs from morning to night, giving diners plenty of options.

360 Jessie St. (at 5th St.)
𝄞 (415) 321-6000 — **WEB:** www.thecavaliersf.com
Lunch & dinner daily

PRICE: $$

COCKSCOMB ⅠO
American • Rustic

MAP: C3

Carnivores will thrill to the offerings at this favored spot from offal-loving Top Chef Masters champ, Chris Cosentino. It doesn't shy away from aggressively rich fare like wood-grilled bruschetta topped with uni butter, sweet Dungeness crab and buttery lardo or smoky butterflied roast quail in a rich, salty tetrazzini gravy. Even veggie-centric celery Victor gets a meaty spin; its tangy vinaigrette accented by crisp chicken-skin chicharrónes.

Thanks to the hearty menu and location in a tech-centric corridor, Cockscomb draws a mostly male crowd that packs in for shellfish platters and intense, boozy cocktails named for SF landmarks. Laid-back, yet attentive service and a soaring, industrial space make it the very picture of a hot spot.

564 4th St. (at Freelon St.)
𝄞 (415) 974-0700 — **WEB:** www.cockscombsf.com
Lunch Mon – Fri Dinner Mon – Sat

PRICE: $$$

HASHIRI ✿

Japanese • Design

◔ ♿ ⊡

MAP: B2

This omakase-only Japanese gem in Mint Plaza may be one of the city's most expensive restaurants, but those who can afford the bill will be rewarded with a truly luxurious culinary experience. Every detail of Hashiri has been finely crafted, from the hand-painted dishes and crystal sake glasses, to the parting seasonal treat presented to diners at the end of their meal. This dining room is home to a host of Asian diners and suits, but don't be surprised if you see a hoodie-clad millionaire or two seated next to you.

Chef Takashi Saito and team offer their own creative hybrid of two classic cuisines—the artistry of sushi fused with the ceremony of a kaiseki meal. Exceptional dishes showcase the best of the season and have included tender pen shell clam with citrus-splashed fava beans and bamboo shoots, as well as lightly grilled A5 Wagyu beef over a celeriac purée and charred ramps. Then move on to some outstanding nigiri like buttery Spanish mackerel enhanced by citrus; aji with minced chives; chutoro; otoro; and Hokkaido uni.

Sake connoisseurs will enjoy the exclusive selection, while novices can rest assured as the helpful staff is happy to steer the way to the right choice.

▨ 4 Mint Plaza (at 5th St.)

✆ (415) 908-1919 — **WEB:** www.hashirisf.com

▨ Dinner Tue – Sat

PRICE: $$$$

IN SITU ❀

International • *Design*

   ♿   ☖

MAP: C2

Like the SF Museum of Modern Art in which it's housed, Corey Lee's "culinary museum" bends notions of time and place to offer a unique array of iconic dishes from top chefs around the world, honoring more than two decades of innovative cooking. Guided by the dishes' creators, Lee has trained his cooks to faithfully replicate more than 100 menu items from a starry lineup that includes Chefs Thomas Keller, Albert Adrià and David Chang.

The concise menu rotates seasonally, ensuring that diners will always have new "exhibits" to sample. They might include David Thompson's intensely spicy Chiang Mai-style guinea fowl larb salad, Mehmet Gürs' luscious lamb shank manti with yogurt mousse and tomato and Hiroshi Sasaki's succulent glazed chicken thigh with a creamy onsen egg. If Adrià's decadent and masterfully prepared Jasper Hill Farm cheesecake with a hazelnut crust and white chocolate cookies is in the lineup, don't hesitate.

In addition to the culinary concept, In Situ's design is in keeping with its museum home, featuring a spare dining room and a few gems from SFMOMA's collection adding pops of color. Be forewarned that a sophisticated but casual crowd fills up this room quickly.

▨   151 Third St. (bet. Howard & Minna Sts.)

☏ (415) 941-6050 — **WEB:** insitu.sfmoma.org

▨   Lunch Thu – Tue Dinner Thu – Sun   **PRICE: $$$$**

INTERNATIONAL SMOKE ⸠⚬

International • *Trendy*

& ⎕

MAP: C1

International Smoke is definitely en fuego. This downtown eatery nails that industrial-chic look with its black brick, copper accents and graffiti-emblazoned pillars. But, it's the buzzing clientele that makes this a smoking-hot spot. Attentive servers make everyone feel like a VIP, though there's a good chance you'll be dining next to a bonafide baller—after all, this is a collaboration between Michael Mina and lifestyle maven/basketball wife, Ayesha Curry.

Expect a meat-centric menu with creative takes on barbecue. Don't pass up the ribs, with three distinct flavors—all equally juicy, and yes, smoky. There's a nice balance here between messy finger food and elevated dishes employing smoke-filled cloches for tableside prep—and a bit of drama.

▦ 301 Mission St. (at Fremont St.)

✆ (415) 543-7474 — **WEB:** www.internationalsmoke.com

▦ Lunch Mon – Fri Dinner nightly   PRICE: $$$

KHAI ⸠⚬

Vietnamese • *Intimate*

&

MAP: C4

A celebrity in his native Vietnam, Chef/owner Khai Duong has chosen to settle down in a strip mall near the Design District, where he offers a ten-course tasting menu with two nightly seatings. The petite dining room is a bit eccentric, with its daytime takeaway counter mostly obscured by curtains. Still, you'll get a lot of face time with the chef, who's an active presence and a great character.

Trained in France, Duong offers beautifully crafted updates on classic Vietnamese dishes, from vermicelli with shredded omelet and pork belly to Hanoi's famous cha ca thang long—turmeric-marinated fish with dill and scallions. Other highlights include rich matsutake mushroom pâté, and for dessert, slippery coconut noodles with durian paste and coconut cream.

▦ 655 Townsend St. (bet. 7th & 8th Sts.)

✆ (415) 724-2325 — **WEB:** www.chefkhai.com

▦ Dinner Tue – Sat   PRICE: $$$$

LUCE ✿

Contemporary · Elegant

MAP: B3

Know that the ambience is pleasant, the space is elegant, the service team is quick and polite and the food is consistently excellent. Also know that you probably won't have a hard time getting a reservation at this InterContinental Hotel restaurant—Luce is often inexplicably empty. Let its lack of popularity be your reminder to come here when looking for a little privacy—think date night.

Soaring ceilings, dark and dramatic spherical lights, a transparent wall of wine bordering the kitchen and shiny cushioned banquettes give the dining room a sumptuous, airy feel that promises the high level of luxury echoed in the cuisine. This may be one of the city's more venerable mainstays, but a contemporary sensibility is clear throughout the décor and menu.

Luce serves breakfast, lunch and brunch, but dinner is when the serious diner arrives for an altogether stellar experience. Highlights include a generous portion of perfectly white halibut poached in California olive oil and placed on a colorful bed of fresh shelling beans with artichokes and clams. Desserts may combine the wonderfully light flavors of sweet corn panna cotta with kernels of honey-caramel popped corn and huckleberry compote.

888 Howard St. (at 5th St.)

℘ (415) 616-6566 — **WEB:** www.lucewinerestaurant.com

Lunch & dinner daily

PRICE: $$$

MOURAD ❀

Moroccan • Chic

This glamorous outpost at the base of the PacBell building introduces the unique soul of Chef/owner Mourad Lahlou's eponymous restaurant. The neighborhood's food-obsessed techies along with tourists flock to this boldly designed space, replete with soaring ceilings, glowing central columns and a superb (suspended) wine cellar. The crowd is contented and lively, and while the servers fit the bill, the sommelier is especially impressive.

Chef Lahlou's expression of Moroccan cuisine is peppered with local and contemporary influences like maple and brown butter, as well as more traditional inflections such as charmoula and preserved lemon. Diners may commence with the basteeya, a traditional Moroccan pastry made modern with finely shredded duck and composed with verjus crème fraîche, compressed pear, edible flowers as well as cocoa paste. Couscous is jazzed up with savory brown butter and a host of vegetables, then hit with spicy harissa for a slight kick.

Even dessert comes packed with flavor. For instance, the slender slice of pistachio cake set with candied pink grapefruit, fresh grapefruit segments, a quenelle of tangerine sorbet and orange-infused cream, is lush and delicious.

◻ 140 New Montgomery St. (bet. Minna & Natoma Sts.)

✆ (415) 660-2500 — **WEB:** www.mouradsf.com

◻ Lunch Mon-Fri Dinner nightly

PRICE: $$$

M.Y. CHINA ☺

Chinese • *Contemporary décor*

 ♿ 🗡️   **MAP:** B2

Need proof that Yan Can Cook? Just snag a table at the famed PBS chef's elegant restaurant. Housed under the dome of the Westfield San Francisco Centre shopping mall, M.Y. China is a dark, sultry space full of posh Chinese furniture, antiques and dramatic lighting. Shopping-weary patrons fill the dining room, whereas chowhounds hit the exhibition counter to watch the staff masterfully hand-pull noodles and toss woks.

The menu reads like an ode to regional Chinese cuisine, spanning chewy scissor-cut noodles with wild boar, fluffy bao stuffed with sweet and smoky barbecue pork and, when it's in season, delectable pepper-dusted whole crab. Be sure to order strategically, as you'll want room for the flaky, buttery, creamy and outright superb Macanese egg tarts.

▫ 845 Market St. (bet. 4th & 5th Sts.)

📞 (415) 580-3001 — **WEB:** www.tastemychina.com

▫ Lunch & dinner daily   **PRICE:** $$

OKANE ☺

Japanese • *Simple*

 ♿   **MAP:** C4

Can't afford to indulge in the exquisite sushi at Omakase? Consider heading to its next-door little sib, where the fish is still top-notch (it's all sourced from Japan) but the atmosphere is more laid-back. Okane draws lots of nearby Adobe and Zynga employees at lunch and big groups at dinner, all sharing bottles of sake and making the most of the small-plates menu.

Sushi is, of course, a must: the nigiri is pristine and delicious, as are more Americanized rolls like the Harajuku (filled with shrimp tempura, avocado and salmon and topped with tuna, eel sauce and lotus root chips). But don't sleep on the non-sushi dishes—cod marinated in sake lees is grilled to perfection, and broiled salmon aburi with avocado and ikura is delicious too.

▫ 669 Townsend St. (bet. 7th & 8th Sts.)

📞 (415) 865-9788 — **WEB:** www.okanesf.com

▫ Lunch & dinner daily   **PRICE:** $$

OMAKASE ✿

Japanese • Simple

&

True, the vibe is friendly and the location is convenient for tech entrepreneurs, but superb Edomae sushi is the real reason why Omakase is always full. Ergo, reservations are required and punctuality is a must. The kimono-clad servers strain to place dishes in front of diners, who usually sit elbow-to-elbow at the tight L-shaped counter, but the chummy young professionals and gourmands don't seem to notice anything but the chefs.

Choose from two omakase menus; the more extensive (and expensive) one offers additional sashimi and nigiri. Begin with buttery ocean trout steamed in sake and presented with a wedge of heirloom black tomato as well as a herb salad in rice wine vinaigrette. Beautifully arranged sashimi features bluefin tuna with red-fleshed sea perch, garnished with cured kombu, shiso leaf, wasabi and a bit of chrysanthemum petal salad. Still, no dish can compare with the exquisite level of nigiri, which may showcase marinated chutoro, cedar-torched sea bream, Hokkaido uni with house-brined ikura and a fluffy piece of lobster-infused tamago.

Extreme attention to detail is the hallmark of dining here, with customized portions of rice and wasabi adjustments for each guest's palate.

▨ 665 Townsend St. (bet. 7th & 8th Sts.)

✆ (415) 865-0633 — **WEB:** www.omakasesf.com

▨ Dinner nightly

PRICE: $$$$

PROSPECT ⅋○

American • *Elegant*

MAP: D1

For a polished and contemporary experience that doesn't sacrifice approachability, FiDi denizens turn to Prospect, a crowd-pleaser for the full-pocketbook crowd. Set on the ground floor of a soaring high-rise, its airy space offers attractive, roomy tables, adept service and a popular, well-stocked cocktail bar.

Simple, well-constructed American fare abounds, with menu mainstays like an heirloom tomato salad with creamy dollops of burrata and crisp, garlicky breadcrumbs; or a perfectly flaky Coho salmon fillet set over earthy black rice, sweet yellow corn and caramelized summer squash. Dessert should not be missed: the butter brickle icebox cake with honey-glazed plums and toasted pecan butter crunch is a truly memorable treat.

▪ 300 Spear St. (at Folsom St.)
✆ (415) 247-7770 — **WEB:** www.prospectsf.com
▪ Lunch Mon – Fri Dinner Mon – Sat   PRICE: $$$

ROOH ⅋○

Indian • *Contemporary décor*

MAP: D3

Amidst a slew of upscale Indian restaurants descending upon San Francisco, Rooh rises to the top, thanks to an innovative menu that fuses the subcontinent's myriad flavors with modern restaurant staples (oysters, pork belly, burrata). The bold India-goes-industrial décor is a bit paint-by-numbers, with vivid jewel tones and an oversized mural depicting a traditionally dressed woman. But the vibe is engaging and the cocktails quite unique.

Rooh's approach is casual, but tabs can grow stratospheric in this pricey tech corridor. For the best value, opt for a meal of delicious small plates like the piquant paneer chili, coated in crispy shreds of kataifi noodles. Wrap up with the exquisite carrot halwa cake, accented by cardamom kulfi and yogurt mousse.

▪ 333 Brannan St. (at Stanford St.)
✆ (415) 525-4174 — **WEB:** www.roohsf.com
▪ Lunch & dinner Mon – Sat   PRICE: $$$

SAISON ✿✿✿

Californian • Chic

🍇 🍸 ♿ 🖐

MAP: D3

Inside this grandiose warehouse, the kitchen's footprint overlaps the dining room, where the cooks themselves can often be seen serving diners. While savoring each course, you may have a full view of Chef Joshua Skenes and his team tending the fiery hearth that is the soul of Saison's culinary philosophy. This enticing chamber combines the original brick ceilings with cushy seats and giant taxidermy that boasts of the chef's hunting prowess. Over at the bar, a salon fills with couples dining at cocktail tables.

The single fixed menu demonstrates a range of skill and flavors. Begin with lightly seared Nova Scotia lobster tails accompanied by house-grown greens to create Vietnamese-inspired lettuce wraps with roasted pineapple and a perfect lime. Tender abalone is then arranged with sauerkraut and mustard seeds, before getting topped with crisp, dehydrated cabbage and dressed tableside with a mussel-crème fraîche sauce. Finally, hearth-roasted yam divulges the intensity of smoke and texture, covered with seeds and set over buttermilk for an absolutely memorable dish.

Flaunting the height of their local ingredients is a creamsicle-stuffed Sumo mandarin and the season's first strawberries.

▨ 178 Townsend St. (bet. 2nd & 3rd Sts.)
☏ (415) 828-7990 — **WEB:** www.saisonsf.com
▨ Dinner Tue – Sat

PRICE: $$$$

Proud sponsor of the 2019 San Francisco Michelin Guide.

1601 BAR & KITCHEN 😊
Sri Lankan • *Contemporary décor*

& **MAP:** A4

Sri Lankan flavors infuse the dishes at this quiet winner, which also employs Western ingredients to arrive at its very own delicious concoctions. For a more extensive exploration of this island nation's cuisine, go for the degustation menu. Or stick to such decidedly untraditional items as lamprais, which might stuff a classically French bacon-wrapped rabbit loin and eggplant curry into a banana leaf. Halibut "ceviche" is more like flavored sashimi, with hints of coconut milk and serrano chilies.

This contemporary space with its wraparound windows and slate walls is a perfect showcase for the cooking. Dine solo at the bar with a bittersweet Dubonnet sangria, or come with friends to share food and wine—the polished staff makes either experience enjoyable.

◻ 1601 Howard St. (at 12th St.)
𝒫 (415) 552-1601 — **WEB:** www.1601sf.com
◻ Dinner Tue – Sat   **PRICE:** $$

YANK SING 😊
Chinese • *Family*

& ⊟ ⚱ **MAP:** D1

With a higher price tag than the average Chinatown joint, Yank Sing is arguably the place in town for dim sum. The upscale setting boasts reasonable prices, but the zigzagging carts can get hectic. While peak hours entail a wait, one can be assured of quality and abundant variety from these carts rolling out of the kitchen.

The signature Peking duck with its crispy lacquered skin and fluffy buns makes for a memorable treat, not unlike the deliciously sweet and salty char siu bao. Of course, dumplings here are the true highlight, and range from fragrant pork xiao long bao to paper-thin har gao concealing chunks of shrimp. Don't see favorites like the flaky egg custard tarts? Just ask the cheerful staff, who'll radio the kitchen for help via headsets.

◻ 101 Spear St. (bet. Howard & Mission Sts.)
𝒫 (415) 781-1111 — **WEB:** www.yanksing.com
◻ Lunch daily   **PRICE:** $$

ZERO ZERO 🏮

Pizza • *Rustic*

Zero Zero may be named for the superlative flour used in its blistered pies, but it is so much more than a pizzeria. While the Castro topped with oozing mozzarella and spicy soppressata is delicious, this casual spot offers far more than just a good slice. Absolute knockouts include a beautifully composed panzanella accompanied by basil pesto, as well as gnocchi tossed in a hearty pork belly ragù, decked with dollops of ricotta making it light and bright, despite the indulgent ingredients.

A mix of families, hipsters and business folk from the Moscone Center fills the warm, bi-level space. Group dining is ideal for sampling more of the menu, and the sizable bar will ensure that everyone's furnished with a terrific cocktail or pint of local draft root beer.

▦ 826 Folsom St. (bet. 4th & 5th Sts.)
📞 (415) 348-8800 — **WEB:** www.zerozerosf.com
▦ Lunch & dinner daily

PRICE: $$

Your opinions are important to us.
Please write to us directly at:
michelin.guides@us.michelin.com

EAST BAY

EAST BAY

A signature mash-up of wealthy families, senior bohemians and college kids, Berkeley is extolled for its liberal politics and lush university campus. Snooty gourmands and reverential foodies consider it to be the Garden of Eden that sprouted American gastronomy's leading purist, Alice Waters. Her **Chez Panisse Foundation** continues to nurture the **Edible Schoolyard**, an organic garden-cum-kitchen classroom for students. Waters also founded Slow Food Nation, the country's largest celebration of sustainable foods; and her influence can be tasted in numerous establishments serving Californian cuisine.

GOURMET GHETTO

Budget-conscious Berkeleyites needn't look to restaurants alone for pristine, local and organic food. Their very own **North Shattuck** corridor (also known as the "gourmet ghetto") gratifies with garden-fresh produce as well as takeout from **Grégoire**. This area is also home to aficionados who frequent co-ops like the **Cheese Board Collective**, **Cheese Board Pizza Collective** and **Acme Bread Company** for first-rate produce and variety. The **Juice Bar Collective** keeps diet-conscious droves coming back for more; whereas meat addicts can't get enough of Chef Paul Bertolli's **Fra' Mani Handcrafted Foods**, where traditional Italian

friendly patio. Cooks on a mission collect routinely at ingredient-driven **Berkeley Bowl**, a grocery store-farmer's market hybrid, to scan their offering of fresh produce, cooked items and health foods. Named after a region in Southwest India, **Udupi Palace** is equally revolutionary in concept, with cooking that is wildly popular for that same region's delicacies. Sample the likes of masala dosas, packed with spiced mashed potatoes and paired with pungent sambar, for an undoubtedly satisfying meal.

flavors mingle with creative techniques. Every Thursday, the **North Shattuck Organic Farmer's Market** draws cooking enthusiasts from near and far who are looking to expand their culinary repertoire with a vast range of regionally sourced produce.

Meanwhile, hungover scholars can't imagine beginning a day without brunch at **La Note**, where the cinnamon-brioche pain perdu packs a walloping punch. Too rich? Test the spread at **Tomate Cafe**, churning out a wholesome Cuban breakfast followed by lunch on the pup-

OAKLAND

Located across the bridge from the city, Oakland may not exude the same culinary flamboyance. Nevertheless, this earnest city has seen a resurgence of its own, thanks to an influx of businesses and residences. With panoramic views of the Bay, terrific restaurants, shops and a hopping nightlife, Jack London Square is not only a tourist draw but revered by locals as well for sunsoaked docks and a **Sunday Farmers' and Artisan Market**. Mornings are busy at **La Farine**, a European-style patisserie, proffering pastries, cakes and buttery croissants. As noon sets in, downtown crowds nosh on po'boys from **Café 15**. But over in Temescal, **Bakesale Betty** caters to big appetites with bulky chicken sandwiches served atop ironing-board tables. Post-work revelry reaches epic status at **The Trappist**, pouring over 160 Belgian and other specialty beers. However, if dessert is the most divine way to end the day, then convene at **Fentons Creamery**, churning handmade ice creams for over 120 years. Not far behind, **Lush Gelato** spotlights homegrown ingredients like Cowgirl Creamery Fromage

Blanc in some of the city's most decadent flavors. **Tara's Organic Ice Cream** continues the craze with unique scoops like beet-balsamic served in compostable cups!

HOME IS WHERE THE HEART IS

Down-home Mexican food fans get their fiesta on at taco trucks parked along International Blvd. But local joints like **Taqueria Sinaloa** continue to flourish as the real deal for these treats. The Art & Soul Festival in August brings a buffet of world flavors; and the **Chinatown Streetfest** adds to the lure with curries and barbecue. Bonus bites await at **Rockridge Market Hall**, featuring **Hapuku Fish Shop** and **Highwire Coffee Roasters**. Set between Oakland and Berkeley, Rockridge boasts a plethora of quaint boutiques and tasty eateries—including **Oaktown Spice Shop** on Grand Avenue, which showcases excellent herbs and exotic spices, available in both small amounts and bulk bags.

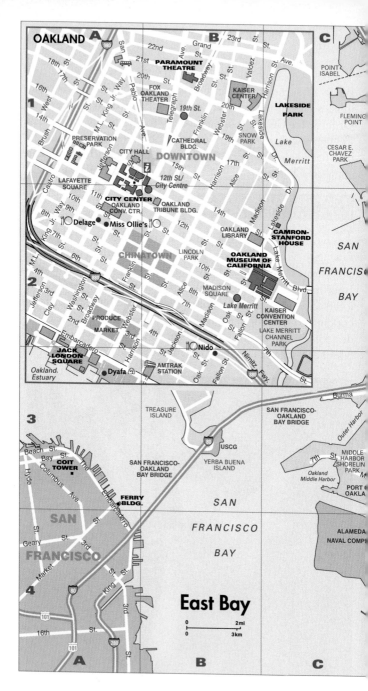

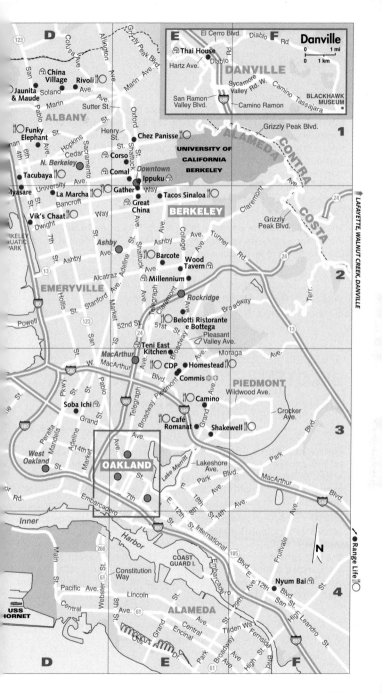

Danville

Thai House

DANVILLE

BLACKHAWK
MUSEUM

El Cerro Blvd.   Diablo   Rd.

Hartz Ave.

Sycamore
Valley Rd. W.   Camino
Tassajara

San Ramon
Valley Blvd.   Camino Ramon

0   1 mi
0   1 km

D

China
Village   Rivoli

Jaunita
& Maude   Solano   Ave.

Marin

ALBANY

Funky
Elephant

N. Berkeley

Tacubaya

Vyasare   La Marcha

Vik's Chaat

EMERYVILLE

West
Oakland

Soba Ichi

Chez Panisse

Corso

Comal   Ippuku

Gather   Tacos Sinaloa

Great
China

BERKELEY

UNIVERSITY OF
CALIFORNIA
BERKELEY

ALAMEDA

CONTRA

COSTA

Grizzly Peak Blvd.

Grizzly
Peak Blvd.

Ashby

Barcote

Wood
Tavern

Millennium

Rockridge

Belotti Ristorante
e Bottega

Pleasant
Valley Ave.

Teni East
Kitchen

CDP   Homestead

Commis

Camino

Café
Romanat   Shakewell

PIEDMONT

Wildwood Ave.

Crocker
Ave.

OAKLAND

Lake Merritt

Lakeshore
Ave.

MacArthur

COAST
GUARD I.

USS
HORNET

ALAMEDA

Nyum Bai

N

Range Life

LAFAYETTE, WALNUT CREEK, DANVILLE

Inner   Harbor

BARCOTE 🍴

Ethiopian · *Simple*

  ♿ ⛱

MAP: E2

The competition may be stiff in Oakland's Ethiopian restaurant row, but thanks to a warm and welcoming team of chef/owners as well as a menu that excels in weaving together the spices and seasonings, the cuisine at Barcote stands out and sparkles like no other. Whether you opt for a meaty plate of kitfo (spiced minced beef cooked in clarified butter); a sampler of vegetarian stews like spicy misir wot (lentils simmered in berbere sauce); or hearty atakilt wot (cabbage, potato, and carrot stew with turmeric); you'll be captivated by the layers of flavor.

The space is clean and simple, but friendly service and a tree-shaded front patio ensure that it's homey, not ho-hum. Don't come in a rush—this is a place to kick back and enjoy a leisurely meal.

◾ 6430 Telegraph Ave. (bet. Alcatraz Ave. & 65th St.), Oakland
📞 (510) 923-6181 — **WEB:** www.barcote.com
◾ Lunch & dinner daily

PRICE: ⬮⬮

BELOTTI RISTORANTE E BOTTEGA 🍴

Italian · *Contemporary décor*

  🥢

MAP: E2

Pasta aficionados will find paradiso in this petite and casual restaurant-turned-enoteca, set on a busy but bucolic stretch of Rockridge's main artery. Boasting an impressive passel of regulars who frequently park at the bar to chat with the owner in Italian between bites, Belotti dabbles in the traditional cuisine of Piemonte.

Envision such hearty dishes as brasato—braised beef with mushrooms served over polenta and finished with a nebbiolo reduction. House-made pastas are also a major attraction here, including the heirloom grain spaghettini in a tomato sauce with creamy burrata. But more unexpected dishes excel as well: try the delicious butter lettuce salad with lemon and pine nuts, or the decadent tortino, a spinach flan with egg yolk and truffle.

◾ 5403 College Ave. (bet. Kales & Manila Aves.), Oakland
📞 (510) 788-7890 — **WEB:** www.belottirb.com
◾ Lunch & dinner Mon – Sat

PRICE: $$

CAFÉ ROMANAT 🍴

Ethiopian • *Regional décor*

MAP: E3

In a stretch of Oakland that teems with Ethiopian restaurants, Café Romanat is a standout, thanks to its deliciously spiced dishes served in generous portions. Locals (including some Ethiopian families) fill the small room that is set with traditional low stools, woven tables and features colorful fabric curtains and artwork.

Order up a homegrown beer, honey wine or a nutty ground flax or sesame seed juice to pair with the sambussas, triangular pastries stuffed with piquant jalapeño-spiked lentils. All the combination platters, served on spongy, slightly sour injera, are perfect for sharing. And the veggie combo, with dishes like sautéed collard greens, lentils in smoky berbere and split peas with turmeric and ginger, will delight any crowd.

▪ 462 Santa Clara Ave. (near Grand Ave.), Oakland
☏ (510) 444-1800 — **WEB:** www.caferomanat.com
▪ Lunch Sat – Sun Dinner Tue – Sun   **PRICE:** 🍜🍜

CAMINO 🍴

Californian • *Rustic*

🍹 ♿

MAP: E3

With its look of a medieval refectory and that central wood-burning hearth, Camino can seem like a trip to the days of yore—but the cool crowd, fun cocktails and innovative food are decidedly modern. Take a seat under wrought-iron chandeliers at one of the long, communal tables (one of them is cut from a single redwood tree!) and expect to make some new friends.

Chef-owner Russell Moore worked at Chez Panisse for many years, and his food is appropriately hyper-seasonal. An egg baked in the wood oven, its yolk still velvety, is nestled in leeks, herbs and cream, while slices of char-grilled sourdough provide the base for a sandwich of juicy pancetta and rustic sauerkraut. Moist, sticky Lardy cake is also grilled, and topped with rich ricotta and honey.

▪ 3917 Grand Ave. (bet. Jean St. & Sunnyslope Ave.), Oakland
☏ (510) 547-5035 — **WEB:** www.caminorestaurant.com
▪ Dinner Wed – Mon   **PRICE:** $$

CDP ⅱ◯

Contemporary • Chic

🍸 ♿

In addition to its entrance, CDP shares a great deal with its sibling, Commis. The name itself is a continuation of classic French kitchen hierarchy nomenclature—the initials stand for Chef de Partie—and it displays the same professional service and elegant cuisine as its counterpart.

While one kitchen serves both restaurants, this menu features affordable, snack-sized portions unlike next door. Those seeking a more hearty meal can opt for the côte du boeuf prix-fixe. Begin with canapés like brown butter blinis topped with smoked trout roe or popcorn dressed with dashi seasoning. The signature egg with a slow-poached yolk is poised delicately atop smoked cream, while a Japanese-style cheesecake is more sweet than tangy, with a scoop of strawberry sorbet.

▨ 3861 Piedmont Ave. (at Rio Vista Ave.), Oakland
☏ (510) 653-3902 — **WEB:** www.commisrestaurant.com
▨ Dinner Wed – Sun   **PRICE: $$$**

CHEZ PANISSE ⅱ◯

Californian • Historic

♿

A legendary address among the foodie set, Alice Waters' Arts and Crafts bungalow continues to flourish as the Bay Area's temple of Californian cuisine. The talented team of chefs here work their magic in a gleaming open kitchen that is set at the very back of the dining room and served by an aromatic wood-burning oven.

Diners are privy to one nightly fixed menu of four rotating courses (three on Mondays). What they will get is a matter of chance, but rest assured it will feature only peak-season produce—from the fresh peas, asparagus and black truffle in a spring risotto, to the sweet corn and squash blossoms served with a summer preparation of pork loin.

Seeking more freedom of choice? Head to the upstairs café, which offers meals á la carte.

▨ 1517 Shattuck Ave. (bet. Cedar & Vine Sts.), Berkeley
☏ (510) 548-5525 — **WEB:** www.chezpanisse.com
▨ Dinner Mon – Sat   **PRICE: $$$$**

CHINA VILLAGE 😄

Chinese • Family

 ⛿ ⌽

It takes a village to feed a big group, and this laid-back spot is a favorite with families. A stylish makeover featured a sleek front bar, contemporary chandeliers and dramatic Chinese art, but one look at the scorching-hot menu options—think spicy Sichuan frog and flaky sautéed fish with pickled chili peppers—confirms the authenticity factor.

Skip the Hunan, Mandarin and Cantonese offerings in favor of the Sichuan specialties like dry-fried, bone-in chicken laced with ground chilies and numbing peppercorns. And be sure to order the five-spice hot and spicy pork shoulder. A house specialty, this mouthwatering dish is fork- (or chopstick) tender and rests atop a deliciously piquant chili-oil jus with baby bok choy, scallions and garlic.

▨ 1335 Solano Ave. (at Ramona Ave.), Albany

☏ (510) 525-2285 — **WEB:** www.chinavillagealbany.com

▨ Lunch & dinner daily

PRICE: ⊜⊜

COMAL 😄

Mexican • Contemporary décor

🍹 ⛿ ☷

For bold and zesty Mexican food crafted with pristine ingredients, Berkeleyites pack this industrial-chic hot spot, where an excellent cocktail program and an extensive tequila and mezcal selection keep things buzzing. The large flat tortilla griddles for which Comal is named are on full display in the open kitchen, while a covered and heated back patio draws locals for year-round outdoor dining

Fryer-fresh warm tortilla chips paired with perfect guacamole are irresistible; summon an order as you peruse other options like the refreshing white shrimp ceviche and earthy hen-of-the-woods mushroom quesadilla. Just make sure that those smoky wood-grilled rock cod tacos, with creamy avocado aïoli and spicy cabbage slaw, are on your must-order list.

▨ 2020 Shattuck Ave. (bet. Addison St. & University Ave.), Berkeley

☏ (510) 926-6300 — **WEB:** www.comalberkeley.com

▨ Dinner nightly

PRICE: $$

COMMIS ❀ ❀
Contemporary • Intimate

&

Oakland continues to evolve and maintain its destination status thanks in large part to Commis and its hard-working troupe. This serene elder from Chef/owner James Syhabout is packed every night for its menu of measured, elegant and well-conceived dishes.

Tucked into colorful Piedmont Avenue, the dining space is long and neat, with a smattering of tables up front; cozy banquette seating in the back; and a lively counter overlooking the humming kitchen. Soft music and a vibrant staff set the mood—cool and contemporary; relaxed but never casual.

In the kitchen, Chef Syhabout pairs local, well-sourced ingredients with precise technique to create his sophisticated nightly tasting menu. Dinner might unveil silky scallops with tangy crème fraîche, poached asparagus and charred lemon granité. That signature slow-poached egg yolk sitting in a bed of onion- and malt-infused cream is a consistent and thrilling revelation; while white sturgeon caviar with creamed potato and beer-marinated onion resembles an exquisitely elevated sour cream-and-onion dip. Perfectly cooked mussels set over porridge-like grains is yet another beautiful plate that reflects this kitchen's keen attention to detail.

▨ 3859 Piedmont Ave. (at Rio Vista Ave.), Oakland
☏ (510) 653-3902 — **WEB:** www.commisrestaurant.com
▨ Dinner Wed – Sun   PRICE: $$$$

CORSO 😎
Italian • Trattoria

♿

MAP: E1

A Tuscan follow-up from the couple behind nearby Rivoli, Corso is every bit the equal of its big sister, thanks to generous, Florentine-inspired dishes like roasted squid panzanella with torn flatbread, buttery white beans and bright dashes of lemon juice and chili oil. Pasta fiends will swoon for house-made tagliatelle in a meaty beef and pork sugo, while butter-roasted chicken boasts juicy meat, golden-brown skin as well as fresh peas and asparagus alongside.

Soul-warming in its hospitality, Corso is the kind of place where servers will bring complimentary pistachio biscotti simply because they're "so good when they're warm." It's no surprise that the tiny trattoria is a favorite among couples, so be sure to reserve in advance and come hungry.

■ 1788 Shattuck Ave. (bet. Delaware & Francisco Sts.), Berkeley
☏ (510) 704-8004 — **WEB:** www.corsoberkeley.com
■ Dinner nightly

PRICE: $$

DELAGE 🍴
Japanese • Rustic

♿

MAP: A2

The word is out about this tiny, omakase-only Japanese gem, located adjacent to Swan's Market in Old Oakland. It's a simple, casual space with a small counter and handful of tables, but it also provides a fine spotlight for a mixture of high-quality nigiri and kaiseki dishes.

Meals typically run about eight courses, with seasonal starters like a grilled apricot and mizuna salad; salmon sashimi adorned with a slice of Saturn peach; or garlic shoots enhancing seared Miyazaki beef.

Excellent nigiri, from tuna to mackerel to fluke, arrive at intervals alongside other captivating items, like seared duck breast with moro miso or scallops with shiso and umeboshi. The only downside is that reservations can be a challenge—so be sure to plan well ahead.

■ 536 9th St. (bet. Clay & Washington Sts.), Oakland
☏ (510) 823-2050 — **WEB:** www.delageoakland.com
■ Dinner Wed – Sun

PRICE: $$$

DYAFA 🐶

Middle Eastern • *Contemporary décor*

MAP: A3

After making a splash with casual Middle Eastern café Reem's, Chef Reem Assil has gone upscale with this big outpost in Jack London Square, a partnership with Daniel Patterson's Alta Group.

"Dyafa" is Arabic for "hospitality," and you'll find plenty of it here, with outstanding service, stunning views of the marina and an array of tempting family-style platters, including braised lamb shanks with garlic yogurt and almonds. Light and fluffy flatbreads are Assil's specialty, and you'll want plenty of her pita to scoop up the delectable dip sampler of creamy hummus, vibrant muhammara and rich labneh. Equally unmissable: the freshly made mana'eesh, which cradles charred and juicy chicken kebabs topped with garlic aïoli and pickled turnips.

▨ 44 Webster St. (at Embarcadero W.), Oakland

☎ (510) 250-9491 — **WEB:** www.dyafaoakland.com

▨ Lunch & dinner daily

PRICE: 🥜🥜

FUNKY ELEPHANT 🍴

Thai • *Simple*

MAP: D1

Look completely past the strip mall location and head into this storefront for some of the more nuanced Thai cooking around. Pop music and colorful plastic tablecloths create a leisurely, relaxed mood, so place your order and head to a table on the patio. This kitchen is helmed by an ex-Hawker Fare chef, so expect spice blends and house-made curry pastes at the base of each dish.

The menu is small but mighty, with items that exude a playful spirit. Nowhere is this clearer than in the "party wings," which sound like a good time but in fact have great depth of flavor. The som tom is an idyllic toss-up of shredded green papaya as well as dried shrimp and long beans pounded together with fish sauce, sugar and lime for a dreamy bite of cool, sweet and heat.

▨ 1313 Ninth St. (bet. Camelia & Gilman Sts.), Berkeley

☎ (510) 356-4855 — **WEB:** www.funkyelephantthai.com

▨ Lunch & dinner Tue – Sun

PRICE: 🥜🥜

GATHER 🍴

Californian • *Family*

♿ 🏠 🛋   **MAP:** E2

With its heavily Californian bill of fare, repurposed décor and Berkeley clientele, Gather is a must for hordes of wholesome foodies of all ages. The aptly named hit serves busy professors during the bustling lunch hour before welcoming a more relaxed evening crowd, who come to sip at the bar and sup en plein air on the patio.

Pescatarians will delight in thick-cut toast spread with albacore tuna rillettes and topped with pan-fried broccoli di cicco, pickled radishes and potatoes, while vegetarians will find it hard to resist a hefty portion of arugula salad tossed with goat cheese, almonds, pomegranate and balsamic dressing. Be sure to try some dessert—specifically the luscious lime curd tart and its thick dollop of meringue. You won't be sorry.

▪ 2200 Oxford St. (at Allston Way), Berkeley
☎ (510) 809-0400 — **WEB:** www.gatherrestaurant.com
▪ Lunch & dinner daily   **PRICE:** $$

GREAT CHINA 😊

Chinese • *Family*

MAP: E2

Chic enough for the style-savvy, cheap enough for students and authentic enough for local Chinese families, Great China is one of the few Berkeley restaurants everyone can (and does) agree on. Spicehounds should look elsewhere, as the food is somewhat mild, but the ingredients are higher quality than the average Chinese spot.

Kick things off with an aromatic bowl of hot and sour soup or an order of vegetarian egg rolls. Then sample generously portioned favorites like the sweet-and-spicy kung pao chicken; beautifully lacquered tea-smoked duck; or the beloved "double skin"—a platter of mung bean noodles tossed with pork, mushrooms, squid and a soy-mustard dressing. Only larger parties can reserve, so be aware there may be lines at peak hours.

▪ 2190 Bancroft Way (at Fulton St.), Berkeley
☎ (510) 843-7996 — **WEB:** www.greatchinaberkeley.com
▪ Lunch & dinner Wed – Mon   **PRICE:** $$

HOMESTEAD ♈️○

American • Rustic

If it wasn't housed in a beautiful Julia Morgan-designed building, this farm-to-table jewel would be defined by the enticing smells that engulf you upon entrance. It's a rustic space, full of large windows peering onto Piedmont Avenue and the jars of dry ingredients, pickling vegetables and cookbooks on the counter create an upscale country-kitchen demeanor.

The menu focuses on the best and freshest of local produce, such as yellowtail ceviche nestled in a tangy aguachile that is interspersed with bits of sweet corn and potato. Roasted duck breast boasts an intensely caramelized skin and is served in its own jus along with maitake mushrooms for a wonderfully woodsy touch. Craving a bright breakfast? Look no further than the homemade pastries or quiche.

4029 Piedmont Ave. (bet. 40th & 41st Sts.), Oakland
(510) 420-6962 — **WEB:** www.homesteadoakland.com
Dinner Tue – Sun

PRICE: $$$

IPPUKU 😊

Japanese • Rustic

Can't swing a ticket to Tokyo? Dinner at Ippuku is the next best thing. With its low Japanese-style tables, extensive woodwork and enormous selection of sake and shochu, it feels like an authentic izakaya transplanted into a corner of downtown Berkeley. The low-profile entrance adds to the feeling that you've lucked upon a special dining secret—assuming you don't stroll right past it, that is.

Yakitori is the big draw here, with smoky, salty chicken thighs, necks, hearts and gizzards arriving fresh off the binchotan. Other excellent small plates include korokke, or golden-brown Dungeness crab croquettes, crisp on the outside and with a creamy interior, or yaki imo, caramelized white sweet potato with a sweet-and-salty glaze.

2130 Center St. (bet. Oxford St. & Shattuck Ave.), Berkeley
(510) 665-1969 — **WEB:** www.ippukuberkeley.com
Dinner Tue – Sun

PRICE: $$

IYASARE 🍴

Japanese • Contemporary décor

 ♿ 🏖

MAP: D2

Japanese techniques and Californian ingredients blend harmoniously at this charming Berkeley getaway, which flaunts a buzzing dining room and a delightful (heated) patio. Start the evening off right with an excellent (and reasonably priced) local wine on tap or a selection from the well-edited sake list. Then, order a variety of their exquisite small plates for sharing.

Every dish is a carefully crafted delight for the senses. Baby kale and mustard greens might not sound very Japanese, but they blend beautifully in a salad with Fuji apple and a sesame-miso dressing. The superb hamachi crudo is dusted with a sprinkle of wasabi snow and lemon-tamari oil, while fresh Manila clams arrive in an aromatic broth of sake, bacon, potatoes and earthy shiitakes.

▪ 1830 4th St. (bet. Hearst Ave. & Virginia St.), Berkeley
☍ (510) 845-8100 — **WEB:** www.iyasare-berkeley.com
▪ Lunch & dinner daily

PRICE: $$$

JUANITA & MAUDE 🍴

Contemporary • Rustic

🍹 ♿ 🏖

MAP: D1

Downtown Albany is abuzz about this chic arrival named for the mother and grandmother of Chef/co-owner Scott Eastman. It has all the accoutrements of a fancy local joint—think unique sculptures from an area artist, rustic plates and fun craft cocktails like the rum- and coconut-based White Picket Fence. And yet, this rookie eschews the tragically hip crowds for an easier, more communal feel.

The roving menu is heavy on odes to seasonal produce, like a succotash of summer squash, corn and cherry tomatoes topped with flaky halibut. You'll also be able to taste the chef's nine years of cooking at Berkeley favorite—Corso—in his perfect veal Bolognese sauce. Creative, well-balanced desserts like a creamy banana custard with coconut granita are menu musts.

▪ 825 San Pablo Ave. (bet. Solano & Washington Aves.), Albany
☍ (510) 526-2233 — **WEB:** www.juanitaandmaude.com
▪ Dinner Tue – Sat

PRICE: $$$

LA MARCHA ⅼⓄ
Spanish • Cozy

   MAP: D2

This Spanish delight from the team behind acclaimed caterer Ñora Cocina Española does double duty as a mecca for both tapas and paella, offered in varieties from the traditional mixta (prawns, chicken, chorizo, garlic, peppers) to the inventive "tres cerditos" (three little pigs) featuring pork chorizo, shoulder and belly. The classic tapas are also out in full force—from grilled head-on garlic shrimp and salt cod croquettes with nutty romesco, to tortilla Española.

Located on busy San Pablo Avenue, the lively space offers enticements for groups of all sizes: foursomes can make the most of the sizable paellas, while a duo of happy hours offer discounts on wine at the L-shaped bar and a selection of free tapas, perfect for solo diners or couples.

◾ 2026 San Pablo Ave. (bet. Addison St. & University Ave.), Berkeley

✆ (510) 269-7374 — **WEB:** www.lamarchaberkeley.com

◾ Lunch Sat – Sun Dinner nightly

PRICE: $$

MILLENNIUM ☺
Vegan • Rustic

   MAP: E2

After more than 20 years in San Francisco, this vegan paradise relocated to Oakland, where it's continuing to put out some of the most unique, delicious plant-based cuisine in the country. This rustic-chic space is laid-back and unfussy, with lots of dark wood, a patio for alfresco dining and a crowd of young families and professionals attended by welcoming servers.

While dedicated vegans are sure to swoon, even hardcore carnivores might reconsider the lifestyle after a dose of Chef/owner Eric Tucker's culinary creativity, showcased best on a five-course "Taste of Millennium" menu. Roasted pumpkin tamales with pumpkin seed pastor and cashew nut crema are knockouts, as are the crunchy king trumpet fritters with chili-persimmon jam.

◾ 5912 College Ave. (bet. Chabot Rd. & Harwood Ave.), Oakland

✆ (510) 735-9459 — **WEB:** www.millenniumrestaurant.com

◾ Lunch Sun Dinner nightly

PRICE: $$

MISS OLLIE'S 🍴

Caribbean • *Rustic*

 ♿

MAP: A2

Even on the coldest (a.k.a. 50-degree) Oakland day, the soul-warming Caribbean cuisine at this little cutie will transport you to the islands. Barbados-born Chef/owner Sarah Kirnon named her restaurant after her grandmother, and it now serves up many of her childhood favorites, including plump, sweet grilled shrimp in a jerk marinade and some of the best fried chicken in town—with a flaky golden-brown crust.

Housed in the historic Swan's Market building in Old Oakland, Miss Ollie's has a particularly loyal crowd of lunchtime regulars, who sip tart ginger limeade as they liberally dose their food with the excellent Scotch bonnet hot sauce. With all the colorful art on the walls as well as a welcoming staff, it's a rustic slice of Caribbean soul.

◻ 901 Washington St. (bet. 9th & 10th Sts.), Oakland
𝒫 (510) 285-6188 — **WEB:** www.realmissolliesoakland.com
◻ Lunch & dinner Tue – Sat   **PRICE: $$**

NIDO 🍴

Mexican • *Rustic*

 ♿ 🛏

MAP: B3

The industrial area west of the I-880 freeway doesn't boast many good restaurants, but this hidden Mexican is an exception. Complete with a hip reclaimed-wood décor and local clientele of suits as well as trendy foodies, it's definitely a cut above a taqueria in terms of quality and price, with fresher, lighter food in smaller—but by no means stingy—portions.

Lunchtime tacos feature handmade corn tortillas perhaps piled high with carnitas and salsa verde, chamoy-glazed grilled chicken or braised beef with chile arbol salsa. Dinner might bring carne asada with black beans and salsa de chile cascabel, or pork pibil panuchos with pickled onion and sikil pak. With a truly relaxed vibe and home-cooked feel to the food, it's worth the extra effort to drop by.

◻ 444 Oak St. (at 5th St.), Oakland
𝒫 (510) 444-6436 — **WEB:** www.nidooakland.com
◻ Lunch Tue – Sun Dinner Tue – Sat   **PRICE: $$**

NYUM BAI 🏮
Cambodian · Simple

♿ ⛱

MAP: F4

Thanks to the support of crowd-funding, Nyum Bai started as a pop-up but grew into this cozy, sun-filled local jewel. Inside, pastel colors and wood accents fashion a retro vibe. Outside, find a beer garden of sorts that is filled with picnic tables for soaking in the sunshine while filling up on Cambodian food.

Chef/owner Nite Yun puts her signature spin on traditional Khmer dishes that layer tangy, sweet, tart and spicy flavors. Some items are so popular that they might run out early, especially the amok—a fish soufflé made with coconut milk. Others like kuy teav cha, a stir-fry of chewy noodles with tamarind, soy, egg and palm sugar, are sure to satisfy. Finish on a sweet note with nom krouch rolled in palm sugar and presented piping-hot from the fryer.

▢ 3340 E. 12th St. Ste. 11 (bet. 33rd & 34th Aves.), Oakland
✆ (510) 500-3338 — **WEB:** www.nyumbai.com
▢ Lunch & dinner Tue – Sun

PRICE: 💰💰

RANGE LIFE 🍴
Californian · Trendy

🍸 ♿

MAP: F4

Livermore may not seem like a go-to spot for inventive California cuisine, but this charming newbie from husband-and-wife chefs Bill and Sarah Niles would be the envy of any city slicker. The rustic space with big arched windows and plenty of succulents screams "hipster hotspot," but few big-city restaurants can offer such an enthusiastic, passionate staff and friendly local crowd.

Order up a refreshing tequila-lime "Range Water" and dive into the appealing menu of beautifully plated bites like duck liver toast with roasted cherries on chewy house-made bread; flavorful artichoke and chickpea curry; as well as rich and creamy chocolate budino with cinnamon whipped cream. A jar of house-made fermented chili sauce from the on-site market makes a delicious souvenir.

▢ 2160 Railroad Ave. (bet. K St. & Livermore Ave.), Livermore
✆ (925) 583-5370 — **WEB:** www.rangelifelivermore.com
▢ Dinner Wed – Mon

PRICE: $$

RIVOLI ✲❒○

Californian • Neighborhood

MAP: D1

Northern Californian cooking with a hint of regional Americana is the main draw at this charmer on the Albany-Berkeley border. It's popular with smartly dressed couples, who come here to savor items like an artfully presented arugula salad with winter citrus, Marcona almonds and avocado, or a highbrow riff on gumbo with chicken confit and andouille sausage perched atop Carolina rice. The excellent gâteau Basque, a caramelized wedge of creamy custard, is a must-order.

Set in an adorable cottage, Rivoli's dining room boasts enormous picture windows overlooking a lush "secret" garden blooming with tender fronds, camellias and magnolia trees. Smartly serviced by an engaging waitstaff, the greenery is a nice contrast to the crisp, white-linen tables.

▨ 1539 Solano Ave. (bet. Neilson St. & Peralta Ave.), Berkeley

☏ (510) 526-2542 — **WEB:** www.rivolirestaurant.com

▨ Dinner nightly

PRICE: $$

SHAKEWELL ✲❒○

Mediterranean • Contemporary décor

MAP: E3

This trendy eatery, the brainchild of Top Chef alums Jen Biesty and Tim Nugent, was made for sipping and supping. Outfitted with a bar up front and several dining nooks on either side of a central walkway, Shakewell keeps things Medi-chic with Moorish accents, reclaimed wood and organic elements.

Service is particularly warm, and an even warmer teal-green wood-fired oven in the back turns out deliciously smoked items like crisp falafel served with romesco. A summer squash salad with heirloom tomatoes, fried bread and feta offers an inspired blend of Greek and Tuscan flavors, and bomba rice with braised fennel, piperade, chicken and prawns is a fluffy take on paella. For a party in your mouth, finish with the caramel syrup-spiked crema Catalana.

▨ 3407 Lakeshore Ave. (bet. Longridge & Trestle Glen Rds.), Oakland

☏ (510) 251-0329 — **WEB:** www.shakewelloakland.com

▨ Lunch Wed – Sun Dinner Tue – Sun

PRICE: $$

SOBA ICHI 😊
Japanese • *Minimalist*

 &♿ 🏮

It takes effort to visit this remarkable little noodle bar, as it's located in deep industrial West Oakland, open only at lunchtime and waits can run upwards of 45 minutes—if the designated 100 daily orders of soba don't sell out first. But rest easy as this delay is happily passed with a drink in the sunny garden, and the warm hospitality rewards the hassle.

Handmade Japanese noodles come in two varieties: 100% or 80% buckwheat, served hot or cold in dishes like tenseiro, chewy cold soba with feather-light tempura shrimp and vegetables alongside a flavorful dipping sauce. For something warmer, kamo nanban, a rich broth with tender slices of duck breast, hits the spot. Be sure to sample the sake, served here in the traditional "overflowing" style.

🔲 2311A Magnolia St. (bet. 24th St. & Grand Ave.), Oakland
🖉 N/A — **WEB:** www.sobaichioakland.com
🔲 Lunch Tue – Sat

PRICE: $$

TACOS SINALOA 🍴
Mexican • *Simple*

East Oakland's taco truck titans have put it in park with this Berkeley taqueria, which is making its name as a Mexican fave in the Bay Area. Sinaloa's logo is a smiling shrimp holding a taco, so your first choice may be the top-notch shrimp tacos (full of plump, succulent, spice-rubbed shrimp). However, rest assured that there's more in store: smoky carnitas with fiery red chili salsa, tender roast chicken and beautifully caramelized al pastor. For the adventurous eater, there's tripe, suadero and pork stomach, too.

Like the truck, this operation is no-frills: pay at the counter, grab some plastic utensils and seat yourself. But with food this good—and prices so low that even a penniless Cal student can afford to dine—who needs frills?

🔲 2384 Telegraph Ave. (bet. Channing Way & Durant Ave.), Berkeley
🖉 (510) 665-7895 — **WEB:** N/A
🔲 Lunch & dinner Mon – Sat

PRICE: 🍪

TACUBAYA 🍴

Mexican • *Colorful*

♿ 🏠 🍽

MAP: D1

Tacubaya is so beloved by locals that they moved a few doors down to an expanded space in an attempt to accommodate its enlarged fan base. This taqueria in the Berkeley shopping complex is where families flock to grab a bite during errands. In fact, there is a perpetual line of patrons ordering limeade at the counter and claiming seats in the festive dining room (look out for the hanging pink papel picados) or sunny front patio.

They are here for chilaquiles and churros at breakfast; then transition into chorizo-and-potato sopes with black bean purée at lunch. Other standbys unveil beef enchiladas doused in a smoky guajillo-tomatillo sauce and covered with melted cheese; followed by tamales de verdure bested with spicy salsa verde and cool crema.

▦ 1782 4th St. (bet. Hearst Ave. & Virginia St.), Berkeley
☏ (510) 525-5160 — **WEB:** www.tacubaya.net
▦ Lunch & dinner daily   **PRICE:** 🍴

TENI EAST KITCHEN 😊

Burmese • *Contemporary décor*

♿

MAP: E3

Burmese food with a California spin is on the menu at Chef/owner Tiyo Shibabaw's cheery spot in Temescal, where the tea leaf salads come with kale and there's plenty of flaky, golden roti bread to go around. Everything's affordable here, but lunchtime specials are an especially good deal: $15 buys both a hot and flavorful entrée (like spicy coconut curry chicken with rice noodles) and a fresh salad—go for the pea shoots topped with radishes and fried garlic in a turmeric dressing.

Bright and airy, with exposed wooden beams on the ceiling, Teni draws a crowd of hipsters of all ages. Its dining room can certainly fill up fast at prime hours, but it's worth the wait for food that's fresh, flavorful, unfussy and generously portioned.

▦ 4015 Broadway (bet. 40 & 41 Sts.), Oakland
☏ (510) 597-1860 — **WEB:** www.tenieastkitchen.com
▦ Lunch & dinner daily   **PRICE:** 🍴

THAI HOUSE ☺

Thai • Elegant

🛖 🍽️

Many a warm evening has been spent on the garden patio of this fantastic Thai restaurant, where potted plants create a leafy retreat. Whether you're dining alfresco or tucked inside the tiny, colorful bungalow, you can be assured of a warm welcome and boldly flavorful food—a secret that's out with the locals, making this house a packed one from noon to night.

The consistently outstanding menu makes it hard for one to go wrong, but you can't miss with the creamy red pumpkin curry, full of tender scallops, prawns and perfectly balanced notes of sweet, spicy, salty and sour. Other showstoppers may reveal pad prik khing, chicken in a spicy peanut-tamarind sauce or the aromatic basil tofu, jam-packed with fresh vegetables, chili and garlic.

▢ 254 Rose Ave. (bet. Diablo Rd. & Linda Mesa Ave.), Danville

✆ (925) 820-0635 — **WEB:** www.thaihouseca.com

▢ Lunch Mon – Fri Dinner nightly　　　　**PRICE: $$**

VIK'S CHAAT 🍴

Indian • Family

♿

This bright orange and yellow building looks big enough to be a warehouse, which makes sense as the inside is not only a counter-service restaurant but also a market. Its namesake chaat may be the star here, but lunch specials are a fantastic bargain. For $12.50, you can get perfectly tender tandoori chicken with a mouthwatering smoky char, served alongside basmati rice, dal, raita and papadum. Family-friendly and casual, this Indo canteen seems to attract everyone with its excellent chaat, authentic flavors and breads— especially the fried and puffy bhature ideal for sopping up spicy chole. A glass case filled with colorful sweets reminds everyone to save room for dessert.

The kitchen closes early at dinner, so unless you're an early bird, go for lunch.

▢ 2390 Fourth St. (at Channing Way), Berkeley

✆ (510) 644-4412 — **WEB:** www.vikschaat.com

▢ Lunch Sun – Sat Dinner Fri – Sun　　　　**PRICE:** 🍴🍴

WOOD TAVERN 😊

American • *Contemporary décor*

&

MAP: E2

There's always a crowd at this lively neighborhood standby, where groups of friends, parents on date night and trendy couples congregate for drinks at the copper-topped bar. Flanked by organic groceries, indie bookstores and antique shops, its surroundings speak of peace, weaving a pleasantly bohemian spell that captivates both regulars and newcomers alike.

Rustic American cooking with a hint of Italian flair dominates this tavern's menu, and the local Belfiore burrata—served atop diced pears, honey-cashew cream and peppery arugula—is a surefire hit. A bit of Calabrian chili adds a welcoming bit of heat to the otherwise earthy pan-roasted Maple Leaf duck breast, while the warm mini Bundt cake bursts with chocolate goodness.

▨ 6317 College Ave. (bet. Alcatraz Ave. & 63rd St.), Oakland

𝒫 (510) 654-6607 — **WEB:** www.woodtavern.net

▨ Lunch Mon – Sat Dinner nightly   **PRICE: $$**

Remember, stars ✿
are awarded for cuisine only! Elements
such as service and décor are not a factor.

MARIN

MARIN

Meandering Marin is located north of the Golden Gate Bridge and draped along breathtaking Highway 1. Coastal climates shower this county with abounding agricultural advantages, which in turn become abundantly apparent as you snake your way through its food oases, always filled with fresh, luscious seafood, including slurpable oysters and cold beer. Farm-to-table cuisine is de rigueur in this liberal-leaning and affluent county, boasting an avalanche of local food suppliers. One of the most celebrated purveyors is the quaint and rustic **Cowgirl Creamery**, whose "cowgirl" employees are charged with churning out delicious, distinctive and hand-crafted cheeses. By specializing in farmstead cheeses alone, they have refined the process of artisan cheesemaking, and ergo, garnered national respect along the way. Continue exploring these fromageries at **Point Reyes Farmstead Cheese Co.**, a popular destination among

natives for the famously lush "Original Blue" and its heady flavor profile. And thanks to such driven, enterprising cheesemakers (who live by terroir, or taste of the earth), surrounding restaurants follow the European standard of offering cheese before, or in lieu, of a dessert course. After so much savory goodness, get your candy crush going at **Munchies of Sausalito**.

If cheese and meat are a match made in heaven, then North Bay must be a thriving intermediary with its myriad ranches. At the crest is **Marin Sun Farms**, a glorified and dedicated butcher shop whose heart and soul lies

in the production of locally raised, natural-fed meats for fine restaurants, small-scale grocers and everything in between. Championing local eating is **Mill Valley Market**, a can't-miss commitment among gourmands for top-quality foods, deli items and other organic goods.

STOP, SIP & SAVOR

To gratify those inevitable pangs of hunger after miles of scenic driving complete with ocean breezes, **The Pelican Inn** makes for an ideal retreat. Serving hearty English country cooking along with a range of brews from their classic "bar," this nostalgic and ever-charming rest stop will leave you yearning for more. But forge ahead by strolling into **Spanish Table**, a shopper's paradise settled in Mill Valley, only to find foodies and locals alike reveling in unique Spanish cookbooks, cookware, specialty foods and drool-worthy wines. Finally, peckish travelers with a sweet craving can also be found at **Three Twins Ice Cream** for their organically produced creamy treats that promise to leave an everlasting impression.

Waters off the coast here provide divers with exceptional hunting ground, and restaurants throughout Marin count on supremely fresh oysters, briny clams

and meaty mussels. The difficulty in (legally) sourcing these large, savory mollusks make the likes of red abalone a treasured species in area (particularly Asian) establishments, though seafood does seem to be the accepted norm among most of the restaurants in town. If fish doesn't float your boat, **Fred's Coffee Shop** in Sausalito is a no-frills find for fulfilling breakfast signatures like deep-fried French toast with a side of calorie-heavy, yet crazy-good caramelized "Millionaire's bacon." Carb addicts routinely pay their respects at **M.H. Bread & Butter**, said to be the best bakery around town. Their crusty loaves make for fantastic sandwiches, but are equally divine just slathered with—you guessed it—butter! While fertile San Rafael county's natural ingredients may be sold in countless farmers' markets, many other celebrations of food and wine continue to pop up throughout—during the spring and summer

months. Given its culinary chops and panoramic views, Marin is one of the most sought-after counties for celebrities and visitors alike. True, some places here can seem touristy. But, these chefs and restaurants are lauded for good reason, and know how to make the most of their choice homegrown produce and food purveyors.

BAR BOCCE 🍴○
Pizza • *Trendy*

  ♿ 🍸   **MAP:** A3

This little bungalow on the Bay draws big crowds for the harbor views from its covered patio, complete with a namesake bocce court. Equipped with beachside benches for watching youngsters at play and toasty fire pits for warding off the late-afternoon fog, it's often packed to the gills on weekend afternoons with locals lingering over a second (or fourth) glass of wine.

Should the buzz get too strong, there's hearty Italian cooking to set you right, including wood-fired pizzas topped with pesto, ricotta and kale; tender meatballs in a rich San Marzano tomato sauce; and rib-sticking eggplant parmesan dolloped with burrata. Perk yourself up for the ride home with a vanilla gelato affogato, drowned in espresso and sprinkled with Heath bar crumble.

■ 1250 Bridgeway (bet. Pine & Turney Sts.), Sausalito
℺ (415) 331-0555 — **WEB:** www.barbocce.com
■ Lunch & dinner daily   PRICE: $$

BARREL HOUSE TAVERN 🍴○
Californian • *Contemporary décor*

  ♿ 🍸 🍷   **MAP:** A3

The former San Francisco-Sausalito ferry terminal has found new life as this lovely Californian restaurant, which gets its name from its barrel-like arched wood ceiling. A front lounge with a crackling fireplace and well-stocked bar is popular with locals, while tourists can't resist the expansive dining room and back deck, which boasts spectacular views of the Bay.

The cocktail and wine offerings are strong, as is the house-made soda program, which produces intriguing, never-too-sweet combinations like yellow peach, basil and ginger. These pair beautifully with meaty Dungeness crab sliders coupled with watermelon-jicama slaw; though they might be too tasty to keep around by the time grilled swordfish and pork belly with white beans hit the table.

■ 660 Bridgeway (at Princess St.), Sausalito
℺ (415) 729-9593 — **WEB:** www.barrelhousetavern.com
■ Lunch & dinner daily   PRICE: $$$

BUCKEYE ROADHOUSE ¡|O
American · *Elegant*

MAP: A2

This hideout has welcomed generations of locals through its doors since 1937, even as its location on Highway 1 gave way to the more bustling 101. Enter the whitewashed Craftsman building, and you'll be given your choice of dining—either at the clubby bar or the grand main room with wood-paneled walls and red leather banquettes.

The food here is classical but never dull, with a simple menu of salads, sandwiches and grilled meats. Oysters bingo set over spinach and topped with garlic aïoli oozes with California panache, while succulent and crisp-skinned chili-lime brick chicken is just as delicious as its accompanying sides—think polenta sticks and cheese-stuffed pasilla peppers. Finish with a slice of pie—the s'mores version or key lime are both winners.

15 Shoreline Hwy. (off Hwy. 101), Mill Valley
(415) 331-2600 — **WEB:** www.buckeyeroadhouse.com
Lunch & dinner daily   **PRICE:** $$

BURMATOWN ¡|O
Burmese · *Cozy*

MAP: C2

Bypass the tired Asian-fusion offerings and head straight for the authentic Burmese dishes at this out-of-the-way cutie. A nutty, crunchy and flavorful tea leaf salad is the perfect answer to a hot summer day, while hearty spiced potato-stuffed samosas and fresh, springy egg noodles tossed with barbecue pork and fried garlic chips will warm your soul in the cooler months.

Given the high quality of its food, it's no surprise that Burmatown is Corte Madera's most popular neighbor: it's big with local families from the surrounding residences who pack every single table, attended to by warm servers. If you're willing to make a special trip to this charming bright-orange bungalow, the laid-back vibe will have you feeling right at home.

60 Corte Madera Ave. (bet. Bahr Ln. & Redwood Ave.), Corte Madera
(415) 945-9096 — **WEB:** www.burmatown.com
Dinner Tue – Sun   **PRICE:** $$

CAFE REYES ⅋○

Pizza • Rustic

MAP: A1

This unassuming charmer in quaint Point Reyes Station is a perfect stop for day-trippers who are sure to enjoy the many delicious dishes that emerge from its duo of wood-fired ovens. Pizza is the focus, with ten varieties ranging from a classic Margherita to meaty classics like fennel sausage and mushroom. The deliciously crusty pies are named after local destinations like the Limantour and Bodega, as well as the Farallon, with its slivers of roasted garlic, mini pepperoni with crisped edges and mushrooms, plus a pile of mozzarella.

Given its cooking method, it's no surprise that Cafe Reyes is stacked high with wood, both against the walls and under the counter. The big, spacious, barn-like dining room is rustic, unfussy and perfect for groups.

- 11101 Shoreline Hwy. (at Mesa Rd.), Point Reyes Station
- (415) 663-9493 — **WEB:** www.cafe-reyes.com
- Lunch & dinner Wed – Sun

PRICE: $$

COPITA ⅋○

Mexican • Family

MAP: A3

Set sail aboard the Sausalito ferry for dinner at this Mexican smash hit that is located just steps from the harbor's bobbing yachts. Colorful and casual, Copita's most coveted seats are on the sidewalk patio (complete with partial views of the water and quaint downtown), but a spot at the exceptionally well-stocked tequila bar or in the brightly tiled dining room is no disappointment.

A light meal of tacos could include seared mahi mahi with pineapple pico de gallo and tomatillo salsa or tomato-accented chicken tinga with avocado and Mexican crema. Options abound for heartier appetites, like 24-hour carnitas and chicken mole enchiladas. And the lively surrounds are a hit with kids, who love sipping on the sweet house-made horchata.

- 739 Bridgeway (at Anchor St.), Sausalito
- (415) 331-7400 — **WEB:** www.copitarestaurant.com
- Lunch & dinner daily

PRICE: $$

INSALATA'S 🐾
Mediterranean • *Contemporary décor*

♿ ⊡ 🛋

MAP: B2

San Anselmo restaurateur, Chef Heidi Krahling honors her late father, Italo Insalata, at this crowd-pleasing Marin hangout. The zucca-orange stucco exterior alludes to the Mediterranean air within. Insalata's upscale setting is framed by lemon-yellow walls hung with grand depictions of nature's bounty, setting the scene for an array of fresh and flavorful cuisine to come.

Sparked by Middle Eastern flavors, the kitchen's specialties include velvety smooth potato-leek soup made brilliantly green from watercress purée. Also sample grilled lamb skewers drizzled with cumin-yogurt atop crunchy salad and flatbread. The takeout area in the back is stocked with salads, sides and sandwiches made with house-baked bread. Boxed lunches are a fun, tasty convenience.

▨ 120 Sir Francis Drake Blvd. (at Barber Ave.), San Anselmo
✆ (415) 457-7700 — **WEB:** www.insalatas.com
▨ Lunch & dinner daily

PRICE: $$

MASA'S SUSHI 🍴
Japanese • *Simple*

MAP: B1

Respected veteran Chef Takatoshi Toshi has returned to his roots and taken over the reins to bring Novato locals hearty and affordable sushi. Don't be surprised to see him behind the counter here, breaking down a whole salmon while making small talk with his neighbors. The space is simple, understated and quiet, which seems to match its quaint downtown location, set amid boutiques and restaurants.

Lunch combinations are an excellent deal, offering chirashi bowls as well as sushi and nigiri with miso soup. Come dinner, the affordable omakase selection unveils nigiri, salmon and tuna tastings. Bigger platters might arrive as lovely amalgamations of avocado and albacore rolls alongside ebi, yellowtail and cherry wood-smoked goldeneye snapper (kinmedai).

▨ 813 Grant Ave. (bet. Reichert & Sherman Aves.), Novato
✆ (415) 892-0081 — **WEB:** www.masasnovato.com
▨ Lunch Mon – Fri Dinner Mon – Sat

PRICE: $$

MARIN

MADCAP ❀
Contemporary · Chic

&♿

MAP: B2

Upscale yet friendly and approachable, Madcap is fast becoming one of the Bay Area's beloved destinations for contemporary dining. The superb culinary skills on display should be no surprise considering that Chef/owner Ron Siegel worked at some of the West Coast's more renowned kitchens, including The French Laundry and Masa's. This is his first solo project and it reflects much of his background as a chef with Californian sensibilities and subtle Japanese influences—note the paper lamps and minimalist décor. At its soul, this is a humble hangout, striving to highlight the best local and seasonal ingredients with little fuss.

Both à la carte and fixed menus are offered and are sure to feature some of the kitchen's more surprising concoctions. While each composition is likely to change with the seasons, every bite remains well crafted, balanced and teeming with unique flavor combinations. Highlights unveil house-made, toothsome tortelloni filled with delicately braised rabbit, resting on a miso-mushroom purée and capped with parmesan espuma.

Desserts are also artful and fun, as seen in a cube of Japanese cheesecake set on a lid over shiso-panna cotta with hot pink huckleberry foam.

▓ 198 Sir Francis Drake Blvd. (bet. Bank St. & Barber Ave.), San Anselmo

✆ (415) 453-9898 — **WEB:** www.madcapmarin.com

▓ Dinner Thu – Mon

PRICE: $$$$

OSTERIA STELLINA ⅰ○

Italian · Family

MAP: A1

Its name is Italian for "little star," and this gem does indeed shine in the heart of tiny Point Reyes Station, a one-horse clapboard town with little more than a filling station and a post office to its name. But the Wild West it's not: this frontier village is Marin-chic, and its saloon is a soothing retreat with wide windows and local produce on the menu.

You'll taste the difference in the pillowy house-made focaccia, the soothing chicken brodo and the crisp salad of little gem lettuce with blue cheese, toasted walnuts and honeycrisp apples. Organic, grass-fed beef stew is packed with spices and served over herbed polenta. Finish with the warm, moist Guinness gingerbread cake with a scoop of lemon ice cream and butterscotch drizzle. Yum!

11285 Hwy. 1 (at 3rd St.), Point Reyes Station
☎ (415) 663-9988 — **WEB:** www.osteriastellina.com
Lunch & dinner daily   PRICE: $$

PICCO ⅰ○

Italian · Contemporary décor

MAP: B2

Picco is Italian for "summit," and this charming Larkspur hilltop home has long been a beacon among Marin County diners. Chef/owner Bruce Hill is a true local-food devotee: his Italian-influenced fare heaps on Marin ingredients like the fresh turnips that dot his silky-smooth duck tortelli, or the Meyer lemon yogurt and beets that sit atop a nourishing kale salad. The "Marin Mondays" menu is a particular steal.

The precise staff moves ably through the busy dining room, carrying bowls of creamy risotto made on the half-hour. With a high ceiling and exposed brick walls, the vibe is graceful but never fussy, making this the perfect setting for couples and groups of friends who congregate here.

Also check out Pizzeria Picco next door.

320 Magnolia Ave. (at King St.), Larkspur
☎ (415) 924-0300 — **WEB:** www.restaurantpicco.com
Dinner nightly   PRICE: $$$

PLAYA 😃
Mexican · *Family*

🍸 ♿ ♨️

MAP: B2

The foggy beaches of Marin County may be a far cry from the sand and surf of Baja, but this lively spot keeps the vacation vibe alive with margaritas, mezcal and madly delicious Mexican cooking. And while Playa feels upmarket with its colorful tiles, blown-glass lights and walls of windows, its food is wonderfully authentic.

The menu makes for tough choices: opt for the outstanding al pastor tacos layered with sweet-spicy caramelized pineapple salsa, or the crispy empanadas stuffed with chorizo, currants and green olives, drizzled with chimichurri. Whether you choose a cocktail and a mushroom-squash blossom quesadilla at the bar or bowls of chips and queso fundido with a big group on the sunny back patio, good times are guaranteed.

▦ 41 Throckmorton Ave. (bet. Blithedale & Miller Aves.), Mill Valley

✆ (415) 384-8871 — **WEB:** www.playamv.com

▦ Lunch Tue – Sun Dinner nightly

PRICE: $$

POGGIO 😃
Italian · *Trattoria*

♿ ♨️ 🚲

MAP: A3

A restaurant of Poggio's vintage could easily rest on its tourist-trap laurels—after all, its alfresco terrace has views of the Sausalito harbor that any starry-eyed visitor would long to savor. But this enduring favorite also provides plenty to enjoy on the plate, as well as a comfortable atmosphere, friendly service and a solid Italian wine selection.

The menu takes some northern California detours, like the Dungeness crab salad with blood oranges and radishes. But even the most die-hard Italian would give a seal of approval to the homemade agnolotti, served in a succulent pork ragù with a dusting of parmesan. Want something a little more special? In season, they're happy to give your pasta a hefty shaving of black or white truffles.

▦ 777 Bridgeway (at Bay St.), Sausalito

✆ (415) 332-7771 — **WEB:** www.poggiotrattoria.com

▦ Lunch & dinner daily

PRICE: $$

SALTWATER 🍴

Seafood • Contemporary décor

 ♿ ⛲   **MAP:** A1

If you love oysters, this coastal-chic spot will have you as happy as a clam. Nearly half its menu features these ultra-fresh bivalves plucked straight from nearby Tomales Bay—whether raw, broiled with chili-garlic butter, or simmered in a creamy leek stew. If oysters aren't your thing, there's also plenty of other local seafood to choose from, including crisp-skinned steelhead trout or risotto with clams and uni. Carnivores can opt for a roasted pork chop with collard greens.

Set in a country-style house, Saltwater is a small town hot spot that attracts casual couples of all ages for local beer and wine on tap. The menu changes often to reflect the best of its markets, so be sure to pounce on such dishes as spicy gingerbread cake before they vanish.

▪ 12781 Sir Francis Drake Blvd. (at Inverness Way), Inverness
☎ (415) 669-1244 — **WEB:** www.saltwateroysterdepot.com
▪ Lunch Sat – Sun Dinner Thu – Mon   **PRICE:** $$$

SIR AND STAR 🍴

Californian • Cozy

 ♿ ⛲ ☕   **MAP:** A1

This quirky roadhouse in the historic Olema Inn is one-of-a-kind, from the displays of branches in the light-flooded dining room to the poetic menu descriptions ("small feast of fishes," otherwise known as mussels). But in the hands of Chef/owners and longtime Marin fixtures Daniel DeLong and Margaret Gradé, you can always expect a fine meal made with painstakingly sourced local ingredients.

Sip a glass of Marin-made mead by the fire; then head to the dining room, where you'll sample dishes like Point Reyes Toma cheese "fondue," golden beet soup and fluffy cardamom sugar beignets with local honey and strawberries—all accompanied by excellent crusty bread.

Come Saturday, there is also a prix-fixe menu, available by reservation only.

▪ 10000 Sir Francis Drake Blvd. (at Hwy. 1), Olema
☎ (415) 663-1034 — **WEB:** www.sirandstar.com
▪ Dinner Wed – Sun   **PRICE:** $$

SOL FOOD 🍴○

Puerto Rican • Family

♿ 🏠

MAP: C2

You won't be able to miss this Puerto Rican favorite, recognizable by its grasshopper-green exterior and overflowing crowds of festive diners. In fact, their comida criolla is so popular that it's taken over the block: a sister bodega does a booming takeout business, while gift store Conchita sells wares from San Juan and beyond.

Sol Food's soul food is hearty and abundant, from tamale-like pasteles of mashed plantain and taro stuffed with garlicky pork to fragrant sautéed shrimp loaded with tomato, onion and spices. Outstanding daily specials, from arroz con pollo to pernil, are also big draws. Wash it all down with a delicious mango iced tea, and don't skip the decadent pineapple bread pudding, soaked in warm, buttery mango sauce, for dessert.

▢ 903 Lincoln Ave. (at 3rd St.), San Rafael

✆ (415) 451-4765 — **WEB:** www.solfoodrestaurant.com

▢ Lunch & dinner daily

PRICE: $$

SUSHI RAN 😊

Japanese • Contemporary décor

🍶 ♿ 🍴

MAP: A3

Chefs have come and gone at this Sausalito staple, but its zen-like atmosphere and exquisite selection of raw fish remain unchanged—and that's just how the regulars like it. With its charming beachside-bungalow ambience, attentive service staff and thoughtfully curated sake selection, Sushi Ran is as dependable as a restaurant can get.

Start off with a small bite like shrimp tempura over crisp veggies, tobiko and asparagus, or a steamed red crab salad mingled with seaweed, cucumber and a sweet soy dressing. Then move on to the main event: meticulously sourced, extraordinarily pure hamachi, big-eye tuna, steamed blue prawns and Santa Barbara uni. Whether you choose sashimi or nigiri, rest assured that these talented chefs will steer you right.

▢ 107 Caledonia St. (bet. Pine & Turney Sts.), Sausalito

✆ (415) 332-3620 — **WEB:** www.sushiran.com

▢ Lunch Mon – Fri Dinner nightly

PRICE: $$

VILLAGE SAKE 👻

Japanese · Rustic

🍶 ♿ ⛱

MAP: B2

Set along a bustling stretch, Village Sake is a mighty hot and mod izakaya delivering authentic goods in the heart of quaint Fairfax. All the classic small plates are in full force here: crisp and creamy takoyaki (octopus croquettes), okonomiyaki, tataki (made with silky smoked hamachi) and coconut mochi cake complete with cardamom gelato. If you must have sushi, there's a small selection of excellent nigiri, too—make sure to sample the shima aji and kinmedai.

The look of the room suggests Tokyo, with closely spaced tables, an array of wood accents (including a live-edge wood counter) as well as a friendly staff, many of them Japanese natives. This is a popular spot that doesn't take reservations, so expect long lines, especially on weekends.

▨ 19 Bolinas Rd. (bet. Broadway Blvd. & Mono Ave.), Fairfax
✆ (415) 521-5790 — **WEB:** www.villagesake.com
▨ Dinner Wed – Sun   **PRICE:** $$

Look for our symbol 🍺
spotlighting restaurants
with a notable beer list.

PENINSULA

PENINSULA

A COLLISION OF CULTURES

Situated to the south of the city, the San Francisco Peninsula separates the Bay from the expansive Pacific Ocean. While it may not be known across the globe for stellar chefs and pioneering Californian cooking, the Peninsula boasts an incredibly diverse and rich Asian culture. Local eateries and numerous markets reflect this region's melting pot and continue to draw residents for authentic international cuisines. Those in need of a taste from the Far East should join Korean natives at **Kukje Super Market** as they scoop up fresh seafood, rolls of gimbap and a host of other prepared delicacies. Alternatively, one may practice the art of chopstick wielding at one of the many Japanese sushi bars, ramen houses and izakayas. Filipino foodies tickle their fancy with an impressive selection of traditional breads and pastries at **Valerio's Tropical Bakeshop** in Daly City. Fittingly set in a Filipino-

dominated quarter referred to as "**Little Manila**," Valerio's is famously revered as *the* best bakery around.

Beyond the Far East, sugar junkies of the Western variety savor classic Danish pastries at Burlingame's **Copenhagen Bakery & Cafe**, also applauded for their creamy special occasion cakes. Over in San Mateo, Italians can't miss a stop at **pasta pasta** for freshly made shapes, homemade sauces and salads that are both fulfilling and easy to put together at home. If your domestic skills leave much to be desired, charming **La Biscotteria** has premium, hand-crafted Italian pastries and cookies on hand, including cannoli, amaretti, sfogliatelle and biscotti in an assortment of flavors. This precious gem in Redwood City also sells beautiful hand-painted Deruta ceramics that are imported directly from Umbria.

The Peninsula is also known for its large Mexican-American population. Their taste for home can be gratified at such authentic taquerias as **El Grullense** in Redwood City; **El Palenque** in San Mateo; and **Mexcal Taqueria** in Menlo Park. Just as **Gabriel & Daniel's Mexican Grill** in the Burlingame Golf Center clubhouse is an ideal place to unwind after playing a round out on the plush course, divey **Back A Yard** in Menlo Park is eternally beloved among foodies yearning for flavorful Caribbean cuisine. Pescetarians know that **Barbara's Fishtrap** in Half Moon Bay is a sought-after "catch" for fish 'n chips by the harbor, whereas pig trumps fish at **Gorilla Barbeque**. Here, fat-frilled pork ribs are all the rage, especially when served out of an orange railroad car parked on Cabrillo Highway in Pacifica.

SUMMER'S BOUNTY

In addition to harboring some of the Bay Area's most authentic Cantonese dens and dim sum houses, Millbrae is a lovely spot to raise one last toast to summer. In fact, **The Millbrae Art & Wine Festival** is a profusion of wicked fairground eats—from meltingly tender cheesesteaks to spicy Cajun-style corndogs and everything in between. Then, motivated home chefs may stop by **Draeger's Market** in San Mateo to pick up some wine and cheese for dinner, while **Wursthall Restaurant & Bierhaus** brings a fun, festive spirit along with a bevy of German beer and bites to this tech center. Finally, those looking for a little instant gratification are bound to revel in the riot of Japanese treats at **Suruki Supermarket**.

Half Moon Bay is a coastal city big on sustainable produce; and in keeping with this philosophy, residents prepare for cozy evenings at home by loading up on local fruits and vegetables from one of the many roadside stands on Route 92. Find them also scanning the bounty at **Coastside Farmer's Market**, which has been known to unveil such Pescadero treasures as **Harley Farms** goat cheese, as well as organic eggs from **Early Bird Ranch**.

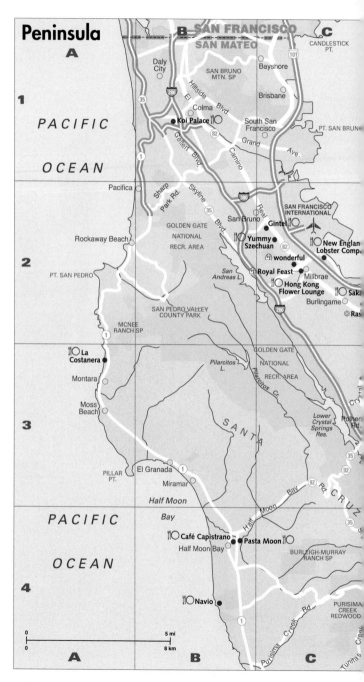

Peninsula

A

PACIFIC

OCEAN

CANDLESTICK PT.

Daly City

SAN BRUNO MTN. SP

Bayshore

Brisbane

Colma

●Koi Palace

South San Francisco

PT. SAN BRUN

Grand

Camino

Ave.

Pacifica

Sharp

Park Rd.

Skyline

Real

SAN FRANCISCO INTERNATIONAL

San Bruno

●Gintei

Rockaway Beach

GOLDEN GATE NATIONAL RECR. AREA

Blvd

●Yummy Szechuan

●New England Lobster Comp.

PT. SAN PEDRO

San Andreas L.

wonderful

●Royal Feast

Millbrae

●Hong Kong Flower Lounge

●Saka

SAN PEDRO VALLEY COUNTY PARK

Burlingame

●Ras

MCNEE RANCH SP

●La Costanera

GOLDEN GATE

Pilarcitos L.

NATIONAL

Montara

Pinarcitos Cr.

RECR. AREA

Moss Beach

Lower Crystal Springs Res.

Rolher Rd.

Crys

SANTA

PILLAR PT.

El Granada

Miramar

Half Moon

CRUZ

Rd.

Bay

Half Moon

Bay

PACIFIC

Bay

●Café Capistrano

●Pasta Moon

OCEAN

Half Moon Bay

BURLEIGH-MURRAY RANCH SP

●Navio

PURISIMA CREEK REDWOOD

Creek Rd.

Purisima Creek

Tunitas

4

0 ——————— 5 mi

0 ——————— 8 km

A

B

C

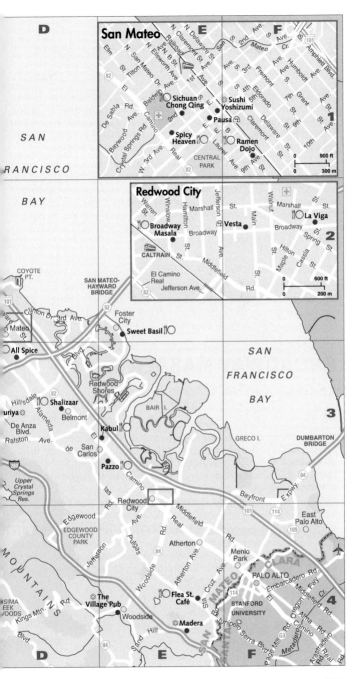

San Mateo

Elm St.
N. San Mateo Dr.
N. Ellsworth Ave.
N. Claremont St.
N. Delaware St.
N. B St.
Railroad Ave.
San Mateo Ave.
2nd Ave.
Amphlett Blvd.
101
Humboldt St.
Cr.
De sabla Rd.
E. Tilton Ave.
El Camino Real
Baldwin Ave.
1st Ave.
3rd Ave.
Fremont Ave.
7th Ave.
Grant St.
Eldorado St.
4th Ave.
Delaware St.

Sichuan Chong Qing
Sushi Yoshizumi
2nd Ave.
Pausa
Claremont St.
9th St.
10th St.
Baywood Ave.
Crystal Springs Rd.
Spicy Heaven
Laurel Ave.
Ramen Dojo
W. 3rd Ave.
82
CENTRAL PARK
9th St.

82

900 ft
300 m

Redwood City

Jefferson St.
Walnut St.
Marshall St.
Winslow St.
Hamilton St.
Marshall St.
Warren St.
Main St.
La Viga
Broadway Masala
Vesta
Broadway
Spring St.
Hilton St.
Maple St.
Cassia St.
CALTRAIN
St.
Middlefield Rd.
El Camino Real
Jefferson Ave.
82

600 ft
200 m

COYOTE PT.

101
Clifton Dr.
3rd Ave.
92
SAN MATEO-HAYWARD BRIDGE
Foster City
n Mateo
Sweet Basil
All Spice

SAN FRANCISCO BAY

Hillsdale Blvd.
82
Shalizaar
Alameda
uriya
Belmont
Redwood Shores
BAIR I.
De Anza Blvd.
Ralston Ave.
Kabul
de
San Carlos
GRECO I.
DUMBARTON BRIDGE
84
280
Pazzo
Camino
las Rd.
Redwood City
Middlefield Rd.
Bayfront Expwy.

Upper Crystal Springs Res.
Edgewood Rd.
EDGEWOOD COUNTY PARK
Real
101
114
East Palo Alto
109
Atherton
84
Pulgas
Atherton Ave.
Menlo Park
SAN MATEO
SANTA CLARA
Woodside Rd.
Jefferson Ave.
Santa Cruz Ave.
Atherton Ave.
114
Embarcadero Rd.
PALO ALTO
Middlefield Rd.
MOUNTAINS
SIMA EEK OODS
Kings Mtn. Rd.
The Village Pub
Flea St. Café
STANFORD UNIVERSITY
Junipero Serra Blvd.
Oregon Expwy.
Alma St.
El Camino Real
Arastradero Rd.
Blvd.
84
Woodside
Madera
Sand Hill Rd.
G3
Page Mill Rd.
Metralbado

ALL SPICE ||O
International • Cozy

Like a bracelet glittering with different jewels, All Spice is home to a bevy of vibrant dining rooms, made extra colorful with artwork and sparkling chandeliers. It's a delightful blend of old-school charm and contemporary verve that appeals to a sophisticated crowd. They're usually here to catch up with friends or celebrate a birthday.

This kitchen offers a variety of creative selections on both the à la carte and five-course tasting menus, which spin to highlight the seasons. Chilled butternut squash soup in a shot glass makes a soigné amuse-bouche and is a delicious way to start a meal; while carrot-date fritters with charred eggplant and mango with carrot curls is accompanied by toasted almonds as well as smoked date chutney for added enrichment.

1602 El Camino Real (bet. Barneson & Borel Aves.), San Mateo
(650) 627-4303 — **WEB:** www.allspicerestaurant.com
Dinner Tue – Sat   PRICE: $$$

BROADWAY MASALA ||O
Indian • Contemporary décor

&

Set in the heart of downtown Redwood City, this contemporary Indian boasts great views onto the main thoroughfare it's named for. In all likelihood though, you might be distracted by what's on your plate as these traditional dishes are executed to precision. Begin with crispy potato-and-pea samosas that exude a nice kick of spice, before moving on to smoky butter chicken served atop basmati rice. Even the warm and flaky naan is an outstanding delight.

While service is distracted, it's hard to argue with a place that has such hefty portions for such reasonable prices. Lunch specials are a steal, and the kitchen does a booming takeout business. Adventurous diners may also enjoy such fusion items as chapatti lamb tacos or Cajun-spiced chicken tikka masala.

2397 Broadway (at Winslow St.), Redwood City
(650) 369-9000 — **WEB:** www.broadwaymasala.net
Lunch & dinner daily   PRICE: $$

CAFÉ CAPISTRANO ⅈ○

Mexican • *Family*

♿ ⛱

Chef/owner Arturo Mul grew up on the Yucatán peninsula, and the traditional Mayan dishes of his youth are now the backbone of this cute café in the heart of Half Moon Bay. Housed in an older home surrounded by gardens and a small side deck, this retreat is warm, inviting and, to the delight of local families, off most tourists' radars.

Start with a plate of fried panuchos (stuffed with earthy black bean purée and topped with achiote-marinated tender pulled chicken). Then dig into the Mayan pork adobo served with fresh salsa, guacamole, a lightly pickled coleslaw and crema. But, save room for the true star of the show—grilled red snapper coupled with warm tortillas for wrapping, as well as queso for rich and creamy goodness.

▨ 523 Church St. (at Miramontes St.), Half Moon Bay
✆ (650) 726-7699 — **WEB:** N/A
▨ Lunch & dinner daily   PRICE: ⊜⊜

FLEA ST. CAFE ⅈ○

Contemporary • *Cozy*

⛲

This classic "café" retains the feeling of being in a house, with dining areas distributed throughout. Interesting artwork adorns each of these rooms, simply adding to the sense of intimacy, not unlike the warm and inviting front bar area, filled with friendly banter and soft tunes.

The team ensures that each item from this kitchen is well conceived and adheres to California's farm-to-table ethos. Everything on this seasonally driven menu strives to emphasize freshness, starting with the warm and buttery biscuits that welcome you to your table. Don't miss the shell bean soup featuring a braised tomato broth complete with summery flavors. On Thursday through Saturday evenings, explore The Oysterette—a changing carte of oysters served at the bar.

▨ 3607 Alameda de las Pulgas (at Avy Ave.), Menlo Park
✆ (650) 854-1226 — **WEB:** www.cooleatz.com
▨ Dinner Tue – Sun   PRICE: $$

GINTEI ⅡО

Japanese • *Minimalist*

🍶 ♿

San Bruno's reputation as a dining wasteland is due for a re-evaluation thanks to this sleek and stylish sushi spot, whose offerings can hang with the best in San Francisco. Bright and contemporary, with dramatic pressed-tin ceilings and a coveted eight-seat counter, it's known as a reservations-required must for omakase enthusiasts, with deeply hospitable service.

Fans of nigiri should make a beeline for the chef's selection, but the more discerning palate will revel in market specials like the silky Hokkaido scallops, sweet and succulent live spot prawns (with the traditional deep-fried heads alongside) as well as firm yet tender octopus. Everything is minimally dressed here—all the better to accentuate the fish's outstanding quality.

▨ 235 El Camino Real (bet. Crystal Springs Rd. & San Felipe Ave.), San Bruno
℘ (650) 636-4135 — **WEB:** www.gintei.co
▨ Lunch Tue – Fri Dinner Tue – Sun   PRICE: $$

HONG KONG FLOWER LOUNGE ⅡО

Chinese • *Family*

♿ 🚇 🍴 🧼

Generations of dim sum diehards have patronized this palace of pork buns, where a small army of servers will surround you with carts from the moment you take your seat. They bear innumerable delights: rich barbecue pork belly with crispy skin, pan-fried pork-and-chive wontons steamed to order and doused in oyster sauce, delicate vegetable dumplings and a best-in-class baked egg custard bun. Evenings are a bit more sedate, emphasizing Cantonese seafood straight from the on-site tanks.

As with all dim sum spots, the early bird gets the best selection (and avoids the non-negligible weekend waits). Thankfully, the super-central Millbrae location, towering over El Camino Real, boasts plenty of parking—and a machine-like staff that knows how to pack them in.

▨ 51 Millbrae Ave. (at El Camino Real), Millbrae
℘ (650) 692-6666 — **WEB:** www.mayflower-seafood.com
▨ Lunch & dinner daily   PRICE: $$

KABUL ⅋○
Afghan • *Family*

♿   **MAP:** E3

Fans of Afghan cuisine flock from miles around to this homestyle spot in San Carlos, tucked away in a deceptively large space within a modest shopping plaza. Kabul's walls are festooned with deep red tapestries and other Afghan embroidery, and even on weekday nights it fills up with local families. There's even a semi-private side dining room for big groups.

The friendly staff is happy to suggest favorite dishes, from smoky chicken and lamb kebabs over spiced basmati rice to sweet, fork-tender sautéed pumpkin served with garlicky yogurt sauce and fluffy flatbread. And though everything comes in generous portions, you'll want to save room for the firnee, a sweet milk pudding flavored with cardamom and rosewater and topped with pistachios.

▨   135 El Camino Real (bet. F & Holly Sts.), San Carlos
✆ (650) 594-2840 — **WEB:** www.kabulcuisine.co
▨   Lunch Mon –Fri Dinner nightly   **PRICE:** $$

KOI PALACE ⅋○
Chinese • *Elegant*

♿   🍴   🥢   **MAP:** B1

Long regarded as one of the Bay Area's best spots for dim sum, Koi Palace continues to earn its serious waits (guaranteed on weekends, and common at weekday lunch). The dining room is a step up from its competition, with shallow koi ponds weaving between tables, high ceilings and huge tables to accommodate the Chinese-American families celebrating big occasions.

They come to share plates of perfectly lacquered, smoky-salty roasted suckling pig or sticky rice noodle rolls encasing plump shrimp, minced ginger and sesame oil. Not far behind, find lotus leaves stuffed with glutinous rice, dried scallop and roast pork, as well as big pots of jasmine tea. Save room for desserts like the fluffy almond cream-steamed buns and flaky, caramelized custard tarts.

▨   365 Gellert Blvd. (bet. Hickey & Serramonte Blvds.), Daly City
✆ (650) 992-9000 — **WEB:** www.koipalace.com
▨   Lunch & dinner daily   **PRICE:** $$

LA COSTANERA ⫶○

Peruvian • *Contemporary décor*

Set atop one of the most beautiful perches in the entire Bay Area, this bungalow boasts a gorgeous patio and a dining room that's walled with windows.

While the panoramas are amazing—endless ocean, spectacular sunsets and even frolicking dolphins if you're lucky—so are the boldly flavored plates produced by Chef Carlos Altamirano and his team. Cebiche pescado bathed in leche de tigre is perhaps the best way to experience Peru's national dish, while succulent langostino crocantes served over silky potatoes, or herb-marinated pollo salvaje accompanied by fried yuca are other treasures worth devouring.

Be sure to sample the creative cocktails. Alternatively, try a delicious and refreshing chicha morada, which is safer for the drive home.

■ 8150 Cabrillo Hwy. (bet. 1st & 2nd Sts.), Montara

✆ (650) 728-1600 — **WEB:** www.lacostanerarestaurant.com

■ Dinner Tue – Sun   PRICE: $$$

LA VIGA ⫶○

Mexican • *Cozy*

Named after Mexico City's massive seafood market, La Viga is a Redwood City favorite for oceanic fare with a Latin twist. Wedged between an industrial area and downtown, the basic but cheerful dining room draws both blue- and white-collar workers for heaping tacos—soft white corn tortillas stuffed with fried snapper fillet, cabbage and chipotle crema; or crisp prawns with tomatillo-garlic sauce and pico de gallo.

At the dinner hour, residents stream in for the famed tallarines con mariscos, a sizable mound of al dente fideos studded with pristine seafood cooked in a spicy tomato sauce. With such fresh ingredients and bold flavors, the low prices and generous portions are particularly pleasing. Don't forget to leave room for a delicate flan to finish.

■ 1772 Broadway (bet. Beech & Maple Sts.), Redwood City

✆ (650) 679-8141 — **WEB:** www.lavigaseafood.com

■ Lunch & dinner Tue – Sun   PRICE: $$

MADERA ✿

Contemporary • Trendy

MAP: E4

As evidenced by all those Teslas parked out front, this is a swanky spot for fine dining in the Rosewood Sand Hill hotel. The grand open kitchen, roaring fireplace and large outdoor patio complete with gorgeous views of the Santa Cruz mountains draw a moneyed crowd of local techies.

While its location may mean it is open for three meals a day, come for dinner to taste this kitchen's ambition and pure talent. The cuisine is contemporary, thoughtfully composed with seasonal ingredients and even surprising at times. An excellent risotto sings with the flavors of roasted butternut squash, Perigord black truffles, airy Lacinato kale chips and the unexpected, wondrous touch of finger lime. The kitchen also flaunts its dexterity in three preparations of guinea hen, including its tender breast meat with crackling-crisp skin, sliced thigh and excellent springy sausages accompanied by charred peaches bursting with sweetness, pickled chanterelles, toasted pecans and green onion soubise.

Desserts are fun, delicious and do not hold back, especially the insanely rich peanut butter and black sesame parfait, layered as fudgy brownie, rich ganache, mousse and brittle in a glass goblet.

2825 Sand Hill Rd. (at I-280), Menlo Park

(650) 561-1540 — **WEB:** www.maderasandhill.com

Lunch & dinner daily

PRICE: $$$

NAVIO ⅋○

Californian · *Contemporary décor*

♻ ♿ ⛲ 🛋 🍽   **MAP:** B4

Nestled inside the luxe Ritz-Carlton, Half Moon Bay, Navio is blessed with a classic northern California setting. Whether you're fresh off the course or arriving just for dinner, settle in with a ruby-red Sassamanash punch before admiring the emerald-green links and crashing surf. Golden sunsets are ripe for romantics, but you're almost as likely to find families with young children as lovebirds here.

Just like the coastal décor that is both polished and casual, this kitchen takes classic Americana and ramps it up. Seafood is underlined—diver scallops with a red wine sauce and boudin basque atop seared pear circles are particularly good. But that spaghetti alla chitarra, punctuated by the delicate sweetness of Dungeness crab, is an absolute show-stealer.

■ 1 Miramontes Point Rd. (at Hwy. 1), Half Moon Bay
☎ (650) 712-7000 — **WEB:** www.ritzcarlton.com
■ Lunch Sat – Sun Dinner Wed – Sun   **PRICE: $$$$**

NEW ENGLAND LOBSTER COMPANY ⅋○

Seafood · *Simple*

♿ ⛱   **MAP:** C2

You'll know your meal is fresh at this Peninsula palace of seafood, where flat-screen TVs showcase the bevy of crustaceans in their huge seawater-holding tanks. Set in an industrial warehouse, NELC is both a fish market and a counter-service restaurant—complete with a nautical theme, picnic tables indoors and out and a happy crowd of young and old diners donning lobster bibs.

Kick things off with the justifiably beloved lobster-corn chowder, thick with sweet, succulent meat in a rich and creamy—but not overly heavy—stock. (For dedicated fans, frozen to-go quarts are offered.) Then go for broke with the outstanding lobster roll, lightly dressed with mayo on a fluffy, buttery roll and accompanied by excellent house-made potato chips.

■ 824 Cowan Rd. (off Old Bayshore Hwy.), Burlingame
☎ (650) 443-1559 — **WEB:** www.newenglandlobster.net
■ Lunch & dinner daily   **PRICE: $$**

PASTA MOON 🍴

Italian • *Trattoria*

♿ ⊡   **MAP:** B4

One of Half Moon Bay's most popular restaurants, Pasta Moon is always packed to the gills with locals and tourists filling up on massive portions of hearty Italian-American fare. With its vaulted ceilings and multiple intimate dining rooms, it's a hit among diners of all ages, especially those seated at tables with a view of the lovely side garden.

House-made pastas steal the show, with tempting options like the delicate 30-layer lasagna filled with ricotta, parmesan and house Sicilian sausage (even the half portion is huge). A grilled pork chop stuffed with peaches, pancetta and caramelized onions then arrives with mascarpone mashed potatoes. The butterscotch pudding (with shards of Ghirardelli chocolate, natch) is bound to send you over the moon.

▪ 315 Main St. (bet. Mill St. & Stone Pine Rd.), Half Moon Bay
✆ (650) 726-5125 — **WEB:** www.pastamoon.com
▪ Lunch & dinner daily   **PRICE:** $$

PAUSA 🐶

Italian • *Contemporary décor*

🍸 🍺 ♿ 🍤   **MAP:** E1

Come to this San Mateo sweetie for authentic Italian eats, where Chef/co-owner Andrea Giuliani dishes up the cuisine of his native Veneto. Thanks to the modern space and late hours (by San Mateo standards, at least), it's a big draw for the growing crowds of young tech types in town.

The dining room has a view of the charcuterie aging room and those enticing cured meats like delicate, fennel-flecked finocchiona or exceptional pork ciccioli terrine. The wood-fired Neapolitan pizzas are equally strong—try the porchetta variation, topped with gorgonzola and radicchio. And of course, the pasta doesn't disappoint either: seafood is a specialty of Veneto, and their perciatelli with a tomato-flecked shrimp and octopus ragù is downright perfect.

▪ 223 E. 4th Ave. (bet. B St. & Ellsworth Ave.), San Mateo
✆ (650) 375-0818 — **WEB:** www.pausasanmateo.com
▪ Lunch Mon – Fri Dinner nightly   **PRICE:** $$

PAZZO 🍴

Pizza • *Family*

&

New Haven transplants longing for the region's signature chewy, charred apizza will find a taste of home at this San Carlos jewel, which churns out authentically blistered pies. Keep it traditional with red sauce topped with house-made fennel sausage and cremini mushrooms. Or go slightly Californian with the garlicky asparagus pie, draped with creamy crescenza cheese.

Pazzo (Italian for "crazy") is anything but, thanks to a relaxed, family-friendly vibe. Kids of all ages will delight in the back counter, with a great view of the chef slipping pizzas into the cherry-red, wood-fired oven. And don't sleep through the house-made pastas: pillowy ricotta gnocchi, tucked into a lemony mascarpone and artichoke sauce, is good enough to steal the show.

▨ 1179 Laurel St. (bet. Brittan & Greenwood Aves.), San Carlos
☎ (650) 591-1075 — **WEB:** www.pazzosancarlos.com
▨ Dinner Tue – Sat   PRICE: $$

RAMEN DOJO 🍴

Japanese • *Simple*

The two-hour lines may have died down, but a 40-minute wait on the sidewalk is still standard at this noodle hot spot. The interior, when you finally reach it, is utterly spare—the better to showcase steaming bowls of tasty and satisfying soup. Customize your broth (soy sauce, garlic pork, soybean), spiciness and toppings (like spicy cod roe and kikurage mushrooms), then dive in.

The ramen arrives in minutes, loaded with the standard fried garlic cloves, hard-boiled quail egg, scallion, chili and two slices of roast pork. Your job is to slurp the chewy, delicious noodles (and maybe some seaweed salad or edamame), then hit the road—the hyper-efficient staff needs to keep the line moving, after all. But for one of the best bowls in town, it's worth it.

▨ 805 S. B St. (bet. 8th & 9th Aves.), San Mateo
☎ (650) 401-6568 — **WEB:** N/A
▨ Lunch & dinner Wed – Mon   PRICE: 🍜

RASA ✿

Indian • Contemporary décor

&

In a bustling tech corridor that's also home to Indian expats with high culinary standards, Rasa has managed to find the perfect middle ground. No-joke dishes that aren't toned down for Western palates cater to both software execs and date-night couples, and though the bi-level space boasts a sleek, minimalist-mod décor with bright splashes of orange, stylish pendant lights and dark wood fittings, the focus here is on food.

The elevated South Indian cuisine draws added elegance from superb ingredients and inventive presentations, like fluffy "Bombay slider" buns stuffed with well-seasoned crushed potatoes and drizzled with spicy, smoky "gunpowder" butter. The dosas are appropriately paper-thin and shatteringly crisp, while uttapams topped with peppers and ground masala lamb are earthy and delicate—but watch out for the punch from the accompanying ghost pepper chutney.

A serious spread could be made just out of Rasa's excellent small plates, but for bigger appetites, the flaky white fish moilee, stewed in a creamy coconut curry, is rich and satisfying. No one should skip the cardamom brûlée for dessert: equal parts bread pudding and crème brûlée, it's dizzyingly delicious.

▨ 209 Park Rd. (bet. Burlingame & Howard Aves.), Burlingame
℘ (650) 340-7272 — **WEB:** www.rasaindian.com
▨ Lunch & dinner daily

PRICE: $$

ROYAL FEAST 😊

Chinese • Family

&

You'll dine like royalty at this Millbrae retreat, which offers an array of Chinese delicacies rarely seen outside banquet menus. Helmed by Chef Zongyi Liu, a onetime Bocuse d'Or China competitor, the décor here is light on regal glamour, opting for a simple, spare interior with well-spaced tables. But the menu teems with sought-after items, from abalone to sea cucumber.

Dishes here run the gamut of China's eight great cuisines, with a special emphasis on spicy Sichuan food like white fish in a rich chili-laced broth, or steamed chicken dusted with peppercorns and served in a pool of chili oil. For those seeking milder flavors, the shredded pork in a sweet garlic sauce as well as fluffy pan-fried sesame cakes, make for ideal choices.

▦ 148 El Camino Real (bet. Linden & Serra Aves.), Millbrae
✆ (650) 692-3388 — **WEB:** www.royalfeastmillbrae.com
▦ Lunch & dinner daily

PRICE: $$

SAKAE ⅰ◯

Japanese • Rustic

&

Its glory days of crowds packed to the rafters have passed, but Sakae is still a solid option for elegant sushi and other Japanese specialties. Adjacent to downtown Burlingame and the Caltrain station, this is a sleek space clad in varying shades of wood, Japanese pottery and fresh flowers. Local families enjoy sitting at the bar, where a friendly and engaging sushi chef is a hit with kids.

Skip the many specialty rolls and stick to appetizing nigiri topped with the likes of albacore, yellowtail, crab, salmon or daily featured fish. Otherwise, go for the whiteboard's changing specials like maitake mushroom tempura or grilled baby octopus. Order a pot of hojicha, a roasted green tea, as it nicely complements the impressive range of fish.

▦ 243 California Dr. (at Highland Ave.), Burlingame
✆ (650) 348-4064 — **WEB:** www.sakaesushi.com
▦ Lunch Mon – Sat Dinner nightly

PRICE: $$$

SHALIZAAR ⅋⃝
Persian • Elegant

 ♿ ⊡   **MAP:** D3

A perennial favorite for Persian flavors, Shalizaar is friendly, charming and authentic. Lunchtime draws a large business crowd, while dinners cater to couples on dates. The upscale space features chandeliers, linen-topped tables, Persian carpets and walls of framed windows that flood everything with light.

Meals here are always a pleasure, thanks to the high quality of every ingredient. Try the signature koobideh, smoky ground beef and chicken kebabs served with char-broiled whole tomatoes and rice. Or, tuck into baghali polo, fork-tender lamb shank over bright green rice studded with dill and young fava beans. For dessert, take the friendly servers' advice and order the zoolbia bamieh, sticky-crisp squiggles of fried cake soaked in rosewater syrup.

◾ 300 El Camino Real (bet. Anita & Belmont Aves.), Belmont
☏ (650) 596-9000 — **WEB:** www.shalizaar.com
◾ Lunch & dinner daily   **PRICE:** $$

SICHUAN CHONG QING ⅋⃝
Chinese • Family

 ♿   **MAP:** E1

The medical staff at the Mills Health Center take plenty of heat in an average day, but that doesn't stop them from piling into this compact neighboring Sichuan restaurant for their fix of spicy chili oil and numbing peppercorns. Both ingredients are featured in the crispy Chong Qing chicken and shrimp, each laden with chili peppers (be sure to watch out for shards of bone in the cleaver-chopped chicken).

Skip the mild Mandarin dishes and stick to the house's fiery specialties, like the nutty, smoky cumin lamb with sliced onion, still more chilies and chili oil. Aside from a few contemporary touches, the décor isn't newsworthy and the staff is more efficient than engaging—but you'll likely be too busy enjoying the flavor-packed food to mind.

◾ 211 S. San Mateo Dr. (bet. 2nd & 3rd Aves.), San Mateo
☏ (650) 343-1144 — **WEB:** N/A
◾ Lunch & dinner Tue - Sun   **PRICE:** $$

SPICY HEAVEN ¶○

Chinese • Simple

MAP: E1

The surroundings are bare enough to qualify as purgatory, but for lovers of spicy fare, this humble eatery in downtown San Mateo is worthy of ascension into the astral plane. In an area with plenty of Sichuan dining options, the mostly Chinese-speaking crowd demands that the flavors are authentic and on point.

As is typical, most dishes here revolve around the interplay of tingling peppercorns, mouth-scorching dried chilies and luscious chili oil, from the delicate pork wontons topped with crushed peanuts and scallions to the silky fish fillets and firm tofu swimming in a delectable bright-red and fiery oil bath. Calm your palate with bites of garlicky sautéed water spinach. Then dive in for another chopstick-full of the spicy, tangy chili pork.

35 E. 3rd Ave. (bet. El Camino Real & San Mateo Dr.), San Mateo

☎ (650) 781-3977 — **WEB:** www.spicyheavensanmateo.com

Lunch & dinner daily

PRICE: $$

SWEET BASIL ¶○

Thai • Simple

&

MAP: E2

Set near a charming bayside walking and biking trail on Foster City's perimeter, Sweet Basil makes for a great meal after a leisurely stroll or strenuous ride. The space is snazzy and contemporary-looking with bamboo floors and colorful hanging lights, but the vibe is casual with the staff hustling to serve the daytime rush of office workers as well as families (at night).

Though you may have to wait for a table, their signature kabocha pumpkin and beef in a flavorful red curry will merit patience. Other delights include moist and well-marinated chicken satay; tofu stir-fried with bell peppers and basil; or sticky rice topped with mango. You can choose your own spice level here, but watch out—when this kitchen says hot, they're not kidding around.

1473 Beach Park Blvd. (at Marlin Ave.), Foster City

☎ (650) 212-5788 — **WEB:** www.sweetbasilfostercity.com

Lunch & dinner daily

PRICE: $$

SUSHI YOSHIZUMI ✿

Japanese • *Minimalist*

&

Reservations may be, at times, hard to secure, but rest assured that it is completely worth the effort to dine here. This is a dining room cherished by expats yearning for a taste of home and sushi purists snapping iPhone shots faster than you can say "omakase." The setting is discreet in every way, with a tidy interior that consists of little more than eight seats, a cypress bar, as well as a chef's work station.

The menu is built around Edomae sushi, a style that Chef Akira Yoshizumi spent years perfecting in both Japan and New York. His training clearly pays off with food that is refined, delicate and beautifully balanced. Employing wild seafood, mostly from Japan, to create an intimate omakase experience, Chef Yoshizumi offers detailed explanations and welcomes questions with his warm and open demeanor.

Clean flavors shine in each course; garnishes and sauces are kept to a minimum. Wonderfully firm and surprisingly mild geoduck sashimi arrives with nothing more than fresh wasabi and a sprinkle of black sea salt. Still, the height of any meal is their nigiri, starring flavorful rice seasoned with akazu (red vinegar) and fish so pristine that its taste seems to name its species.

▩ 325 E. 4th Ave. (bet. B St. & Railroad Ave.), San Mateo
℘ (650) 437-2282 — **WEB:** www.sushiyoshizumi.com
▩ Dinner Wed – Sun

PRICE: $$$$

VESTA 😊

Pizza · *Contemporary décor*

  ⚿ 🍽

Whether they're rolling in from their offices at lunch or their condos at dinner, Redwood City locals are always up for a wood-fired pie at this stylish downtown pizzeria. With an airy, mosaic-filled dining room extending into a large front patio, this is a relaxed, roomy space perfect for groups and families.

The menu is divided into red and white pies, and they're equally delicious: zesty tomato sauce enlivens a combo of peppery soppressata, smoked mozzarella and spinach, while a white version with crumbled French feta, fresh slices of garlic, cherry tomatoes and chopped applewood-smoked bacon is irresistible. Get your greens in with the arugula salad, tossed with shaved Parmigiano Reggiano, toasted hazelnuts and a delicious apricot vinaigrette.

▨ 2022 Broadway St. (bet. Jefferson Ave. & Main St.), Redwood City

✆ (650) 362-5052 — **WEB:** www.vestarwc.com

▨ Lunch & dinner Tue – Sat

PRICE: $$

WONDERFUL 😊

Chinese · *Simple*

  ⚿

Hunanese cuisine often takes a back seat to the Bay Area's bumper crop of Cantonese and Sichuanese restaurants, so it's no wonder that this hot spot has caught on with the area's Chinese transplants seeking Hunan dishes. Expect a wait at peak meal hours—especially for large parties, as the dining room is compact.

The boldly flavored dishes incorporate oodles of smoked, cured and fermented ingredients—from the bacon-like pork wok-tossed with leeks, garlic and soy, to the pungent pork, black bean and pickled chili mixture that tops those spicy, chewy, hand-cut Godfather's noodles. The whole chili-braised fish, fresh and flaky in its bath of bright red chili sauce flecked with scallions and garlic, is an absolute must.

▨ 270 Broadway (bet. La Cruz & Victoria Aves.), Millbrae

✆ (650) 651-8888 — **WEB:** www.wonderful.restaurant

▨ Lunch & dinner Wed – Mon

PRICE: $$

THE VILLAGE PUB ✿

Gastropub • Elegant

MAP: E4

Though it has the feel of a chichi private club, this attractive restaurant is open to all—provided they can live up to the style standards set by its fan base of tech tycoons and ladies-who-lunch. Draw your eyes away from those Teslas in the lot, and head inside for fine dining that exceeds this sophisticated restaurant's humble name.

Despite the glitz, the cuisine here is surprisingly approachable, from platters of house charcuterie served with fire-warmed artisan bread to the superb Pub burger, available in both the cozy front lounge and more formal main dining area. It's there that the kitchen shines its brightest, with more elaborate entrées like the almond wood-grilled pork loin, adorned with crispy shrimp-and-pork croquettes, pungent black garlic and caramelized Brussels sprouts. The signature chocolate soufflé is an equally impressive display—its intense, not-too-sweet flavor cut by drizzles of crème anglaise infused with Earl Grey tea.

Given the clientele, the wine list is designed to court the deepest of pockets, with an outstanding selection of French vintages, particularly Bordeaux. On a budget? Aim for lunch, which is lighter not only in approach, but also on the wallet.

■ 2967 Woodside Rd. (off Whiskey Hill Rd.), Woodside

☎ (650) 851-9888 — **WEB:** www.thevillagepub.net

■ Lunch Sun – Fri Dinner nightly

PRICE: $$$

WAKURIYA &

Japanese • Contemporary décor

MAP: D3

Innovative, serious and very well-established, Wakuriya successfully combines a deep respect for the kaiseki tradition with a contemporary touch. This is largely thanks to the lone chef behind the counter, Katsuhiro Yamasaki; his wife is the one so deftly managing and serving the dining room. The location is charmless, but there is a sober elegance here that is enhanced by the kitchen's quiet confidence. The room books a month in advance—set your alarm for midnight, phone them exactly 30 days ahead and pray for a callback.

Each month brings a new, refined menu that combines the chef's personal style with superlative Japanese and Californian ingredients. Course after course arrives uniquely presented, perhaps on handcrafted ceramics or even a silver spoon, cradling chunks of poached lobster with intensely smoky dashi gelée, soft-boiled Jidori egg, crisp asparagus and fried kombu.

This may not be a sushi-ya, but the sashimi course is nonetheless excellent. Find that same level of talent in the yamaimo gratin with silky morsels of black cod and tender Brussels sprouts that are crisp, yet light as air and so delicious. The shirako tofu topped with Kabocha squash tempura is beyond delightful.

---

115 De Anza Blvd. (at Parrot Dr.), San Mateo
(650) 286-0410 — **WEB:** www.wakuriya.com
Dinner Wed – Sun

PRICE: $$$$

YUMMY SZECHUAN ⅋○

Chinese • Simple

&

Long waits for a great Chinese meal are common in the Peninsula, which makes this as yet line-free favorite doubly special. The space is no-frills, but the kitchen is all-thrills, knocking out classic dish after classic dish: crisp Chongqing-style fried chicken buried under a mound of dried chilies and numbing peppercorns, tender pork wontons swimming in gloriously mouth-searing chili oil and chewy dan dan noodles tossed with ground pork, peanuts and plenty of chili oil.

As with all Sichuan restaurants, those who can't stand the heat will have a hard go of it, but non-fiery options include a flaky rolled beef pancake and garlicky pea shoots. The moral of this story: while Yummy may not be anyone's idea of high style, the food assuredly lives up to its name.

🔲 1661 El Camino Real (bet. Park Blvd. & Park Pl.), Millbrae
📞 (650) 615-9648 — **WEB:** www.yummy1661.com
🔲 Lunch & dinner daily

PRICE: $$

Share the journey with us!
🐦 @MichelinGuideSF
📷 @MichelinInspectors

SOUTH BAY

SOUTH BAY

SILICON VALLEY

Silicon Valley has long been revered as the tech capital of the world, but it's really so much more. Combine all that tech money with a diverse, international population and you get an exceptionally dynamic culinary scene. If that doesn't sound like an outstanding (read: successful) formula on its own, think of the area's rich wine culture descending from the Santa Cruz Mountains, where a burgeoning vintner community takes great pride in its work, and realize that the South Bay may as well be sitting on a gold mine. Visitors should be sure to see everything the area has to offer, with a sojourn to **Mountain Winery** in Saratoga—part-outdoor concert venue, part-event space and part-winery—that offers stunning views of the vineyards and valley below.

FESTIVALS GALORE

The Valley is proud of its tech-minded reputation, but don't judge this book by its cover, as South Bay locals definitely know how to party. In San Jose, celebrations kick off every May at the wildly popular **San Jose Greek Festival** featuring music, eats, drinks and dance. Similarly, and with little time to recover, buckets of cornhusks wait to be stuffed and sold at the **Story Road Tamale Festival**, also held every summer. Come July, **Japantown** breathes new life for the two-day **Obon Festival & Bazaar**, and as August rolls around, the Italian-American Heritage Foundation celebrates its annual **Family Festa**. This is a year-long shindig, and **Santana Row** (a sleek shopping village housing numerous upscale restaurants and a fantastic farmer's market) plays a pivotal role in these festivities. One of San Jose's most notable destinations is **San Pedro Square Market**, whose four walls harbor a spectrum of artisanal merchants at historic Peralta Adobe downtown. Farmers and specialty markets are a way of life for South Bay residents and these locals cannot imagine living elsewhere.

CULTURAL DYNASTY

As further testimony to its international reputation, the capital of Silicon Valley is also a melting pot of global culinary influences. Neighborhood pho shops and bánh mì hangouts like **Huong Lan** gratify the growing Vietnamese community. They can also be found gracing the intersection of King and Tully streets (home to some of the city's finest Vietnamese flavors) sampling decadent cream puffs at **Hong-Van Bakery**. **Lion Plaza** is yet another hub for bakeries, markets and canteens paying homage to this eighth most populated Asian country. Neighboring Cambodia makes an appearance by way of delicious noodle soups at **Nam Vang Restaurant** or **F&D Yummy**. And Chinese food makes its formidable presence known at lofty **Dynasty Chinese Seafood Restaurant**. Located on Story Road, this is a popular arena for big parties and favored destination for dim sum. **Nijiya Market**, for instance, is a jewel with several locations, all of which sparkle with specialty goods, top ingredients and other things Far East. Long before it was cool to be organic in America, Nijiya was focused on bringing the taste of Japan by way of high-quality, seasonal and local ingredients to the California coast. Today it continues to tantalize with some of the area's most pristine seafood and meat, as well as an array of tasty sushi and bento boxes. Also available via their website are sumptuous, homespun recipes for a variety of noodle dishes, fried rice signatures and other regional specialties. Encompassing the globe and traveling from this Eastern tip to South America, Mexican food enthusiasts in San Jose seem eternally smitten by the still-warm tortillas at **Tropicana**, as well as the surprisingly tasty tacos from one of the area's many **Mi Pueblo Food Centers**.

A STUDENT'S DREAM

And yet there is more to the South Bay than just San Jose. Los Gatos is home to prized patisseries like **Fleur de Cocoa** and such historic, continually operating and specialized wineries like **Testarossa**. Meanwhile, cool and casual Palo Alto is home base for celebrated Stanford University, its countless students and impressive faculty. Find locals lining up for homemade frozen yogurt at **Fraîche**. Others fulfill a Korean fantasy in Santa Clara, where these same settlers enjoy a range of authentic nibbles and tasty spreads at food court favorite—**Lawrence Plaza**. Just as foodies favor the soondubu jjigae at **SGD Tofu House**, more conservative palates have a field day over caramelized sweet potatoes at **Sweet Potato Stall**, just outside the Galleria. Fill your belly with impeccable produce

along El Camino Real near the Lawrence Expressway intersection. Then treat your senses to a feast at Mountain View's **Milk Pail Market**, showcasing over 300 varieties of cheese. Have your pick among such splendid choices as Camembert, Bleu d'Auvergne, Morbier and Cabriquet, as well as imported Mamie Nova Yogurt. Despite the fast pace of technology in Silicon Valley, Slow Food—the grassroots movement dedicated to local food traditions—has a thriving South Bay chapter. Even Google in Mountain View feeds its massive staff three nourishing, square meals a day. For a wider range of delicacies, they may frequent surrounding eateries or stores selling ethnic eats. Residents of Los Altos also have their German food cravings covered between **Esther's German Bakery** and **Dittmer's Gourmet Meats & Wurst-Haus**. In fact, Dittmer's sausages are made extra special when served on a salted pretzel roll from Esther's. **Los Gatos Meats & Smokehouse** is another stalwart serving

these meat-loving mortals an embarrassment of riches. Think poultry, fish and freshly butchered meat sandwiches served alongside savory beef jerky, prime rib roasts, pork loin, corned beef and, of course, bacon. But wait…did you want it regular, pepper, country-style or Canadian? Pair all these salty licks with a sip from Mountain View's **Savvy Cellar Wine Bar & Wine Shop** only to discover that it's a picnic in the making. Smokers looking to wind down in luxury may head to the handsome, upscale and members-only **Los Gatos Cigar Club**, where the choices are exceptional and conversation intriguing.

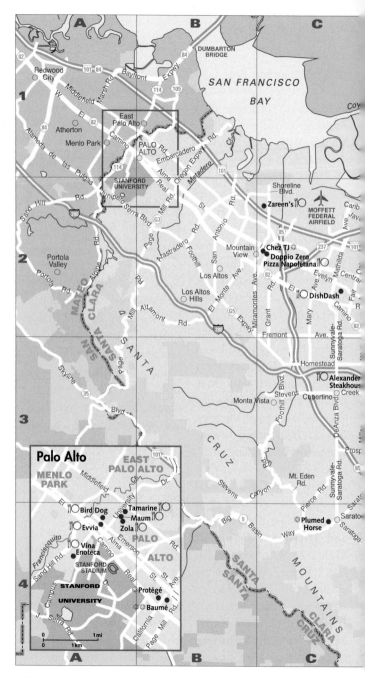

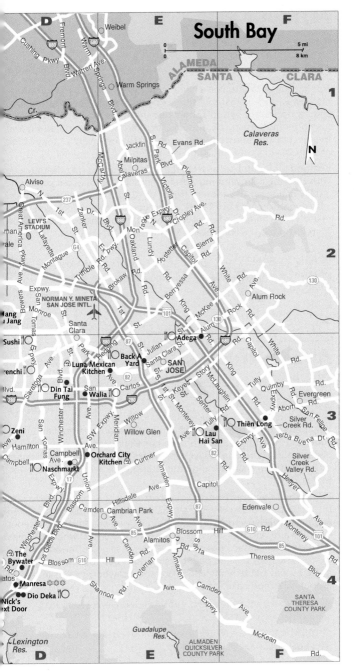

South Bay

N

ADEGA ♚⚬
Portuguese • Neighborhood

MAP: E3

Adega may be located on a commercial strip, but its busy surrounds melt away once you step inside. Exposed wood beams, farmhouse sliding doors and wood tables dominate the scene and thereby fashion a modern-rustic appeal. There are three- and five-course menus, but the seven-course tasting is the best way to take stock of Chef David Costa's Portuguese cooking.

Seafood is plentiful here—from the house favorite arroz de mariscos with shrimp, clams and mussels to the peixe do dia com espargos, a daily changing selection of fresh fish. Codfish croquettes topped with confit tomato have terrific textures with creamy centers, while caldo verde flaunts a tempting presentation. Desserts too are on theme and toe the line between traditional and retro.

▨ 1614 Alum Rock Ave. (bet. 33rd & 34th Sts.), San Jose
✆ (408) 926-9075 — **WEB:** www.adegarest.com
▨ Dinner Wed – Sun

PRICE: $$$

ALEXANDER'S STEAKHOUSE ♚⚬
Steakhouse • Contemporary décor

MAP: C3

This behemoth and swanky flagship steakhouse is housed in the suburban Main Street Cupertino center. But make your way inside to unearth this sharp and stylish dining room done up with sleek grey hues, beautiful floral arrangements and thick white linen-topped tables.

Pricey steaks emerge from the glass enclosed dry-aging room to sate the executives doing deals over their meals. They may range from Japanese Wagyu variations to dry-aged domestic Porterhouse, but let the warm and well-dressed servers take the lead when it comes to these impeccable cuts of meat. Other luscious offerings like icy oysters and fiery shishito peppers simply prepare you for a delightful finale by way of the white chocolate and strawberry mousse served atop devil's food cake.

▨ 19379 Stevens Creek Blvd. (bet. Tantau Ave. & Wolfe Rd.), Cupertino
✆ (408) 446-2222 — **WEB:** www.alexanderssteakhouse.com
▨ Lunch Tue – Sat Dinner nightly

PRICE: $$$$

BACK A YARD ꭥO

Caribbean • *Colorful*

&

MAP: E3

Though this Caribbean spot is located in the heart of downtown San Jose, dining here feels like a vacation thanks to cheerful murals, a lively soundtrack and hospitable servers. Unlike its Menlo Park predecessor, which mainly does to-go orders, this location boasts a capacious brick dining room.

Back A Yard is a Jamaican term meaning "the way things are done back home," and the food doesn't disappoint on that count. Specialties include smoky, spicy and tender jerk chicken, flavorful curry goat and vinegar-marinated escovitch fish fillets, all accompanied by coconut rice and red beans, a side salad and caramelized fried plantains. Cool off your palate with a glass of coconut water, then order a slice of dense, flan-like sweet potato pudding.

▨ 80 N. Market St. (bet. Santa Clara & St. John Sts.), San Jose
✆ (408) 294-8626 — **WEB:** www.backayard.net
▨ Lunch & dinner Mon – Sat   **PRICE:** ⬤⬤

BIRD DOG ꭥO

Contemporary • *Chic*

🍸 & ⬚   **MAP:** A4

Anyone on the hunt for a happening scene in Palo Alto should follow the scent to Chef Robbie Wilson's Bird Dog, where the décor is sleek and the cocktails flow freely.

The food is ambitious, and while it may misstep here and there, it gets points for a modern approach. Delicious options abound; start with a wood-grilled avocado filled with ponzu and a dab of fresh wasabi before tucking in to the KFC, three bone-in Jidori chicken thighs coated in a thick, crunchy batter and served with a kicky chickpea gochujang. House-made sodas, with flavors like blueberry lemon, banana lime and ginger cinnamon-chai, are especially refreshing. Finish with the doughnuts and coffee, a trio of warm and dainty coffee-glazed, sugar-dipped and chocolatey delights.

▨ 420 Ramona St. (bet. Lytton & University Aves.), Palo Alto
✆ (650) 656-8180 — **WEB:** www.birddogpa.com
▨ Lunch Mon –Fri Dinner nightly   **PRICE:** $$

BAUMÉ ✿ ✿

Contemporary • Elegant

&

A bold and bright glass door in an otherwise nondescript building along Palo Alto's main thoroughfare marks the entrance to the mystical Baumé. Inside, find a dining room with a modernist sensibility that carries through with orange-hued walls and fabric room dividers. Chef Bruno Chemel offers a select number of seatings. Tables are spaced widely for privacy and never rushed. Mrs. Chemel oversees this luxurious enclave, adding warmth, detailed knowledge and clear enthusiasm for her husband's progressive (albeit pricey) cuisine. It's a family affair indeed, as the couple's young son, decked out in whites, assists in the kitchen as well.

Each contemporary dish is refined, balanced and demonstrates an enormous attention to detail. The kitchen focuses on seasonal ingredients and coaxing flavor to profound levels. Roasted California squab with its caramelized, ever-so-perfect crispy skin and light dusting of fennel is an absolute showstopper in all of its velvety, well-seasoned glory.

Desserts include a pear bavarois artfully crested with delicious cassis jam and a frozen flower composed with grape sorbet. A plate of perfectly ripe stone fruit is a wonderfully seasonal send-off.

▨ 201 S. California Ave. (at Park Blvd.), Palo Alto

✆ (650) 328-8899 — **WEB:** www.maisonbaume.com

▨ Lunch Thu – Sat Dinner Wed – Sat   **PRICE: $$$$**

THE BYWATER 😊
Southern · *Family*

 ♿   🏠   🛋

MAP: D4

If dining at Manresa is like a weeklong stay at a luxury resort, this New Orleans-inspired little sib from Chef/owner David Kinch is more like a weekend of partying in the Big Easy. With its zinc bar, pressed ceilings and open kitchen stacked with bottles of Crystal hot sauce, it might just fool you into thinking you're in Louisiana—right down to the zydeco and jazz playing on the stereo.

Reservations aren't accepted, so locals (some with kids in tow) line up early to get a taste of spicy, andouille-flecked gumbo z'herbes, golden-brown hushpuppies, oyster po'boys and other Cajun and Creole classics. For the finale, a luscious butterscotch pot de crème may sound less traditional, but rest assured that it tastes like heaven.

▨ 532 N. Santa Cruz Ave. (bet. Andrews St. & Roberts Rd.), Los Gatos

℘ (408) 560-9639 — **WEB:** www.thebywaterca.com

▨ Lunch & dinner Tue – Sun

PRICE: $$

DIN TAI FUNG 🍴○
Chinese · *Contemporary décor*

MAP: D3

You'll need to wait (and wait, and wait) to get a taste of the much-coveted dumplings at the first Bay Area outpost of this acclaimed international chain, which has drawn crazy crowds to the Westfield Valley Fair mall since day one.

With only a handful of reservations taken a month in advance, expect to cool your heels for anywhere from 45 minutes to two hours. Is the wait worth it? Depends on how much you love xiao long bao, the Shanghai-style soup dumplings that are offered here in outstanding pork-crab and utterly decadent black truffle variations. Bring a crew so you can sample the non-dumpling offerings as well: delectably spicy wontons, top-flight barbecue pork buns, springy house-made noodles and lightly sweetened black sesame buns for dessert.

▨ 2855 Stevens Creek Blvd. (bet. Monroe St. & Winchester Blvd.), Santa Clara

℘ (408) 248-1688 — **WEB:** www.dintaifungusa.com

▨ Lunch & dinner daily

PRICE: $$

CHEZ TJ ✿
Contemporary • *Elegant*

MAP: C2

Nestled into a charming 19th-century Victorian in the heart of downtown Mountain View, Chez TJ likes to kick it old-school. This elder statesman in the fine-dining scene flaunts an elegant and welcoming streak thanks to antique pictures and Venetian blown-glass table lamps that infuse the space with a romantic feel. And the waitstaff is formally suited—naturally.

Having launched the career of many a culinary legend, including its current leader—Jarad Gallagher—this kitchen showcases contemporary French cuisine by way of one tasting. Featuring a number of courses, the menu aims at highlighting ingredients sourced from within 100 miles of the restaurant as well as exploring global territory.

Dinner might begin with a fried yuba skin beggar's purse stuffed with Kumamoto oysters bobbing in spicy kimchi juice and served atop a porcelain soup spoon. Later, a delicate French onion soup, crowned with a Gruyère crostini and paired with homemade sourdough levain, makes its way to your table. Sashimi courses typically precede richer items, including a duo of veal, served beneath paper-thin shingles of turnip and slipped into a small crispy croquette set over sautéed Bloomsdale spinach.

---

938 Villa St. (bet. Bryant & Franklin Sts.), Mountain View

℘ (650) 964-7466 — **WEB:** www.cheztj.com

Dinner Tue – Sat

PRICE: $$$$

DIO DEKA ♟🍽

Greek • Elegant

☸ ♿ 🏠 🖥 ✋   **MAP:** D4

Dio Deka may specialize in Greek food, but this is no typical taverna, as the stylish dining room (complete with a roaring fireplace) ably demonstrates. A wealthy, well-dressed Los Gatos crowd flocks to the front patio on warm evenings, dining and people-watching within the vine-covered walls of the Hotel Los Gatos. The bar also draws a brace of cheery regulars.

Skip the dull mesquite-grilled steaks and keep your order Greek: think stuffed grape leaves with tender braised beef cheek, or a bright pan-seared local salmon with roasted yellow peppers, potatoes and artichokes. The adventurous shouldn't miss out on the fun offering of Greek wines, and sweet buffs should allow space for the crema me meli, a fantastic burnt-honey mousse with almond and lemon.

⬛ 210 E. Main St. (bet. Jackson St. & Villa Ave.), Los Gatos
✆ (408) 354-7700 — **WEB:** www.diodeka.com
⬛ Dinner nightly   **PRICE:** $$$

DISHDASH ♟🍽

Middle Eastern • Regional décor

♿ 🏠   **MAP:** C2

Dining on the run is certainly possible at this Mid-East gem on historic Murphy Avenue—just ask the techies who rush in to take food back to their desks. Families and groups congregate in the colorful dining room; and even though the space has expanded to include five outposts, you might want to linger on the front sidewalk patio— all the better to people-watch while savoring a bright, tangy tabbouleh, tender-crisp falafel or baba ghanoush topped with black olives and roasted garlic cloves.

Served on griddled bread and enriched with a garlicky yogurt-parsley sauce, wraps like the incredibly smoky and juicy chicken shawarma are full-flavored and downright memorable. For dessert, go for the m'halabieh, a creamy and fragrant rosewater-and-pistachio pudding.

⬛ 190 S. Murphy Ave. (bet. Evelyn & Washington Aves.),
Sunnyvale
✆ (408) 774-1889 — **WEB:** www.dishdash.com
⬛ Lunch & dinner Mon – Sat   **PRICE:** $$

DOPPIO ZERO PIZZA NAPOLETANA 🍴○

Italian • *Neighborhood*

 ♿ ⛱

MAP: C2

It's easy to overlook pizza as a way to quell hunger pangs, but sink your teeth into the selections here and you're quickly reminded that it's an art form unto itself. The pies are, well, epic (and certified by the Associazione Verace Pizza Napoletana, one of just a few in the state), and well-seasoned—topped with a zesty tomato sauce and bold ingredients. Then there is that crust—chewy and blistered with just the right amount of char. You could come just for pizza, but that would mean missing out on such delicious dishes as polpo—smoky octopus dressed with anchovy vinaigrette and set atop tomatoes. It's so much more than just a "salad."

The bustling interior doesn't distract from the goods. On a nice day, grab a seat on the sidewalk to imbibe the bliss.

🔲 160 Castro St. (bet. Evelyn Ave. & Vista St.), Mountain View
📞 (408) 863-0308 — **WEB:** www.dzpizzeria.com
🔲 Lunch & dinner daily

PRICE: $$

EVVIA 🍴○

Greek • *Mediterranean décor*

 ♿ 🖐

MAP: A4

Inviting with its rustic wood beams, hanging copper pots and roaring wood-burning fireplace, this central Palo Alto spot is a draw for Maserati-driving tech billionaires by day and couples in the evening. Dress to impress here, where the scene dictates high prices (though lunch features lighter dishes and more palatable pricing).

Much of the menu emerges from the wood-fired grill, including smoky, tender artichoke and eggplant skewers drizzled in olive oil and paired with garlicky Greek yogurt. The rustic, impossibly moist lamb souvlaki is nicely contrasted by a refreshing tomato, cucumber and red onion salad. For dessert, pumpkin cheesecake is subtle, sweet and accented with syrup-poached chunks of pumpkin.

🔲 420 Emerson St. (bet. Lytton & University Aves.), Palo Alto
📞 (650) 326-0983 — **WEB:** www.evvia.net
🔲 Lunch Mon – Fri Dinner nightly

PRICE: $$$

JANG SU JANG 🍴◯
Korean • Family

♿ ⬚   **MAP:** D2

Smoky Korean barbecue, luscious soft tofu stews and enormous seafood pancakes are among the standards at this Santa Clara classic and Koreatown jewel. Its strip-mall façade may not seem enticing, but the interior is classier than expected, thanks to granite tables equipped with grill tops and ventilation hoods, and a glass-enclosed exhibition kitchen located in the back.

This is fiery-flavored cuisine for gourmands who can stand the heat. A heavy-handed dose of kimchi flavors soft beef and pork dumplings, while the fierce red chili paste that slicks garlicky slices of marinated pork may actually cook the meat in daeji bulgogi. Cool down with mul naengmyun, a cold beef broth with tender, nutty buckwheat noodles and a pot of boricha.

▨ 3561 El Camino Real, Ste. 10 (bet. Flora Vista Ave. & Lawrence Expwy.), Santa Clara
✆ (408) 246-1212 — **WEB:** www.jangsujang.com
▨ Lunch & dinner daily   **PRICE:** $$

LAU HAI SAN 🍴◯
Vietnamese • Simple

                                           MAP: E3

Most Westerners don't think of hot pot when they're craving Vietnamese food, but it's actually a traditional favorite well worth sampling—and the proof is in this sunny spot. The overstuffed menu boasts 20 different variations on the theme, including a spicy seafood version with shrimp, mussels, squid, fish balls stuffed with salmon roe and other aquatic delights. Dip them into the sour, tangy broth; twirl them with noodles; garnish with herbs—the choice is yours.

If hot pot isn't adventurous enough, bring a group to sample delicacies like chewy, flavorful curried coconut snails and crispy fried pork intestine. The diner-like space and strip-mall setting are nothing special, but the hot pot is so outstanding that lines are to be expected.

▨ 2597 Senter Rd. (bet. Feldspar Dr. & Umbarger Rd.), San Jose
✆ (408) 938-0650 — **WEB:** N/A
▨ Lunch & dinner Thu – Tue   **PRICE:** $$

LUNA MEXICAN KITCHEN 😋

Mexican · *Colorful*

♿ 🪑 🚪 🛋️   **MAP:** E3

The name means "moon" in Spanish, and this Mexican kitchen also uses it as an acronym to reflect its philosophy of "L(local) U(unrefined) N(natural) A(authentic)" cooking. The food is decidedly highbrow, thanks to special ingredients like Rancho Gordo beans, Mary's free-range chickens and everything else that's made from scratch. Chef/owner Jo Lerma-Lopez's love for cooking is clear in every single bite, especially the fire-roasted chiles rellenos, generously stuffed with a fragrant beef stew and deep-fried to perfection. Ask for extra handmade tortillas to go with your simmered charro beans.

The dining room seems to burst with color. A full-service bar lures with backlit tequila bottles and vibrant tiles. Come summer, the back patio is the place to be.

▨ 1495 The Alameda (at Magnolia Ave.), San Jose
☎ (408) 320-2654 — **WEB:** www.lunamexicankitchen.com
▨ Lunch & dinner daily   PRICE: $$

MAUM 🍴

Korean · *Contemporary décor*

🍸 ♿   **MAP:** A4

Originally founded as a private dining club for a Korean venture capitalist's family and friends, Maum still feels exclusive, with seating for just 16 at a communal table available only a few nights a week. Though the setting is spare, the vibe is social and exuberant, as patrons mingle over cocktails and canapés before coming together tableside for a set menu of upscale Korean food.

Both Chef Michael Kim and his wife, Meichih, who trained at some of the Bay Area's most exclusive spots, dazzle diners with dishes like caramelized duck "galbi" over scallion salad; or oysters with kimchi snow and sablefish dressed with a gochujang broth. Wine lovers should opt for the pairing as the sommeliers have assembled a particularly thoughtful selection.

▨ 322 University Ave. (bet. Bryant & Waverly Sts.), Palo Alto
☎ (650) 656-8161 — **WEB:** www.maumpaloalto.com
▨ Dinner Wed – Fri   PRICE: $$$$

MANRESA ✿✿✿

Contemporary • Elegant

✿ 🍸 ♿ 🍽️

MAP: D4

It may have a reputation for being one of the Bay Area's most well-regarded restaurants, but Manresa is welcoming, distinctively stylish and extraordinarily hospitable for a fine-dining operation. Chef David Kinch works with some of the region's most revered growers, turning products from Andy's Orchard, Pistils & Petals Farm and Dirty Girl, among others, into works of art.

The nightly compositions are unknown until they arrive on the table (a souvenir copy of the menu will be handed to you at the end). The food is at once cerebral and luxurious, approachable and thoroughly delicious. Each course is likely to represent a moment within a season, beginning with savory petit fours that are an illusory play on the palate. Sample red-pepper pâtes de fruits or black olive madeleines along with excellent bread baked at the offshoot bakery made with house-milled flour. Tender striped bass in a saffron bouillabaisse is topped with a crisp wafer of brioche, while juicy duck is sided by buttery foie gras. Even something as simple as asparagus is elevated here with a charred beurre blanc and its fantastic smokiness.

Don't miss those excellent vanilla-bean caramels offered on your way out.

🟦 320 Village Ln. (bet. Santa Cruz & University Aves.), Los Gatos
📞 (408) 354-4330 — **WEB:** www.manresarestaurant.com
🟦 Dinner Wed – Sun   PRICE: $$$$

NASCHMARKT 🍴

Austrian • *Simple*

 &♿ 🏠

MAP: D3

A slice of Vienna in downtown Campbell, Naschmarkt scores high marks for its authentic flavors, inviting space and friendly service. The cozy, brick-walled dining room is a favorite among couples, and solo diners will have a ball at the wraparound counter, which has a great view of the busy open kitchen.

Most of the menu is traditional: think bratwurst, krautrouladen and Wiener schnitzel. The pan-roasted chicken breast, moist and juicy with a golden-brown seared crust, is served over a "napkin dumpling" made with compressed bread, tomato and herbs. But, rest easy as there are a few items that have lighter Californian twists, like spätzle made with quark (a fresh white cheese) and tossed with smoked chicken, yellow corn, English peas and wild mushrooms.

▦ 384 E. Campbell Ave. (bet. Central & Railway Aves.), Campbell
✆ (408) 378-0335 — **WEB:** www.naschmarkt-restaurant.com
▦ Dinner Tue – Sun   **PRICE:** $$

NICK'S NEXT DOOR 🍴

American • *Contemporary décor*

 &♿ 🏠

MAP: D4

There is a loyal crowd of locals flooding Nick's Next Door, but this delightful haunt is as welcoming to rookies as it is to regulars. Inside, the bar and semi-open kitchen beckon; while outside, there's plenty of space to linger just a little bit longer.

The mood, thanks to a chic black-and-gray palette, and the food scream upscale American bistro. Pan-fried abalone served with creamy risotto and crispy Brussels sprouts leans edgy, while Nani's meatloaf, a thick slab of juicy meat in a savory mushroom gravy and resting atop fluffy, buttery mashed potatoes, is straight-up comfort. Finish with the apple bread pudding, a blend of sourdough and brioche, a variety of apples as well as a decadent caramel sauce that smacks of pure pleasure—and joy.

▦ 11 College Ave. (at Main St.), Los Gatos
✆ (408) 402-5053 — **WEB:** www.nicksnextdoor.com
▦ Lunch & dinner Tue – Sat   **PRICE:** $$

ORCHARD CITY KITCHEN ☺

International • *Rustic*

                                                MAP: D3

Jeffrey Stout is at the helm of this international small-plates spot, where a wall-to-wall crowd of loyal followers flock despite the humble shopping-center environs. Polished yet casual with a big front bar and patio, a meal here is best enjoyed with a group—so come prepared to max out the menu.

The menu spins in a number of directions, but this team won't steer your wrong. Kick it off with a cocktail, then tuck into a hodge-podge of dishes, including a riff on poutine with tater tots, muenster cheese, bacon and fried egg; and a spicy budae jjigae with slurpy ramen noodles and Spam. Served in a cast iron pan, the orange dream pulls together orange soft serve, kiwi, honey cream and poppy seed for an unusual twist on the ice cream truck favorite.

◾ 1875 S. Bascom Ave., Ste. 190 (off Campisi Way), Campbell
☏ (408) 340-5285 — **WEB:** www.orchardcitykitchen.com
◾ Lunch & dinner daily   **PRICE: $$**

ORENCHI ¶〇

Japanese • *Simple*

                                                MAP: D3

Whether at lunch or dinner, this ramen specialist is known for its lines of waiting diners that curl like noodles outside its door. Even those who arrive before they open may face a long wait, so don't come if you're in a rush. Once inside, you'll be seated at a simple wood table or at the bar, collaged with Polaroid portraits of guests savoring their ramen.

The reason for the wait becomes clear when you're presented with a rich and utterly delicious bowl of tonkotsu ramen full of chewy noodles, roasted pork and scallions. Shoyu ramen is equally delish, but make a point to show up early if you want to try the tsukemen (dipping noodles), as there is a limited number of servings available daily.

Orenchi Beyond is an equally busy younger sib in SF.

◾ 3540 Homestead Rd. (near Lawrence Expy.), Santa Clara
☏ (408) 246-2955 — **WEB:** www.orenchi-ramen.com
◾ Lunch & dinner daily   **PRICE:** ⌾

PLUMED HORSE ✿
Contemporary • Elegant

This handsome stallion is certainly a feather in the cap of the inviting, if slightly sleepy, Saratoga. There has been a Plumed Horse in this spot since 1952, though this decade-old iteration is by far the best. The décor inside exudes warmth, first in the fireplace-warmed lounge, then in the stunning dining room, with its arched barrel ceiling. From shimmering Venetian plaster to striking chandeliers that emit a colorful glow, these rich details create a sensational backdrop that is at once elegant and comfortable.

The kitchen turns out modern and upscale cooking with an Asian bent. Duck consommé, poured tableside and enhanced with meaty mushrooms as well as a bright English pea flan, is as impressive to the eye as it is to the palate. Locally sourced abalone is finished with XO sauce for a pop of flavor, while the decadent black pepper- and parmesan-soufflé accompanied by a delicate petal of uni is of the dive-right-in variety.

Almond cake with cocoa-nib mousse and orange foam is delightful, but wait until those chocolates arrive. Wheeled over in a glass-domed cart with row-upon-row of beauties from Chocolaterie by Angelica, they are nothing less than exquisite.

▨ 14555 Big Basin Way (bet. 4th & 5th Sts.), Saratoga
✆ (408) 867-4711 — **WEB:** www.plumedhorse.com
▨ Dinner Mon – Sat

PRICE: $$$$

PROTÉGÉ ⌘
Contemporary • *Chic*

🍇 🍷 ♿ 🪑 ⬜

MAP: B4

This Palo Alto hit boasts an envious pedigree—Chef Anthony Secviar, Pastry Chef Eddie Lopez and Master Sommelier Dennis Kelly all trained under Chef Thomas Keller at The French Laundry. However, Protégé offers an experience that is far from weighty. In fact, the staff aims to keep things more lenient in this dining room, which sports cushy leather booths, beautifully laid tables and even the occasional diner donning flip-flops.

Hungry techies from around the enclave can expect cooking with a suave, edgy panache—reviving such tired players as Alaskan king crab (a seasonal delight here with sweet corn purée and bacon-tinged corn succotash); or beef tenderloin accompanied by buttery potatoes with a sharp horseradish mousseline. One might even be hard-pressed to find better foie gras around—light and exquisite with fennel relish and a slice of perfect vanilla brioche. Such keen attention to detail and surprisingly well-balanced flavors continue through to dessert—as in the dulce de leche mousse coated with salted hazelnuts, toasted honey and dark chocolate.

In keeping with its accessible slant, the kitchen also offers a lounge menu, which thanks to its popularity, requires reservations.

■ 250 California Ave. (bet. Birch St. & Park Blvd.), Palo Alto
☏ (650) 494-4181 — **WEB:** www.protegepaloalto.com
■ Dinner Tue – Sat   **PRICE:** $$$

SAWA SUSHI ¶○

Japanese • *Simple*

&

Strict rules and big rewards unite at this zany, unusual and randomly located (in a mall) dive, where Chef Steve Sawa rules the roost. After going through the rigamarole of landing a reservation for his omakase-only affair, throw all caution to the wind and just go with the flow. Yes, the décor is nothing special; however, the food is anything but so-so, and the ad hoc prices are quite high.

So what draws such a host of regulars? Their pristine and very sublime fish, of course—from creamy Hokkaido sea scallops to delicious toro ribbons. Sawa is also an expert on sauces: imagine the likes of yuzukosho topping kanpachi or a sweet-spicy tamarind glaze on ocean trout. Accompany these with a top sake or cold beer and feel the joy seep in.

▦ 1042 E. El Camino Real (at Henderson Ave.), Sunnyvale
℘ (408) 241-7292 — **WEB:** www.sawasushi.net
▦ Dinner Mon – Sat   PRICE: $$$$

TAMARINE ¶○

Vietnamese • *Simple*

🍹 & 🗔

Tamarine has long been a Palo Alto standby for its refined take on Vietnamese food that doesn't sacrifice authentic flavor. There's nearly always a corporate lunch happening in the private dining room, and techies, families and couples alike fill the rest of its linen-topped tables.

Family-style sharing of dishes is encouraged, which is good because deciding on just one entrée is nearly impossible. To start, make like the regulars and order one of the "Tamarine Taste" appetizer platters with a round of tropical fruit-infused cocktails. Then move on to the fresh shrimp spring rolls, full of bean sprouts and mint; the springy ginger-chili seitan with steamed coconut rice; and curried long beans, sautéed with fragrant Makrut lime leaves and chili.

▦ 546 University Ave. (bet. Cowper & Webster Sts.), Palo Alto
℘ (650) 325-8500 — **WEB:** www.tamarinerestaurant.com
▦ Lunch Mon – Fri Dinner nightly   PRICE: $$$

THIÊN LONG ¶○
Vietnamese • *Simple*

& ⑤   **MAP:** F3

There are plenty of Vietnamese restaurants catering to the local expats in San Jose, but Thiên Long stands out for its pleasant dining room presenting delicious cooking—as the numerous families filling the large space will attest. Tile floors and rosewood-tinted chairs decorate the space, while walls hung with photos of Vietnamese dishes keep the focus on food.

Begin with sweet-salty barbecued prawns paired with smoky grilled pork and served atop rice noodles. But, it is really the pho with a broth of star anise, clove and ginger, topped with perfectly rare beef that is a true gem—even the regular-sized portion is enormous. English is a challenge among the staff, but they are very friendly; plus the authentic flavors make up for any inadequacies.

▨ 3005 Silver Creek Rd., Ste. 138 (bet. Aborn Rd. & Lexann Ave.), San Jose
✆ (408) 223-6188 — **WEB:** www.thienlongrestaurant.com
▨ Lunch & dinner daily   **PRICE:** 🍲

VINA ENOTECA ¶○
Italian • *Contemporary décor*

❀ 🍸 & 🛖 ⛲   **MAP:** A4

It has been made more than apparent by now that this owner, Rocco Scordella who is a native of Italy, succeeded in bringing a delicious taste of his homeland to Palo Alto. Look around and note that pasta tops everyone's table for good reason. If offered, be sure to try the toothsome spinach tagliatelle in a meaty ragù that's composed with local pork and naturally raised beef. This kitchen clearly prioritizes sourcing—a majority of the greens and vegetables are grown at Stanford Education Farm—and pastas, pizzas and bread are all crafted in-house.

The industrial-chic décor features high ceilings, arches and soft leather chairs. Whether you pop in for snacks and cocktails at the bar or plan on savoring a full meal, service is always friendly and quick.

▨ 700 Welch Rd. Unit 110 (at Arboretum Rd.), Palo Alto
✆ (650) 257-4819 — **WEB:** www.vinaenoteca.com
▨ Lunch & dinner daily   **PRICE:** $$

WALIA ♨○
Ethiopian • *Simple*

&

Authentic Ethiopian flavors are delivered without pretense at this easygoing, affordable restaurant housed in a strip mall just off Bascom Avenue. Though the space is basic, the service is friendly and it's casual enough for kids in tow.

Start things off with an order of sambussas, fried dough triangles filled with lentil, onion and chilies. Then choose from an all-meat, all-veggie or mixed selection of warming stews, like tibs firfir, featuring lamb in a garlicky berbere sauce dolloped on spongy injera. Vegetarians will particularly love dining here, as all of the plant-based options including alicha wot or split peas in turmeric sauce, shiro (spiced chickpeas) and gomen (wilted collard greens with onion and spices), are big winners.

▨ 2208 Business Cir. (at Bascom Ave.), San Jose
✆ (408) 645-5001 — **WEB:** www.waliaethiopian.com
▨ Lunch & dinner Wed – Mon

PRICE: ⊜

ZAREEN'S ♨○
Indian • *Simple*

&

Taking up residence just steps from the Googleplex, it's no surprise that this wholesome little South Asian restaurant is absolutely packed with tech employees seeking a taste of their homelands. But local families love Zareen's as well, perusing books from the lending library or doodling their heartfelt thanks on the wall. An added bonus: the space is set in a small shopping plaza with a big lot out front, making parking a non-issue.

The chicken Memoni samosas, supposedly made from a recipe known to only a select number of grandmothers worldwide, are a must-order: crispy, well-spiced and flavorful, they're so good they don't need chutney. Follow these with the outstanding chicken shami kebabs, juicy and caramelized on their bed of fluffy basmati rice.

▨ 1477 Plymouth St. (off Shoreline Blvd.), Mountain View
✆ (650) 641-0335 — **WEB:** www.zareensrestaurant.com
▨ Lunch & dinner Tue – Sun

PRICE: ⊜

ZENI ⅋○

Ethiopian • Simple

 ♿

MAP: D3

From its home at the end of a shopping plaza, Zeni caters to expats, tech types and families alike. The interior has a standard dining area decorated with colorful portraits and tapestries as well as traditional seating on low stools at woven tables. Either way, group dining is encouraged.

Relish the spongy, enticingly sour injera used to scoop up delicious yemisir wot (red lentils with spicy berbere); kik alicha (yellow peas tinged with garlic and ginger); or beef kitfo (available raw or cooked) tossed with that aromatic spice blend, mitmita, and crowned by crumbled ayib cheese. Here, injera is your only utensil, but be assured as there's a sink in the back to tidy up. Balance the fiery food with cool honey wine, or opt for an after-dinner Ethiopian coffee.

▪ 1320 Saratoga Ave. (at Payne Ave.), San Jose
☎ (408) 615-8282 — **WEB:** www.zeniethiopianrestaurant.com
▪ Lunch & dinner Tue – Sun   **PRICE:** ⬭⬭

ZOLA ⅋○

French • Bistro

 ♿

MAP: A4

A Palo Alto sparkler, Zola charms its way into diners' hearts via a seductive French bistro menu with Californian flair. Whether you're spreading smoky salmon rillettes on toasted artisan levain, twirling pillowy caramelized ricotta gnocchi into the yolk of a soft-cooked egg in brown butter or tucking into tender filet de boeuf with creamy sauce béarnaise and golden-brown fingerling potatoes, you're sure to fall hard for the food.

The stylish space updates a few classics (wood tables, bistro chairs, pressed ceilings) with a dark teal color scheme and enticingly low lighting, and the well-chosen wine list is equal parts Gallic and Golden State. Crème caramel for dessert may be traditional, but it's also perfectly executed and decadently rich.

▪ 565 Bryant St. (bet. Hamilton & University Aves.), Palo Alto
☎ (650) 521-0651 — **WEB:** www.zolapaloalto.com
▪ Dinner Tue – Sat   **PRICE:** $$

WINE COUNTRY

NAPA VALLEY

GRAPES GALORE

Revered as one of the most exalted wine growing regions in the world, Napa Valley is a 30 mile-long and luscious basin where wine is king. Given its grape-friendly climate and prime location (north from San Pablo Bay to Mount St. Helena, between the Mayacama and Vaca mountains), Napa ranks with California's most prestigious wineries. Here, powerfully hot summer days and cool nights provide the perfect environment for cabernet sauvignon grapes, a varietal for which the county is justifiably famous. But, it's not about just vino here. Top chefs also have a bounty of exceptional ingredients to choose from, including a range of locally grown and pressed extra virgin olive oils. **The Brasswood Bakery**, a deli and culinary emporium, is primo for excursion essentials like market-driven salads, hearty sandwiches, flaky pastries and so much more. Moving on to other savory spreads, culinary enthusiasts and cooks make their annual expedition to the **Napa Truffle Festival**, a veritable shindig of all things earthy. Also on offer here are cooking demos, seminars and foraging. Among the region's many winemakers are names like **Robert Mondavi**, **Francis Ford Coppola** and **Miljenko**

"Mike" Grgich. Originally from Croatia, Grgich rose to fame as the winemaker at **Chateau Montelena** when his 1973 chardonnay took the top prize at the Judgment of Paris in 1976, outshining France's best white Burgundies. This triumph turned the wine world on its ear, and put California on the map as a bona fide producer. Since then, Napa's indisputable success with premium wines has fostered endless pride, country-wide. American Viticultural Areas (AVAs) currently regulate the boundaries for districts such as Calistoga, Stags Leap, Rutherford and Los Carneros.

SPECIALTY FINDS

The Valley's wine-rich culture coupled with its illustrious restaurants that are destinations in themselves, make this region one of the world's most popular tourist attractions. Reclaimed 19th-century stone wineries and gorgeous Victorian homes punctuate the rolling landscape and serve as a constant reminder that there were some 140 wineries here prior to 1890. Up from a Prohibition-era low of perhaps a dozen, the area today boasts over 400 growers and producers. However, this is not to say that there aren't stellar alfresco dining spots and specialty stores situated along its picturesque streets. Gourmands never fail to make the trek to **Rancho Gordo**, headquartered here, for heirloom beans of the highest quality. Serving as the main supplier to area chefs, it is also open to the public—who seem smitten by their divine selection. Looking for some inspiration? They can also instruct you on how best to cook them! Picnic supplies are the main draw at **Oakville**

Grocery, the oldest operating store in town on Route 29; while **Model Bakery** in St. Helena or **Bouchon Bakery** in Yountville are wildly popular for fresh-baked breads and finger-licking pastries.

Napa's continued growth in wine production has spawned a special kind of food and wine tourism in this county, and tasting rooms, tours, as well as farm-fresh cuisine are de rigueur here. **Olivier Napa Valley** is a quaint and historic retail shop in St. Helena that proffers oils, vinegars and other local food products alongside beautiful handcrafted tableware and ceramics from Provence. Megawatt personalities like

Thomas Keller, Richard Reddington, Cindy Pawlcyn and Philippe Jeanty also hail from around the way, and may be found rubbing elbows at the flagship location of gourmet grocer, **Dean & Deluca**.

SHOPPING TREATS

Visitors touring the Valley will spot fields of fennel, silvery olive trees and rows of wild mustard that bloom between the grapevines in February and March. Mustard season kicks off each year with the **Napa Valley Mustard Festival** paying homage to the food, wine, art and agricultural bounty of this region. Likewise, several towns host seasonal farmer's markets from May through October, including one in Napa (held near the **Oxbow Public Market** on Tuesdays and Saturdays); St. Helena (Fridays in Crane Park); and Calistoga (on Saturdays at Sharpsteen Museum Plaza on Washington Street). Launched in early 2008, the **Oxbow Public Market** is a block-long, 40,000-square-foot facility meant to rival the **Ferry**

Building Marketplace that is housed across the Bay. Packed to the rafters with food artisans and wine vendors from within a 100-mile radius of the market, and cradled inside a barn-like building, Oxbow keeps fans returning for everything under the sun. Think cheese, charcuterie and spices; or olive oils, organic ice cream and specialty teas. Shoppers who work up an appetite while perusing these shelves can rest assured as there are numerous snacks also available to take home.

SIGHTS TO BEHOLD

Regional products such as **St. Helena Olive Oil** and **Woodhouse Chocolates** on Main Street, also in St. Helena, have similarly gained a large-scale nation-wide following. Three generations of one family run the latter, very charming chocolatier, which is most cherished for its handmade toffees. Just north of downtown St. Helena, the massive stone building that was erected in 1889 as Greystone Cellars now inhabits the West Coast campus of the renowned **Culinary Institute of America (CIA)**. Their intensive training and syllabus ensure a striking lineup of hot chefs in the making.

With all this going for the wine-rich valley, one thing is for certain—from the city of Napa (the county's largest population center) north to the town of Calistoga, known for its mineral mud baths and clean, spa cuisine, this narrow yet noteworthy region is nothing less than pure nirvana for lovers of great food and fine wine.

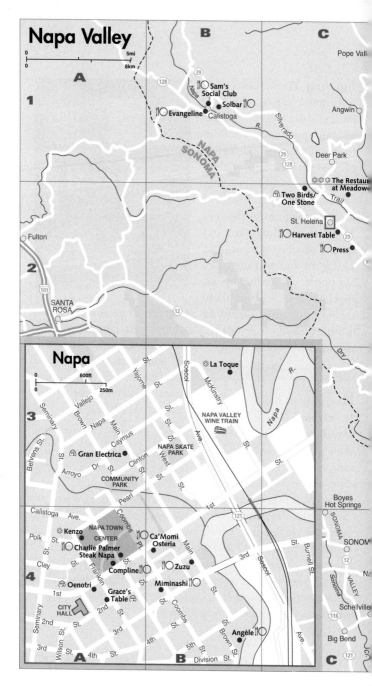

Napa Valley

0 —— 5mi
0 —— 8km

A

B

C

Pope Vall

1

(29)
(128)

Napa

🍴○ **Sam's Social Club**

○ **Solbar** 🍴○

🍴○ **Evangeline**

Calistoga

Silverado

Angwin

NAPA
SONOMA

(29)
(128)

Deer Park

R.

❀❀❀ **The Restau at Meadow**

🍴 **Two Birds/One Stone**

Trail

St. Helena ○

🍴○ **Harvest Table**

(29)

🍴○ **Press**

○ Fulton

2

(101)

SANTA
ROSA

(12)

Dry

Napa

0 —— 600ft
0 —— 250m

Bosco

❀ **La Toque**

Napa

R.

3

Seminary

Vallejo

Brown

Napa

Main

Caymus

Clinton

West

St.

McKinstry

Ave.

NAPA VALLEY
WINE TRAIN

St.

❀ **Gran Electrica**

Behrens St.

Arroyo

Dr.

St.

NAPA SKATE
PARK

1st

St.

COMMUNITY
PARK

Pearl

Calistoga Ave.

(121)

Boyes
Hot Springs

Polk
St.

Clay

❀ **Kenzo**

🍴○ **Charlie Palmer Steak Napa**

NAPA TOWN
CENTER

Coombs

Pl.

🍴○ **Ca'Momi
Osteria**

Main

SONOMA

SONOM

(12)

4

❀ **Oenotri**

1st

Franklin

St.

Compline 🍴○

🍴○ **Zuzu**

3rd

Burnell St.

Sonoma

SONOMA
VALLEY

Seminary

2nd

**Grace's
Table** ❀

🍴○ **Miminashi**

Coombs

2nd

St.

3rd

Schellville

3rd

Wilson St.

St.

4th

St.

4th

Division

5th

Brown St.

🍴○ **Angèle**

Ave.

Big Bend

(116)

(121)

A

B

C

248

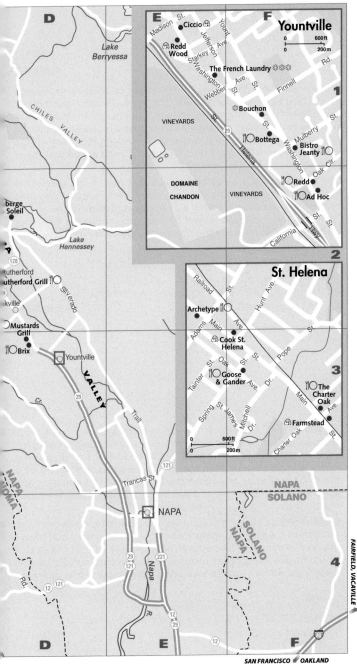

Yountville

0 — 600 ft
0 — 200 m

- Madison St.
- Ciccio
- Redd Wood
- The French Laundry ❀❀❀
- Bouchon ❀
- Bottega ❦
- Bistro Jeanty ❦
- Redd ❦
- Ad Hoc ❦

Yount Mill Rd.
Jefferson St.
Starkey Ave.
Washington St.
Webber Ave.
Finnell
Mulberry St.
Washington St.
Oak Cir.

VINEYARDS

DOMAINE CHANDON

VINEYARDS

St. Helena Hwy.
California Dr.

CHILES VALLEY

Lake Berryessa

Lake Hennessey

berge Soleil

128

utherford
Rutherford Grill ❦

Silverado Trail

kville

Mustards Grill ❦

Brix ❦

VALLEY

Cr.

29

Trail

Trancas St.

121

St. Helena

- Archetype ❦
- Cook St. Helena ❦
- Goose & Gander ❦
- The Charter Oak ❦
- Farmstead ❦

Railroad St.
Adams St.
Main St.
Hunt Ave.
Pope St.
Oak Ave.
Tainter St.
Spring St.
St. James
Mitchell Dr.
Main St.
Charter Oak Ave.
Charter Oak St.

0 — 600 ft
0 — 200 m

Yountville

NAPA

121

NAPA SOLANO

SOLANO NAPA

NAPA

29
121

Napa R.

221

12
29

12

12 121

Rd.

4

80

FAIRFIELD, VACAVILLE

AD HOC ⑪

American · *Rustic*

If you've ever wondered how Thomas Keller cooks at home, Ad Hoc is your best bet. The most casual of Chef Keller's restaurants, it offers accessible fare served family style in a bright and inviting wood-paneled room. Waits are inevitable without a reservation, but the engaging staff keep things hopping. The dining room feels like a country home, with that iconic blue awning and a sign that reads "for temporary relief from hunger."

The food is worth the wait and while dishes may sound simple, the crafting is not—come every other Monday for the outstanding fried chicken. A salad of sautéed red bliss potatoes tossed in Sriracha aïoli is beyond par; and even the humble cheese course dazzles. Generous portions may warrant sharing chocolate mousse for dessert.

6476 Washington St. (bet. California Dr. & Oak Circle), Yountville

℘ (707) 944-2487 — **WEB:** www.adhocrestaurant.com

Lunch Sun Dinner Thu – Mon   PRICE: $$$

ANGÈLE ⑪

French · *Rustic*

This airy French charmer, housed inside a century-old brick warehouse, is the perfect place to while away a warm afternoon—complete with an attentive staff, a chic Edith Piaf soundtrack and lovely view of the Napa River from the spacious outdoor dining area. No need to shy away on a cooler day either as the rustic interior, with its wood A-frame ceiling and polished concrete floors, is equally compelling.

Order a glass of a local white and savor the bistro food inflected with Californian flavor, from plump, garlicky escargot in flaky puff pastry to a croque monsieur, layered with ham, Gruyère and béchamel, that would do any Frenchman proud. Finish with caramelized banana gratin, heaped with crisp streusel and a big scoop of vanilla ice cream.

540 Main St. (at 5th St.), Napa

℘ (707) 252-8115 — **WEB:** www.angelerestaurant.com

Lunch & dinner daily   PRICE: $$

ARCHETYPE ⅋🍴

American • Elegant

♿ ⛱ 🛋

MAP: E2

Even by the standards of luxuriously appointed Napa Valley restaurants, Archetype is quite the looker. Blending farmhouse comfort with luxurious modern touches, it's just as glamorous for an evening meal by the fireplace as it is for brunch on the covered, screened-in patio strewn with climbing yellow rose bushes.

During the day, the menu focuses on comfort food like velvety artichoke soup with parmesan foam and flaky cheddar biscuits with sausage gravy. At night, things get more ambitious with such satisfying plates as oak-grilled duck breast with scallion pancakes and gochujang; or curry-braised red snapper with crab dumplings. There are also plenty of fun theme nights for locals—from fish taco Thursdays to fried chicken and waffle Sundays.

🔲 1429 Main St. (bet. Adams & Pine Sts.), St. Helena
📞 (707) 968-9200 — **WEB:** www.archetypenapa.com
🔲 Lunch & dinner Thu – Mon   **PRICE:** $$

BISTRO JEANTY ⅋🍴

French • Bistro

♿ ⛱

MAP: F1

Napa transforms into the French countryside via a meal at Bistro Jeanty, which serves rib-sticking favorites like coq au vin, boeuf Bourguignon and a sinfully rich milk-fed veal chop with chanterelle mushrooms and Camembert sauce. But California's lighter side is here, too: a salad of silken smoked trout and frisée is garden-fresh, and daily specials highlight the best in local produce.

The classic bistro accoutrements (yellow walls, wooden tables, framed retro posters) are present and accounted for, but there's an element of quirky fun here as well—from the flower-bedecked bicycle out front to the porcelain hens and hogs that dot the dining room. Like the flaky, caramelized and unmissable tarte Tatin, this is a gorgeous update on a classic.

🔲 6510 Washington St. (at Mulberry St.), Yountville
📞 (707) 944-0103 — **WEB:** www.bistrojeanty.com
🔲 Lunch & dinner daily   **PRICE:** $$$

AUBERGE DU SOLEIL ✿
Californian • *Luxury*

This is one of the first restaurants to elevate the Napa Valley to greatness. For the past decade, Chef Robert Curry has been ensuring its legacy with cooking that is the very definition of Californian cuisine: global flavors expressed through local and seasonal ingredients. The kitchen's work is as impressive as the setting, although it is during brunch or lunch when its creations truly come to life. It's when everything seems just a bit more beautiful from this extraordinary perch, overlooking the vineyards and mountains. Those terrace tables have some of the best views around.

Meals may be inspired by the comforting flavors of Sacramento Delta asparagus soup bobbing with lobster bits lurking at the bowl's base. Then Kurobuta pork chop set atop a red wine-Meyer lemon sauce is cooked to a perfect blush and served alongside intensely charred rapini for refreshing bitterness. A warm pineapple tart surrounded by a swirl of salted caramel makes for a sweet, savory and deliciously fruity bite.

Servers are stylish, polite and manage to refill your glass after each sip, without seeming intrusive. Their wine list is one of the most notable in the valley and proudly showcases local growers.

▦ 180 Rutherford Hill Rd. (off the Silverado Trail), Rutherford
✆ (707) 967-3111 — WEB: www.aubergedusoleil.com
▦ Lunch & dinner daily

PRICE: $$$$

BOTTEGA 🍴

Italian • *Elegant*

Michael Chiarello is one of the original celebrity chefs, and his higher-end Napa Valley outpost draws fans from around the globe. Hopefuls are indeed likely to see him in the kitchen, drizzling olive oil on plates of creamy, almost liquid-fresh burrata and marinated mushrooms; or pouring persimmon purée across thick slices of yellowfin tuna crudo. Even the wine list features his house blends, which pair delightfully with pastas like the whole-wheat tagliarini tossed in a pitch-perfect Bolognese.

Large and boisterous, Bottega's autumn-hued dining room welcomes crowds with comfy banquettes and terra-cotta accents. One will also find lovely outdoor seating by the firepit. A well-made tiramisu and espresso offer a fine Italiano end to the festivities.

▨ 6525 Washington St. (near Yount St.), Yountville
✆ (707) 945-1050 — **WEB:** www.botteganapavalley.com
▨ Lunch Tue – Sun Dinner nightly　　　　**PRICE: $$**

BRIX 🍴

Californian • *Elegant*

This roadside treat overlooking the Mayacamas Mountains is almost as lauded for its 16-acre produce garden (which provides many of the ingredients seen on your plate) and vineyard, as it is for its ultra-seasonal and eclectic-Californian cuisine. Dishes are wide-ranging and often refined as verified by ricotta gnocchi cooked to a gentle gold in rosemary-browned butter with squash, plump Medjool dates and almonds; or saffron and orange salmon that arrives firm and pink with quail eggs, dill aïoli and potato salad. An extensive Sunday brunch buffet highlights offerings from the wood-fired oven and charcoal grill.

The interior feels like a mountain ranch with its stone walls, fireplaces and chandeliers cleverly crafted from cutlery. Service is finely tuned.

▨ 7377 St. Helena Hwy. (at Washington St.), Napa
✆ (707) 944-2749 — **WEB:** www.brix.com
▨ Lunch & dinner daily　　　　**PRICE: $$$**

BOUCHON ✿
French • Bistro

♿ 🍴 🛏️

Timeless French food is recreated with great regard for quality and technique at Thomas Keller's exuberant bistro, set down the street from his iconic The French Laundry. Complete with lush potted plants, shimmering brass accents and enormous mirrors, this dining room is the spitting image of Parisian chic. A theatrical crowd uplifts the space with conviviality, and every lavish banquette or stool at the bustling bar is full. Always.

Thanks to the house bakery next door, the bread here is ace, so grab an extra hunk of the supremely fresh and crusty pain d'epi to slather with butter. The menu lists well-executed classics, including that beloved platter of escargot, each coated with intensely flavorful and rich garlic-parsley butter and crowned by addictive little toques of flaky puff pastry. Moving on, braised lamb demonstrates the power of rustic French cooking, set over polenta with grilled young leeks and carrots.

Desserts are quite literally the icing on the cake and often the very definition of decadence. Even the humble pie is elevated here, to be served as an almond-spiced pear, glazed with juice and set over a tiny round of puff pastry matched with rich vanilla ice cream.

▦ 6534 Washington St. (at Yount St.), Yountville

📞 (707) 944-8037 — **WEB:** www.thomaskeller.com

▦ Lunch & dinner daily

PRICE: $$$

CA'MOMI OSTERIA ⵍⵔ

Italian • *Rustic*

MAP: B4

A spinoff of the beloved Ca'Momi Enoteca kiosk in the nearby Oxbow Public Market, this stand-alone spot aims to promote buon gusto with its "heartcrafted" food (as indicated in a sign above the bar). Big and airy, with exposed brick and wooden beams, it is abuzz with pizzaioli turning out Neapolitan pies from the wood-burning oven (note that the counter opposite the fire is the best seat in the house).

The massive menu is inspired by every region of Italy featuring crispy Piemontese sunchoke chips dusted with salt and fried parsley, as well as Tuscan spinach-ricotta gnudi in a creamy butter-and-sage sauce. Finish with the delicious Campanian angioletti, which is basically fried pizza dough packed with that beloved combo of chocolate and hazelnut.

1141 1st St. (bet. Coombs & Main Sts.), Napa
☎ (707) 224-6664 — **WEB:** www.camomiosteria.com
Lunch Fri – Sun Dinner Tue – Sun   **PRICE: $$**

CHARLIE PALMER STEAK NAPA ⵍⵔ

Steakhouse • *Elegant*

MAP: A4

Chef Charlie Palmer may have only recently brought his eponymous steakhouse to the boutique Archer Hotel in downtown Napa, but it already fits seamlessly into these environs and feels like it's been here forever. Service is superb, as you would expect of any restaurant in this chain. The sleek interior features dark woods, stone columns and tables that are on the small side for a steakhouse. The kitchen focuses on classic fare, such as freshly shucked oysters, Caesar salad with fried quail eggs and steaks with a choice of standout sauces, particularly the béarnaise. Non-traditional offerings include sweet pea ravioli or a rack of lamb.

After dinner, head to the rooftop, where a bar and expansive lounge surrounding fireplaces attract long weekend lines.

1260 1st St. (at Napa Town Center), Napa
☎ (707) 819-2500 — **WEB:** www.charliepalmersteak.com
Lunch & dinner daily   **PRICE: $$$$**

THE CHARTER OAK 🍴

Californian • *Rustic*

🍇 🍸 ♿ ⛱ 🎦 🛋

MAP: F3

Courtesy of The Restaurant at Meadowood's team, this approachable retreat is already highly regarded and rightly applauded as a Napa mainstay. It presents a rustic method to dining that centers on hearth-roasted food, and the beautifully restored room's design and large tables seem to promote sharing platters of roasted beef ribs or broccolini.

Their garden's bounty is on full display in a simple, but beautiful bowl of just-plucked veggies, bettered with a swipe of the savory fermented soy dip. The hearth is indeed the heart of this kitchen, and everything from mains to sides bears traces of the flames. Smashed then grilled into little coins, the potato tostones have a terrific char and smoky flavor—enhanced by the caramel quality of brown butter.

▨ 1050 Charter Oak Ave. (off St. Helena Hwy.), St. Helena
✆ (707) 302-6996 — **WEB:** www.thecharteroak.com
▨ Lunch & dinner daily
PRICE: $$$

CICCIO 😋

Italian • *Trattoria*

🍇

MAP: E1

A pleasant contrast to the sleek new spots around town, Ciccio's country-style curtains and slatted front porch are a ticket to another era (and a hot ticket at that, since tables are hard to come by). Its location inside a wood-framed 1916-era grocery could pass as some John Wayne film set, but Ciccio is more of a spaghetti Western, thanks to the focused Italian-influenced menu revolving around pastas and pizzas. Highlights include the feathery ricotta dumplings in a homey veal-and pork Sunday red sauce. Spicy mortadella, fiery cherry peppers and creamy fontina are a winning trio atop crispy pizza, but don't miss the signature sponge cake, soaked in citrus liqueur.

The wine list is a delight, as those behind Ciccio also own Altamura winery.

▨ 6770 Washington St. (bet. Madison & Pedroni Sts.), Yountville
✆ (707) 945-1000 — **WEB:** www.ciccionapavalley.com
▨ Dinner Wed – Sun
PRICE: $$

COMPLINE 🍴

American • Trendy

♿ ♿ 🚲

This cool wine bar clearly takes pride in the mastery of its sommelier by pouring a lengthy and thoughtful array of wines from the world over. At the same time, Compline serves a focused menu of appealingly hearty food that pairs well with this list. Find a perch at the bar so you can chat with the staff about their vast selection, but tables in the dining room or patio are just as pleasant.

Savor a glass of champagne with duck fat fries—to whet the appetite—before perusing the menu. Juicy half-pound burgers on brioche are a great way to get going here, especially when layered with Gruyère and mushrooms. Less casual items feature a Liberty Farms duck breast or rustic hanger steak.

Keep an eye on the calendar for themed tasting events and seminars.

▪ 1300 First St. (at Napa Town Center), Napa
☎ (707) 492-8150 — **WEB:** www.complinewine.com
▪ Lunch & dinner daily

PRICE: $$$

COOK ST. HELENA ☺

Italian • Neighborhood

It's true—solid cooking and sane prices can be hard to come by—but this Italian haven located on St. Helena's main drag appears to have mastered that formula. The cozy space has two seating options: a gleaming marble counter up front, as well as tables that stretch from front to back (the ones up front are lighter, airier and preferable).

The food is thoughtful and refined with a daily rotating risotto, house-stretched mozzarella and burrata and glorious pastas like ricotta fazzoletti with a deeply flavored Bolognese. Grilled octopus salad with potatoes, olives and tomato dressing is boosted by prime ingredients and careful seasoning. The wine list tempts at dinner, but Bloody Marys are all the rage at brunch, served at Cook Tavern next door.

▪ 1310 Main St. (bet. Adams St. & Hunt Ave.), St. Helena
☎ (707) 963-7088 — **WEB:** www.cooksthelena.com
▪ Lunch Mon – Sat Dinner nightly

PRICE: $$

EVANGELINE ◍⚬

American · Rustic

    MAP: B1

Jazzy New Orleans flair infuses every inch of this Southern charmer, which adds just a hint of spice to the easy Californian charm of quaint Calistoga. A trellised garden patio (a must-visit on a warm day) blooms with fragrant jasmine, while the cozy indoor dining room provides an intimate retreat complete with midnight-blue banquettes.

A collection of French bistro- Californian- and Cajun-inspired dishes abound on the approachable menu. Rich, creamy duck rillettes arrive with toasted baguette and red pepper jelly. Shrimp étouffée is spicy and complex, its thick, dark roux coating a heap of fluffy white rice. And melt-in-your-mouth tarte Tatin slathered with locally made Three Twins vanilla ice cream is as good as any beignet.

  1226 Washington St. (bet. 1st St. & Lincoln Ave.), Calistoga
  (707) 341-3131 — WEB: www.evangelinenapa.com
  Lunch Sat – Sun Dinner nightly

PRICE: $$

FARMSTEAD ◉

Californian · Rustic

    MAP: F3

For a down-home (but still Napa-chic) alternative to the Cal-Ital wine country grind, follow your nose to this Long Meadow Ranch-owned farmhouse, whose intoxicating smoker is parked right in the front yard. The cathedral ceiling, old-school country music and boisterous locals give Farmstead a permanent buzz; for quieter dining, hit the front terrace.

Dishes are laden with ranch-grown products (from veggies to olive oil), utilized in outstanding preparations like wood-grilled artichoke with sauce gribiche, meatballs with caramelized onions and tomato marmalade or a smoked chicken sandwich with avocado, sweet onion rings and a side of herb-fried potatoes. Try the ranch's own wine, or splurge on a fancy bottle at a shockingly reasonable markup.

  738 Main St. (at Charter Oak Ave.), St. Helena
  (707) 963-9181 — WEB: www.longmeadowranch.com
  Lunch & dinner daily

PRICE: $$

THE FRENCH LAUNDRY ✿✿✿

Contemporary · Elegant

✿ ♿ 🍴

Over 20 years old and topping every foodie's bucket list, Thomas Keller's legendary destination still doesn't miss a beat. The cuisine, staff and a state-of-the-art kitchen embedded with the chef's renowned sense of purpose and functionality continue to remain at their pinnacle. In fact this may be known as the greatest cooking space in America, as every aspect of the setting is carefully determined—from the counter height to the flowing lines in the ceiling. It's a meeting point of the past, present and future.

Chef Keller continues to pair classic French techniques with wildly fresh ingredients in a setting that is a perfect storm of restaurant greatness—we should all be so lucky to score a reservation here in our lifetime. Choose from two seasonal tasting menus, including a vegetarian option. Both feature products from boutique purveyors. Dinners may highlight signature oysters with white sturgeon caviar in a warm sabayon studded with tapioca pearls, or Scottish sea trout with avocado mousse and a sorrel- and sesame-miso vinaigrette.

Located along a winding road, it is the very picture of bucolic charm with ivy creeping up its stone façade and a tastefully decorated dining room.

■ 6640 Washington St. (at Creek St.), Yountville

☏ (707) 944-2380 — **WEB:** www.thomaskeller.com

■ Lunch Fri – Sun Dinner nightly

PRICE: $$$$

GOOSE & GANDER 🍴

American · Chic

🍸 🍽 🎲

MAP: F3

With its mountain-lodge feel, this clubby retreat has been a favorite among Napa Valley diners since its bygone days as the Martini House. Those classic libations may have long since made way for elaborate concoctions from acclaimed mixologist Scott Beattie, but this gander retains all the charm of the goose—as well as the recipe for its justly famous mushroom soup, which could win over even the staunchest foe of fungi.

Elsewhere on the menu, you'll find hearty dishes like fettuccini carbonara, a bone marrow-topped burger and fried chicken sandwich with charred jalapeño aïoli as well as duck-fat fries. Whether you're soaking up summer on the spacious patio or relaxing by the fireplace in the cavernous downstairs bar, you'll quickly feel at home here.

▪ 1245 Spring St. (at Oak Ave.), St. Helena
☏ (707) 967-8779 — **WEB:** www.goosegander.com
▪ Lunch & dinner daily

PRICE: $$

GRACE'S TABLE 😊

International · Family

♿ 🛋

MAP: A4

Around the world in four courses without leaving wine country? It's possible at this bright, contemporary downtown Napa space that balances fun with excellence. Only here can a top-notch tamale filled with chipotle-pulled pork, green chile and black beans be followed by cassoulet that would do any Frenchman proud—thanks to its decadent mélange of butter beans, duck confit and two kinds of sausage.

With Italian and American staples in the mix as well, it might sound too eclectic for one meal, but Grace's Table earns its name with charming service and a thoughtful, well-priced wine list to bridge any gaps between cuisines. Regardless, make sure you don't miss the satiny, ganache-layered devil's food chocolate cake—a slice is big enough to split.

▪ 1400 2nd St. (at Franklin St.), Napa
☏ (707) 226-6200 — **WEB:** www.gracestable.net
▪ Lunch & dinner daily

PRICE: $$

GRAN ELECTRICA 🐶
Mexican • Colorful

 ♿ ⛱ 🛋

Welcome to Mexico by way of Brooklyn (home to the original location) right in the heart of Napa. Gran Electrica is already a neighborhood hit—particularly during happy hour. Servers are always welcoming and ensure a steady meal. Inside this breezy space, find a long bar stocked with mezcal and tequila as well as floor-to-ceiling windows that practically open onto the sidewalk. The massive outdoor patio is just as popular.

Over in the kitchen, tacos, tostadas and larger plates are all made with great care and top ingredients. Be sure to try the ceviche tostada, a starter filled with clean, bright flavors and lime-cured shrimp. Red snapper mojo de ajo is another highpoint, sautéed in a garlicky red sauce of chile morita, lemon and a bit of paprika heat.

 🔲 1313 Main St. (bet. Caymus & Clinton Sts.), Napa
🕿 (707) 258-1313 — **WEB:** www.granelectrica.com
 🔲 Dinner nightly

PRICE: $$

HARVEST TABLE 🍴
Californian • Neighborhood

 ♿ ⛱ 🛋 🧼

Charlie Palmer's Harvest Inn is a culinary destination thanks to the thriving presence of Harvest Table. Its Californian menu relies on local purveyors and the inn's own gardens for ingredients. Guests are encouraged to tour these grounds before or after meals. The space is simple and appealingly rustic thanks in part to the large fireplace. Two covered patios offer a comfy perch to enjoy the natural beauty of the inn.

Dark wood tables can be seen groaning under the weight of such enjoyable items as smoked Mt. Lassen trout with Meyer lemon gel. Scallops are then set atop savory cauliflower florets and sweet red grapes for a delightful balance in flavors; while a tropical fruit panna cotta with mango and roasted cashew praline is relished at the end.

 🔲 1 Main St. (bet. Lewelling Ln. & Sulphur Springs Ave.), St. Helena
🕿 (707) 967-4695 — **WEB:** www.harvesttablenapa.com
 🔲 Lunch Wed – Sun Dinner Tue – Sun

PRICE: $$$

KENZO ✿

Japanese • Minimalist

Kenzo Tsujimoto made his fortune developing thrilling video games like Resident Evil and Street Fighter, but his Napa temple of traditional Japanese cuisine is a place to hit pause and wash away worldly cares. Designed by Tsujimoto's wife Natsuko, this 25-seat arena is spare and minimal, incorporating traditional woods, maple trees and river rocks to create a peaceful sanctuary.

Though Kenzo offers a handful of tables, the best seats are at the lengthy counter, where diners can chat with the chefs and see their sushi made firsthand. There are two menus: Sushi Kaiseki presents edomae-style bites that are beautifully composed and elegantly paced (and product is sourced from Tokyo's Tsukiji market), while the kaiseki menu features cooked presentations like Wagyu tenderloin with a reduction of the estate's own Bordeaux-style blend. Exceptional servers thoughtfully explain more unusual dishes like shinjo, a gently poached dumpling made from egg whites and chopped scallops that is served in a delicate dashi.

There is an outstanding variety of sake showcased here, but adventurous diners may want to sample Kenzo Estate's own California-grown wines, which are available by the flight.

1339 Pearl St. (at Franklin St.), Napa

℘ (707) 294-2049 — **WEB:** www.kenzonapa.com

Dinner Tue – Sun

PRICE: $$$$

LA TOQUE ✿
Contemporary • Elegant

MAP: B3

You'll want to tip your own toque in appreciation after a meal at this downtown fine-dining palace in the Westin Verasa Napa, which blends a serious approach to cuisine and service that has just enough cheek to keep things lively.

La Toque may display an oversized inflatable chef's hat hanging above its walkway, but the interior is the soul of modern sophistication, with leather-topped tables, a fireplace and an extensive wine list—proffered on an iPad. The cadre of staff is notable, and the well-trained, knowledgeable waiters move in synchronicity within the celebratory crowd.

Choose from a four- or five-course à la carte, beginning with exquisite canapés like perfectly seasoned tuna tartare, clams with apple vinaigrette or crostini with a terrine of foie gras. Thin slices of beef loin carpaccio are lightly smoked, then artfully presented to resemble a flower, topped with creamy tuna sauce, sautéed wild mushrooms and dried tomato. Intense Lebanese spices come to life in wonderfully tender braised squid with dates, almond, cauliflower and a spoonful of Greek yogurt. Desserts, like the butter-crunch cake with apple, underscore the glamorous and delicious character of the restaurant itself.

◻ 1314 McKinstry St. (at Soscol Ave.), Napa

✆ (707) 257-5157 — **WEB:** www.latoque.com

◻ Dinner nightly

PRICE: $$$$

MIMINASHI ⅃○

Japanese • *Minimalist*

♿

Izakaya fare gets Californian flair at this downtown Napa site, which has a distinctive and minimalist look inspired by several trips to Japan. A buzzy crowd of locals fills the wooden booths and tables, while an arrow-shaped bar is a major draw for solo diners.

A variety of skewered chicken parts grilled over the white-hot binchotan are the highlight of the menu—imagine the likes of succulent and smoky chicken thighs, or springy tsukune in an umami-rich tare glaze. A handful of seats at the narrow counter allow guests to chat with the grill cook. The rest of the menu emphasizes local produce, including rice and noodle bowls stuffed with seasonal vegetables; crunchy sweet corn fritters with Kewpie mayo; as well as gingery pan-fried chicken gyoza.

▪ 821 Coombs St. (bet. 2nd & 3rd Sts.), Napa

✆ (707) 254-9464 — **WEB:** www.miminashi.com

▪ Lunch Mon – Fri Dinner nightly   PRICE: $$

MUSTARDS GRILL ⅃○

American • *Neighborhood*

⅗ ♿

At Cindy Pawlcyn's iconic roadhouse, it's a joy to eat your greens. Lettuces are freshly plucked from the restaurant's bountiful garden boxes and tossed with tasty dressings including a shallot- and Dijon mustard-spiked Banyuls vinaigrette. The fish of the day may unveil grilled halibut sauced with oxtail reduction and plated with silken leeks, fingerling potatoes and baby carrots. But, save room as this is not the place to skip dessert, and the lemon-lime tart capped with brown sugar meringue that is fittingly described on the menu as "ridiculously tall," doesn't disappoint. It should come as no surprise that there's usually a wait for a table here. But no matter; use the time to take a stroll on the grounds for a preview of what the kitchen has in store.

▪ 7399 St. Helena Hwy. (at Hwy. 29), Yountville

✆ (707) 944-2424 — **WEB:** www.mustardsgrill.com

▪ Lunch & dinner daily   PRICE: $$$

OENOTRI 😊

Italian • Trattoria

♿ 🏕 🛏️

There's no sweeter greeting than the aroma of wood smoke that beckons diners into this downtown standout. And with its Neapolitan pizza oven, sunny textiles and exposed brick, Oenotri—from an ancient Italian word for "wine cultivator"—looks as good as it smells.

Chef/owner Tyler Rodde imbues the cooking of Southern Italy with a dash of Californian spirit. From the pasta to the herbs, nearly everything is made from scratch or from the garden. Bountiful salads top every table, but those seeking meatier eats should start with the charcuterie, cured in-house. Options change seasonally, but pizza is a must. Torchio, or corkscrew pasta, with diced roasted winter squash, toasted pine nuts, fried sage and a drizzle of brown butter is a close second.

◾ 1425 1st St. (bet. Franklin & School Sts.), Napa
☎ (707) 252-1022 — **WEB:** www.oenotri.com
◾ Lunch Sat – Sun Dinner nightly

PRICE: $$

PRESS 🍴

Steakhouse • Elegant

🕶️ ♿ 🏕 ⬜

The classic steakhouse gets a wine country twist at this standby, where the G&Ts are designed to specifications and the dry-aged USDA Prime steaks hold equal standing with the "vegetable cocktail"—a stunning edible still life of local produce. But indulgence is still the name of the game, from a take on the classic wedge salad made with local Pt. Reyes blue cheese to a decadent mashed potato pancake.

With a bucolic location off Highway 29, Press combines traditional dark wood, cozy booths and a flickering fireplace with lofty and soaring ceilings. The well-to-do crowd marvels at decorative wonders like a massive ceramic clock sourced from a bygone New York train station, all the while sipping full-bodied Napa reds that pair perfectly with the rich food.

◾ 587 St. Helena Hwy. (near Inglewood Ave.), St. Helena
☎ (707) 967-0550 — **WEB:** www.presssthelena.com
◾ Dinner Wed – Mon

PRICE: $$$$

REDD ⅋○

Contemporary · Chic

😎 🍸 ♿ ☂ 🛋

MAP: F2

In this quaint hamlet, Redd stands out both for its modern look and contemporary approach to cuisine, with flavors from around the globe. A meal here might begin with bright hamachi sashimi with a soy lime ginger dressing; then veer into scallops on a bed of cauliflower purée, golden raisins, salty capers, swirls of balsamic reduction, and slivered almonds for a hint of sweetness in flavor and divine texture. A creamy-dreamy passion fruit-panna cotta with coconut flakes, rhubarb and Brazilian nuts tastes of the tropics.

The sleek, modernist décor attracts a sedate crowd, attended to by professional servers. This space really shines at lunch, when sunlight streams through the windows, but on nice days, head outdoors for a seat on the serene patio.

🔲 6480 Washington St. (at Oak Circle), Yountville
📞 (707) 944-2222 — **WEB:** www.reddnapavalley.com
🔲 Lunch Fri – Sun Dinner nightly

PRICE: $$$

REDD WOOD 👓

Italian · Trendy

♿ ☂ 📱

MAP: E1

Napa Valley's answer to the hip Cal-Ital hot spots of San Francisco, Redd Wood boasts an edgy indie soundtrack and a parade of bearded, tattooed waiters. But unlike some cityside establishments, the waitstaff here is personable and enthusiastic, and there's plenty of breathing room (including a private area that's popular for events).

Artisan pizzas are the main attraction of this kitchen and sometimes simplest is best—like the fresh mozzarella, basil and tomato. Another topped with pancetta, asiago, taleggio and black garlic is equally enticing. But, don't let that limit your choices. The house-cured salumi, fresh pastas and appealing antipasti are also winners—just be sure to save some room for their outstanding toffee cannoli dessert.

🔲 6755 Washington St. (bet. Madison & Pedroni Sts.), Yountville
📞 (707) 299-5030 — **WEB:** www.redd-wood.com
🔲 Lunch & dinner daily

PRICE: $$

THE RESTAURANT AT MEADOWOOD ✿✿✿

Contemporary • Luxury

MAP: C2

With its elusive balance of rustic luxury, this is the kind of property that will floor you with its understated beauty. Everything here exudes California-style wealth and comfort, from those cottages dotting the Napa hills to the front lounge's stone fireplace. Beyond this, the dining room is a sophisticated barn of sorts, decked with polished stone tables, wood columns and bucolic splendor.

All of this makes for an elegant backdrop for romantic evenings or family celebrations, as long as everyone is willing to splurge. Servers are impeccable, professional and know how to keep their guests happy and at ease.

The kitchen's magic is its ability to take just-picked produce and create dishes that are the very essence of laid-back luxury. Take the avocado creation for instance, elevated to the next level thanks to a center filled with coal-roasted foie gras. Vichyssoise, with fermented potatoes and leeks and house-made buttermilk, is an absolute work of art, but wait, there's more. The pine cone—a giant one beautifully plated with greenery—hides a seductive chocolate cream within. Garnished with tiny slivers of crystallized baby pine cones cooked in honey, it's pure genius.

---

900 Meadowood Ln. (off Silverado Trail), St. Helena

☎ (707) 967-1205 — **WEB:** www.therestaurantatmeadowood.com

Dinner Tue – Sat   **PRICE: $$$$**

RUTHERFORD GRILL ⅛○

American • *Chic*

As the crowds filter out of neighboring Beaulieu Vineyards and other Highway 29 wineries, they head straight to this upscale chain, which boasts long lines at even the earliest hours. Kudos to the amiable host staff for handling them smoothly. The dark wood interior is clubby yet accommodating, and a large patio offers drinks for waiting diners.

Every portion here can easily serve two, beginning with a seasonal vegetable platter boasting buttery Brussels sprouts, a wild rice salad and braised red cabbage. For those looking to stave off tasting-induced hangovers, the steak and enchilada platter is the ticket with plenty of juicy tri-tip, yellow and red escabeche sauce and a poached egg. A wedge of classic banana cream pie delivers the knockout punch.

   1180 Rutherford Rd. (at Hwy. 29), Rutherford

   (707) 963-1792 — **WEB:** www.hillstone.com

   Lunch & dinner daily

PRICE: $$

SAM'S SOCIAL CLUB ⅛○

American • *Elegant*

Lauded as the main restaurant for the Indian Springs resort, Sam's Social Club is a supremely beloved destination, thanks in large part to its Spanish colonial look and soothing, bucolic vibe. Named for resort founder Samuel Brannan, this Mission Revival dining room boasts lofty ceilings, plush couches, bright murals and a big patio complete with a geyser-fed water feature.

The unpretentious atmosphere extends to the plates, from grilled octopus endowed with a peppy romesco sauce and crispy new potatoes. Specials may include pan-seared duck served with bright green broccoli rabe and sweetly acidic piquillo. Tourists have already caught on: you'll find them happily sharing bottles of wine and digging into plates of strawberry-rhubarb crisp.

   1712 Lincoln Ave. (at Indian Springs Resort), Calistoga

   (707) 942-4969 — **WEB:** www.samssocialclub.com

   Lunch & dinner daily

PRICE: $$

SOLBAR 🍴◯
Californian • *Contemporary décor*

MAP: B1

It may take a few twists and turns around the palatial Solage Calistoga property to locate this bijou, but once inside, you'll find a romantic dining room decked out with banquettes and a contemporary fireplace.

The cuisine may be proudly Californian, but the kitchen is well-versed in classic technique, as evidenced by dishes such as the octopus with Ibérico ham reduction. Dainty and tender faro gnocchetti with a briny-sweet asparagus and clam velouté, coupled with the fett'unta's crispy crust and soft crumb is spot on with an appealing balance of flavors and texture. Eureka lemon and blackberry croccante, with its thin layers of pastry tucked with blood orange gelée, pistachio and Satsuma mandarin sorbet, is a lovely finale.

▢ 755 Silverado Trail (at Rosedale Rd.), Calistoga
✆ (707) 226-0860 — **WEB:** solage.aubergeresorts.com
▢ Lunch & dinner daily   **PRICE:** $$$

TWO BIRDS/ONE STONE 😊
Fusion • *Rustic*

MAP: C2

Acclaimed Chefs Douglas Keane and Sang Yoon join forces at this hip respite, located within the striking Freemark Abbey Winery. The space blends the original stone walls with steel trusses, overhead skylights as well as a spacious patio— reflecting the menu's Californian take on traditional Japanese kushiyaki.

Meals start with seasonal small plates like "Ham & Eggs," featuring a small stone jar filled with savory egg custard, topped with smoked duck ham, onsen jidori egg and shaved scallions. Then shift into a selection of meats, like Ibérico de Bellota—tender, rosy pork shoulder glazed with spiced Vietnamese caramel and grouped with kimchi. Pair one of their wines with sweet Peony grapes accompanied by white miso custard for a singular finish.

▢ 3020 St. Helena Hwy. (bet. Ehlers & Lodi Lns.), St. Helena
✆ (707) 302-3777 — **WEB:** www.twobirdsonestonenapa.com
▢ Dinner Thu – Mon   **PRICE:** $$

ZUZU 🍴

Spanish • Rustic

&

MAP: B4

This Mediterranean-inspired cutie was dishing out small plates long before it was cool, and its rustic bi-level space still draws a steady crowd of local regulars. Upstairs, long picnic tables are ideal for those who come with a crowd. Spanish-style tile floors, a pressed-tin ceiling and honey-colored walls give Zuzu an enchanting old-world vibe, setting the scene for sharing the more than two-dozen tapas, both frio and caliente.

They include the fantastic shrimp ceviche with bright cara cara oranges, chili oil and shaved red onions; plump Gulf coast shrimp with a smoky pimento sauce; and fried Tolenas Ranch quail over rich, smoky Rancho Gordo posole.

For similar cuisine in a more modern atmosphere, sister restaurant La Taberna is also worth a visit.

▨ 829 Main St. (bet. 2nd & 3rd Sts.), Napa

✆ (707) 224-8555 — **WEB:** www.zuzunapa.com

▨ Lunch Mon – Fri Dinner nightly

PRICE: $$

Sunday brunch plans?
Look for the 🥞!

SONOMA COUNTY

Bordering the North Bay, Sonoma County boasts around 76 miles of Pacific coastline and over 400 wineries. Eclipsed as a wine region by neighboring Napa Valley, this county's wineries know how to take full advantage of some of California's best grape-growing conditions. Today, 17 distinct wine appellations (AVAs) have been assigned in this area, which is slightly larger than the state of Rhode Island itself, and produce a groundbreaking range of fine varietals. This region however is also cherished for its culinary destinations starting with **The Naked Pig**, an amazing pit-stop for brunch or lunch. Reinforcing the wine country's ethos of farm-to-table dining, the items on offer here ooze with all things local and sustainable—maybe bacon waffles with Santa Rosa wildflower honey? But, there are plenty of big and bold bites to be had in town. **Bar-B-Que Smokehouse** in Sebastopol is quite literally award-winning, as their 'cue took home the crown at the **Sonoma County Harvest Fair** in 2010. Other premium pleasures include **Screamin' Mimi's**, a local but nationally known ice cream shop that has been preparing its 300-plus recipes since 1995, as well as **Moustache Baked**

Goods, a boutique operation churning out exceptional, all-American baked goods with quirky names. In fact, cupcakes (like The Outlaw or even The Vintner) have been known to cultivate a sizable following. The North American headquarters of the South American energy-boosting beverage line, **Guayaki Yerba Mate Cafe**, is also settled here as a café-cum-community center, while **The National Heirloom Exposition** is commended among epicureans for its sustainable farming and healthy food practices. Along Highway 12 heading north, byroads lead to isolated wineries, each of which puts its own unique stamp on the business of winemaking. Named after the river that enabled Russian trading outposts along the coast, **The Russian River Valley** is one of the coolest growing regions in Sonoma, largely due to the river basin that acts as a conduit for coastal climates. At the upper end of the Russian River, **Dry Creek Valley** yields excellent sauvignon blanc, chardonnay and pinot noir. This region is also justifiably famous for zinfandel—a grape that does especially well in the valley's rock-strewn soil. And for snacks to go with these notable sips, Sonoma's eight-acre plaza is occupied by restaurants, shops and other such stops. Of epicurean note is building contractor Chuck Williams who bought a hardware store here in 1956. He gradually converted his stock to a selection of exceptionally unique French cookware and kitchen tools, and today, **Williams-Sonoma** has over 600 stores nationwide. Following in his footsteps, **Bram** is similarly beloved for their handmade earthenware that is inspired by the Egyptian clay pots of yore. And located on the same square, **Sign of the Bear** is yet another specialty shop (as well as an essential stop) for all types of table- and cook-ware.

BEST IN LIFE

Throughout scenic and bucolic Sonoma County (also known locally as SoCo), vineyards rub shoulders with orchards and farms. The words "sustainable" and "organic" headline these local farmers' markets, where one may find every item imaginable—from

just-picked heirloom vegetables to uni so fresh that it still appears to be moving. Of course, freshness comes first at **Amy's Drive Thru**, where organic veggie burgers and the plant-covered "living rooftop" are well-worth a visit. In business since 2010, **Petaluma Pie Company** keeps picky palates sated and happy with both sweet and savory pies crafted from organic ingredients. And over on Petaluma Blvd., find a cult of carb fans at **Della Fattoria**—drooling over their lineup of just-baked bread.

This very fertile territory also has more than just a fair share of great seafood. In fact, some of the best oysters can be found off the Sonoma coast and enthusiasts drive along Highway 1 to sample as many varieties as possible— from **Tomales Bay Oyster Company** and **The Marshall Store**, to **Hog Island Oyster Co.** Naturally there are much more than just mollusks to be relished here. Start your day right with a serious breakfast at **Dierk's Parkside Cafe**, where "Gompa's Pancake Breakfas" served with two eggs, bacon, ham or sausage is a hearty revelation. Similarly, comfort food is the name of the game at local sensation **Bear Republic Brewing Company Pub & Restaurant**—a family-owned Healdsburg hot spot favored for unique, award-winning brews and tours (by appointment only); just as top-notch IPAs are all the rage at **Lagunitas Brewing Company**—a taproom for the Petaluma-based brewery. For a different kind of buzz, coffee shops are fast becoming the new tasting room in these parts, featuring ethically sourced beans from the world's best growing regions that are roasted locally and expertly brewed to order. **Acre Coffee** and **Flying Goat Coffee** are two such highly regarded options with outposts located throughout this county.

Numerous ethnic food stands bring global cuisines to this wine-centric community, with offerings that have their roots as close as Mexico and far off as India and Afghanistan. Thanks to Sonoma County's natural bounty, farm-to-table cuisine takes on new heights in many of its surrounding restaurants and some chefs need to go no farther than their own on-site gardens for delicious fruits, vegetables and aromatic herbs. With such easy access to local products like Dungeness crab from Bodega Bay, poultry from Petaluma and cheeses from the **Sonoma Cheese Factory**, it's no wonder that the cooking in this town has attracted such high levels of national attention. Serious home gardeners should make sure to scour the shelves of **Petaluma Seed Bank**, located in the historic Sonoma County Bank Building, as it happily counts motivated farmers among its clientele. Find them along

with a host of other visitors rejoicing at the Bank's selection of over 1500 heirloom seeds, after which a luscious scoop or slice from stylish **Noble Folk Ice Cream & Pie Bar** seems completely in order.

Finally, both area residents and tourists can't seem to get enough of the local and handcrafted bounty found inside the original **Powell's Sweet Shoppe** in Windsor. This old-fashioned candy store carries an impressive spectrum of old-world classics, modern (gluten-free) items and "sweet gift boxes" that are big during the holidays. All you have to do is walk in, pick up a pail and start filling up! If that doesn't result in a sugar rush, there's no going wrong with a scoop of creamy gelato.

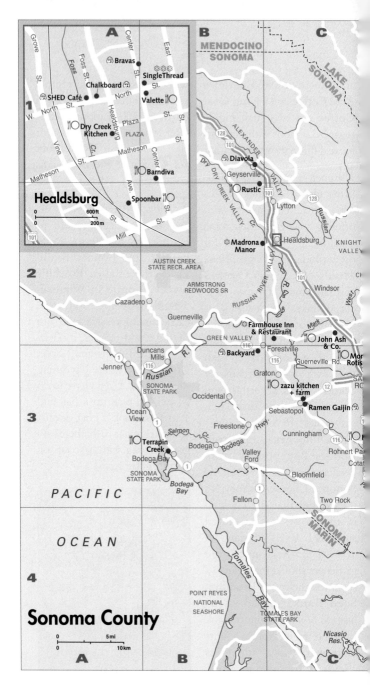

Healdsburg

Bravas
SingleThread
Chalkboard
SHED Café
Valette
Dry Creek Kitchen
Barndiva
Spoonbar

0   600ft
0   200m

Sonoma County

MENDOCINO
SONOMA

LAKE SONOMA

Diavola
Geyserville
Rustic
Lytton

Madrona Manor   Healdsburg

KNIGHT VALLEY

AUSTIN CREEK
STATE RECR. AREA

ARMSTRONG
REDWOODS SR

Windsor

Cazadero

RUSSIAN RIVER VALLEY

Guerneville

Farmhouse Inn & Restaurant

GREEN VALLEY

John Ash & Co.

Backyard   Forestville

Duncans
Mills

Guerneville Rd.

Mor Rotis

Jenner

Graton

zazu kitchen + farm

SONOMA
STATE PARK

Occidental

Sebastopol

Ramen Gaijin

Ocean
View

Freestone

Cunningham

Rohnert Par

Terrapin Creek

Bodega   Bodega

Valley
Ford

Cotat

SONOMA
STATE PARK

Bodega Bay

Bloomfield

PACIFIC

Fallon

Two Rock

OCEAN

SONOMA
MARIN

POINT REYES
NATIONAL
SEASHORE

TOMALES BAY
STATE PARK

Nicasio
Res.

0   5mi
0   10km

A   B   C

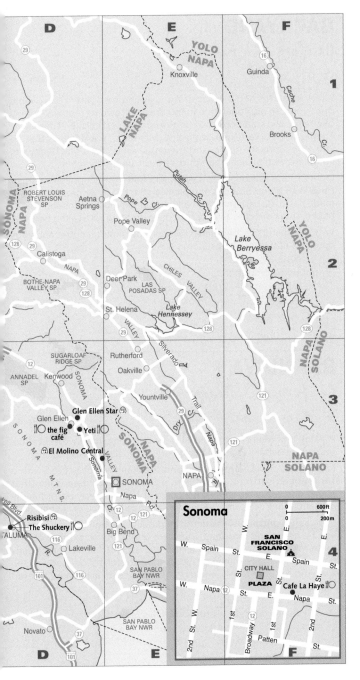

BACKYARD 🏵

Californian • Family

    ♿ 🚻 🛋

MAP: B3

Savvy locals flock to this out-of-the-way charmer, where reasonable prices and an approachable menu draw a crowd of regulars—many of whom have standing dates for the famed fried chicken Thursdays. Thanks to Backyard's husband-and-wife team, you'll feel as though you're in a private home, and the patio looks like a real backyard, complete with picnic tables and a tree strung with lights.

Dishes rotate seasonally, but you might find a tender grilled calamari salad with blood oranges and pickled sunchokes; or creamy house-made pasta à la carbonara with black trumpet mushrooms and smoky bacon. Don't miss the velvety chocolate pudding with salted caramel.

With doughnuts accompanied by apple-persimmon butter and eggs benedict atop biscuits, brunch is a hit.

    ▦ 6566 Front St. (bet. 1st & 2nd Sts.), Forestville
    📞 (707) 820-8445 — **WEB:** www.backyardforestville.com
    ▦ Lunch & dinner Thu – Mon   **PRICE: $$**

BARNDIVA 🍴

Californian • Elegant

    🍸 🍸 ♿ 🚻 🛋

MAP: B1

Pristine ingredients are the real stars at this decidedly un-diva-like restaurant, where the only thing barn-like is the soaring ceiling.

From goat cheese croquettes and Alaskan halibut served with a spring pea risotto to a giant macaron the size of a pancake (that makes an equally big impression), their dishes show wonderful finesse and abundant creativity, yet never sacrifice balance or technique.

With a thoughtfully constructed cocktail menu boasting an array of spirits, herbs and infusions, Barndiva offers lots to explore off the plate. Witty decorative touches like two-story green velvet curtains and a wall-hanging made of wood shoe stretchers only add to the fun. And for post-meal perusing, there's even an art gallery located right next door.

    ▦ 231 Center St. (bet. Matheson & Mills Sts.), Healdsburg
    📞 (707) 431-0100 — **WEB:** www.barndiva.com
    ▦ Lunch & dinner Wed – Sun   **PRICE: $$$**

BRAVAS 🐷
Spanish • Cozy

🍽

MAP: A1

"Jamón in" says the cheeky neon sign at this lively tapas bar, set in a former home full of sunny accents and 1970s psychedelic posters. While there's a small bar inside, most visitors make a beeline to the huge backyard with its outdoor porch and garden. Thanks to a welcoming cocktail-party vibe, this is the kind of place where big groups of tourists and locals can be found in abundance.

Whether you like your tapas traditional or with a little added flair, there's plenty to sample and share, from plancha-seared sea scallops with creamy romesco to a classic tortilla Española. Lighter appetites will enjoy the chilled tuna belly salad packed with crisp fennel and buttery green olives—it's practically made for washing down with a glass of cava-spiked sangria.

🔲 420 Center St. (bet. North & Piper Sts.), Healdsburg
📞 (707) 433-7700 — **WEB:** www.starkrestaurants.com
🔲 Lunch & dinner daily   PRICE: $$

CAFE LA HAYE 🍴
Californian • Neighborhood

♿

MAP: F4

For years, Cafe La Haye has been a standby off the square in downtown Sonoma. One bite of its luscious burrata, surrounded by Early Girl tomatoes and crispy squash blossoms in the summer, or vinaigrette-dressed pea shoots in spring, proves it hasn't aged a day. The small, modern space is still charming, with large windows and lots of mirrors. Stunning local artwork for sale decorates the walls.

The food spans cultural influences, including a delicate risotto with pine nuts in a cauliflower broth, or soy-sesame glazed halibut atop whipped potatoes and braised kale. A postage stamp-sized bar pours glasses of Sonoma chardonnay and cabernet, perfect with rich strozzapreti tossed with braised pork ragù, Grana Padano and toasted breadcrumbs.

🔲 140 E. Napa St. (bet. 1st & 2nd Sts.), Sonoma
📞 (707) 935-5994 — **WEB:** www.cafelahaye.com
🔲 Dinner Tue – Sat   PRICE: $$

CHALKBOARD 🐷

American • *Elegant*

 ♿ 🍽️

MAP: A1

Located in the luxury boutique Hotel Les Mars, Chalkboard is a surprisingly laid-back boîte, with a casual vibe and a buzzing bar that offer a refreshing counterpoint to a day of wine tasting. The dining room's low vaulted ceilings and marble tables might feel a touch austere if not for the rustic wooden chairs, open kitchen and warm, easygoing service. Sip a little wine as you nosh on sweet, tender pork belly biscuits in the cozy backyard.

The menu of small plates spans every cuisine and appetite. Be sure to sample at least one of the homemade pastas; bucatini with pepperoni and Meyer lemon is fresh and delightful. English peas with truffled chevre, mint, potatoes and pickled red onions are a tasty, and visually appealing, celebration of spring.

 ▪️ 29 North St. (bet. Foss St. & Healdsburg Ave.), Healdsburg
 📞 (707) 473-8030 — **WEB:** www.chalkboardhealdsburg.com
 ▪️ Lunch Sat – Sun Dinner nightly

PRICE: $$

DIAVOLA 🐷

Italian • *Trattoria*

 ♿ ⛱️

MAP: B1

Its home in downtown Geyserville may look like the Wild West, but this devilishly good Italian restaurant can hold its own with any city slicker. Festooned with statues of saints, boar tusks and stacks of cookbooks, it has a playful yet smart vibe.

Excellent pizzas, like the signature combo of spicy meatballs, red peppers, provolone, pine nuts and raisins, are the reason why crowds pack this spot. And top-notch house ingredients like salumi, lardo and cured olives elevate each and every dish. But, that's not to count out their exquisite pastas, including linguine tossed with baby octopus, bone marrow, zucchini and bottarga. Desserts, like the chocolate pistachio semifreddo paired with a perfectly pulled Blue Bottle espresso, are yet another treat.

 ▪️ 21021 Geyserville Ave. (at Hwy. 128), Geyserville
 📞 (707) 814-0111 — **WEB:** www.diavolapizzeria.com
 ▪️ Lunch & dinner daily

PRICE: $$

DRY CREEK KITCHEN 🍴

American • Elegant

Attached to the sleek hotel Healdsburg, find this upscale haunt of famed Chef Charlie Palmer. The wine list beams with Sonoma pride, and each month highlights top vintners from the region. The vaulted room is airy and refined, with white tablecloths and windows overlooking the downtown square. This kitchen may serve American classics, but each has a unique edge, making the five-course tasting a major draw. Indulge in gnocchi with a succulent lamb ragù, black garlic purée and watercress for a bit of pungent fun. The pastry chef's talent is formidable, resulting in beautifully delicate lemon tarts with pistachio sable or strawberry mousse buried under its own unique world of toppings.

If you're lucky, textbook canelé will arrive as a grand finale.

◾ 317 Healdsburg Ave. (bet. Matheson & Plaza Sts.), Healdsburg
☏ (707) 431-0330 — **WEB:** www.drycreekkitchen.com
◾ Dinner nightly

PRICE: $$$

EL MOLINO CENTRAL 😊

Mexican • Simple

Lovers of regional Mexican food will swoon for this laid-back charmer, which offers full-throttle fare made with quality ingredients. The colorful little building has a strange layout (order at the counter, then pass through the kitchen to dine on the patio), but it still draws a large following—expect to chat with fellow diners hungry for intel on the day's best dishes.

Entrées shift with the seasons, but the preparations are always expert: try the halibut ceviche with house-made chips or the red mole tamales chockablock with chicken and just a touch of masa. The Bohemia beer-battered fish tacos featuring handmade tortillas are a must, as are the addictive poblano-tomatillo nachos verdes. Of course, spice fans can't get enough of the crispy chilaquiles.

◾ 11 Central Ave. (at Sonoma Hwy.), Sonoma
☏ (707) 939-1010 — **WEB:** www.elmolinocentral.com
◾ Lunch & dinner daily

PRICE: 🍤

FARMHOUSE INN & RESTAURANT ✿

Californian • Rustic

❀ ♿

Urbanites seeking an escape from the fray head to this charming inn, nestled in a quiet, woodsy corner of Sonoma, for fine cooking, upscale accommodations or both. Dinner guests will find themselves charmed by the dining room's soothing colors, rustic-elegant décor, crackling fireplace and numerous intimate nooks—including an enclosed patio.

The protein-centric menu reads like an ode to California's purveyors, and a focus on seasonality is in keeping with the area's ethos.

Unsurprisingly, the results are often rewarding: succulent, perfectly balanced heirloom tomatoes are twirled with crunchy seaweed, briny clams and mirin dressing, while flaky halibut arrives atop a richly flavored fennel-tomato beurre blanc, dotted with corn and huitlacoche pudding. The signature "rabbit, rabbit, rabbit" showcases the kitchen's creativity, bringing together a confit rabbit leg, an applewood-smoked bacon-wrapped loin and a minuscule rack of chops rounded out with Yukon Gold potatoes and a whole grain mustard-cream sauce.

Pair your meal with a bottle from the impressive list of local and European wines. Then complete the seduction with an airy soufflé concealing a treasure of Blenheim apricot preserves.

▨ 7871 River Rd. (at Wohler Rd.), Forestville

✆ (707) 887-3300 — **WEB:** www.farmhouseinn.com

▨ Dinner Thu – Mon

PRICE: $$$$

GLEN ELLEN STAR 🐤
Californian • *Neighborhood*

&

MAP: D3

The country charm of this quaint cottage belies the level of culinary chops that will impress even a hardened city slicker. With knotty pine tables, well-worn plank floors and a wood-burning oven, the space is delightful. A perch at the chef's counter affords a great view of the action.

Here, Chef Ari Weiswasser showcases his signature style via the use of Mediterranean and Middle Eastern ingredients. Imagine wood-roasted asparagus with lavash crackers and shaved radish over a tangy hen egg emulsion; or chicken cooked under a brick with coconut curry and sticky rice. Daily pizzas like the tomato-cream pie with Turkish chilies are also a thrill. Save room for house-made ice cream in flavors like vanilla maple Bourbon, salted peanut butter or peach verbena.

▦ 13648 Arnold Dr. (at Warm Springs Rd.), Glen Ellen
✆ (707) 343-1384 — **WEB:** www.glenellenstar.com
▦ Dinner nightly

PRICE: $$

HANA ⅱ○
Japanese • *Simple*

🍶 &

MAP: C3

Rohnert Park denizens continue their love affair with this spacious gem featuring semi-private nooks and a lounge. Tucked in a hotel plaza next to the 101, Hana is run by affable Chef/owner Ken Tominaga, who sees to his guests' every whim. For the full experience, park it at the bar where the obliging staff can steer you through the best offerings of the day. Top quality fish flown in from Tsukiji Market (ask for the daily specials), traditional sushi and small plates are the secret to their success, though mains like pan-seared pork loin with ginger-soy jus also hit the spot.

The omakase is a fine way to go—six pieces of nigiri, which may include toro, hamachi belly, kampachi, tai, halibut with ponzu sauce or sardine sprinkled with Hawaiian lava salt.

▦ 101 Golf Course Dr. (at Roberts Lake Rd.), Rohnert Park
✆ (707) 586-0270 — **WEB:** www.hanajapanese.com
▦ Lunch Mon – Sat Dinner nightly

PRICE: $$

JOHN ASH & CO. ⅋⍩

Californian • *Elegant*

A pioneer in farm-to-table dining, this stalwart in the Vintners Inn (owned by Ferrari-Carano) is 35+ years strong and still serving the region's best, much of it grown in the on-site gardens. The rustic Front Room is a popular happy-hour spot with its menu of bar snacks, while the Tuscan-inspired dining room boasts plush booths, a stone fireplace and Italian landscapes on the walls.

Chef Tom Schmidt has broadened the restaurant's focus, incorporating Latin touches like a halibut ceviche with aji amarillo and creamy sweet potato. But there are still indulgent classics aplenty, like the dry-aged beef filet, cooked to a buttery medium rare and accompanied by decadent Point Reyes blue cheese-mashed potatoes, or even the rich chocolate truffle cake for dessert.

4330 Barnes Rd. (off River Rd.), Santa Rosa
(707) 527-7687 — **WEB:** www.vintnersinn.com
Dinner nightly

PRICE: $$$

MONTI'S ROTISSERIE ⅋⍩

American • *Family*

With the scent of wood smoke hanging in the air, it seems impossible to resist ordering the day's offering hot off the rotisserie. Those smoked prime ribs or pomegranate-glazed pork ribs do not disappoint either. But the oak-roasted chicken is a perennial favorite and deserves a visit on its own. Succulent auburn skin, seasoned flesh, heirloom carrots, smashed fingerling potatoes and crisped pancetta render this dish a thing of beauty. End your meal over baby lettuces with Point Reyes blue cheese and candied walnuts; or butterscotch pudding for lip-smacking comfort food—Monti's-style.

Set within Santa Rosa's Montgomery Village, this is your quintessential wine country hangout, dressed with rustic tables and centered around a roaring fireplace—natch.

714 Village Court (at Sonoma Ave.), Santa Rosa
(707) 568-4404 — **WEB:** www.starkrestaurants.com
Lunch & dinner daily

PRICE: $$

MADRONA MANOR ✿
Contemporary · *Historic*

MAP: B2

This romantic Victorian mansion is the unexpected home of a forward-looking kitchen. It's the kind of place that makes one want to dress up—at least a little bit—to fully engage in the art of dining. Arrive early to enjoy a sunset drink out on the terrace. You can either stay there to dine, or head inside to settle into one of several timelessly elegant dining rooms cloaked in sleek marble, plush silk and old-world grandeur.

The showmanship here extends to the artistic, often theatrical plates that make the most of herbs and flowers to create novel and very focused flavors throughout the carte. Tasting menus begin with a smoked egg amuse-bouche whereby a smoke-filled cloche unveils a delicate eggshell filled with a feather-light sabayon and watercress purée that looks and tastes of magic. The kitchen is also particularly adept with raw vegetables, as may be found in the roasted quail that is cut and served with olive oil-fried chard and onion soubise.

A green profiterole stuffed with apple mousse leads to a "morning breakfast dessert" of Turkish figs, apple sorbet, thin and crunchy melba toast as well as a host of garnishes like chocolate, jelly, raisins and corn caramels.

■ 1001 Westside Rd. (at W. Dry Creek Rd.), Healdsburg
✆ (707) 433-4231 — **WEB:** www.madronamanor.com
■ Dinner Wed - Sun   **PRICE: $$$$**

RAMEN GAIJIN 😀

Japanese • Rustic

 ♿ 🛖

MAP: C3

"Gaijin" is the none-too-polite Japanese term for a foreigner, but the American chefs of this noodle joint clearly take pride in their outsider status, fusing local ingredients with traditional technique. It's surely one of the best bowls of ramen around, and you can smell the soup before you're even past the front door.

The best seats are at the counter, where you can chat with the chef as he assembles bowls of light, fresh shoyu ramen filled with thick house-made rye noodles and caramelized pork belly chashu. Appetizers are also notable, like the karaage: crunchy-coated, tender chicken thighs with miso ranch. Desserts, such as the black-sesame ice cream over miso-salted caramel, matcha meringue and coconut flakes, mix sweet and savory for the win.

 ▨ 6948 Sebastopol Ave. (bet. Main St. & Petaluma Ave.), Sebastopol

 ✆ (707) 827-3609 — **WEB:** www.ramengaijin.com

 ▨ Lunch & dinner Tues – Sat

PRICE: $$

RISIBISI 😀

Italian • Cozy

 ♿ 🛖 🪑

MAP: D4

Though it's named for a comforting dish of rice and peas, Risibisi's seafood-heavy take on Italian cuisine is a bit more sophisticated. This kitchen excels at both land and sea. Meaty highlights include the fork-tender, delicate braised pork and ricotta meatballs and the winning crispy duck confit salad with bittersweet arugula. All of the pastas are made in house and desserts entice with house-made tiramisu and cannoli with bits of candied fruit, caramel and strawberry sauce vying for your attention.

A makeshift picture gallery constructed out of salvaged Tuscan chestnut window frames, wine barrels and wagon wheels brings character to this inviting brick-walled dining room. A back patio offers views of the Petaluma river and old train tracks.

 ▨ 154 Petaluma Blvd. N. (bet. Washington St. & Western Ave.), Petaluma

 ✆ (707) 766-7600 — **WEB:** www.risibisirestaurant.com

 ▨ Lunch & dinner daily

PRICE: $$

RUSTIC ⓘⓄ
Italian · Rustic

 ♿ ⌂   **MAP:** B2

Those Godfather Oscars certainly could have funded a posh restaurant for Francis Ford Coppola, but the director has kept it relatively simple at his enormous Geyserville eatery, offering Italian classics from his childhood. Savory pettole doughnuts in a paper bag kick off the meal, followed by crispy chicken al mattone sautéed in olive oil with strips of red pepper. Coppola's personality is a big part of Rustic's appeal, and these walls are covered with his film memorabilia as well as his own wines. Crowds also cherish the Italian-American music, games and nostalgia that define Coppola's past as well as those of his customers.

Come on Tuesdays to find a special prix-fixe, as well as the sociable staff donning vintage garb.

■ 300 Via Archimedes (off Independence Ln.), Geyserville
☎ (707) 857-1485 — **WEB:** www.franciscoppolawinery.com
■ Lunch & dinner daily   **PRICE:** $$

SHED CAFÉ 🐤
Californian · Minimalist

 ♿ ⌂ 🛏   **MAP:** A1

Despite its humble "café" moniker, this is the jewel in the crown of the ambitious Healdsburg SHED complex, a foodie wonderland with an in-house market, coffee bar, housewares shop and even its own farm. The eatery's location is a bit odd—it's in the rear of the complex with little barrier to those milling about shopping for gadgets—but the food is good enough that you might not notice.

The well-arranged, generously portioned plates vary with the seasons, but you might find yellowtail sashimi with seaweed and kimchi powder; roasted potatoes with green garlic and chicharrónes; as well as the luscious braised pork cheeks, dusted with fennel pollen and served over thyme spätzle. For dessert, the Meyer lemon pavlova is a crunchy, creamy delight.

■ 25 North St. (at Foss St.), Healdsburg
☎ (707) 431-7433 — **WEB:** www.healdsburgshed.com
■ Lunch daily Dinner Wed – Mon   **PRICE:** $$

THE SHUCKERY ⁏◯
Seafood · Simple

&

MAP: D4

It is a wonder that this easygoing oyster bar is Petaluma's first. The breezy vibe is amplified through oversized windows that let in plenty of natural light.

Everything here seems to be focused on raw delicacies, from minerally Hog Island oysters to meatier Hammersley ones from the Puget Sound. All of these are shucked right at the bar before arriving at your table, so the action and entertainment are constant. Raw items may be the focus, but a handful of fried or baked classics are not to be missed, like oysters Rockefeller laden with parmesan, Pernod, spinach and cured ham. Round out your feast with something more substantive, like puffy golden hushpuppies filled with shrimp morsels in a light corn batter. Fish tacos are yet another big hit.

▧ 100 Washington St. (at Kentucky St.), Petaluma
✆ (707) 981-7891 — **WEB:** www.theshuckeryca.com
▧ Dinner nightly

PRICE: $$

SPOONBAR ⁏◯
Contemporary · Chic

🍸 & 🏠

MAP: A2

Seeking a modern departure from wine country's faux-rustic aesthetic? This restaurant in the eco-chic h2hotel will fit the bill with reclaimed wood tables and 3-D artwork. Its bar is a local haunt, with wine-weary tasters arriving to palate-cleanse via an extensive list of cocktails. In the kitchen, a husband-and-wife chef team successfully guides the menu in a sophisticated, vegetable-driven direction. Find such inventive dishes as Meyer lemon-ricotta gnudi in a parmesan-mushroom broth; or seared scallops with roasted and pickled brassicas and black garlic purée.

Should you order dessert, like the honey-crème fraîche panna cotta, don't be surprised if a second arrives gratis—the chef likes to test out her latest experiments on an all-too-willing public.

▧ 219 Healdsburg Ave. (bet. Matheson & Mill Sts.), Healdsburg
✆ (707) 433-7222 — **WEB:** www.spoonbar.com
▧ Dinner nightly

PRICE: $$

SINGLETHREAD ✿✿✿

Contemporary · Luxury

🍷 🍸 ♿

"Exquisite" barely begins to describe a meal at this Healdsburg jewel, where every detail has been considered, from the moss and flowers cradling the amuse-bouche presentation to the packets of heirloom seeds that are sent home as parting gifts. Trained in Japan, Chef Kyle Connaughton adheres to the philosophy of omotenashi, or anticipating a guest's every need.

The menu is acutely tuned to each micro-season in Sonoma County, thanks to the bounty provided by farmer and co-owner, Katina Connaughton. For instance, late spring might bring poached foie gras with dried, fermented beets and wild greens, while winter showcases pumpkin tartare with Dungeness crab and a miso-Makrut lime foam. An expert in donabe (Japanese clay pot) cooking, the chef proclaims his skills with brilliant fish dishes like "fukkura-san"—black cod that is served over a broth of ember-grilled cod bones. Desserts include a Japanese cheesecake, or a delicate snowfall of buttermilk-thyme sherbet.

The service and wine selection are every bit the equal of their thoughtful food and décor, to the point where guests may never want to leave. For them, there's an on-site inn, where lovely breakfasts await the next day.

◻ 131 North St. (at Center St.), Healdsburg

✆ (707) 723-4646 — **WEB:** www.singlethreadfarms.com

◻ Lunch Sat – Sun Dinner Tue – Sun   PRICE: $$$$

TERRAPIN CREEK 🍴

Californian • *Cozy*

MAP: B3

Whether it's the ochre walls, the bold artwork or the fireplace, Terrapin Creek emits palpable warmth. Liya Lin and Andrew Truong, partners and co-chefs, have created an alluring sanctum where everyone feels like a regular, whether you're a resident or simply here to spot the migrating whales.

The menu is concise, so expect a spectrum of bites that may include grilled Monterey sardines set over shaved radishes and cabbage dressed in a refreshing lime-curry vinaigrette. Pasta is made in house, so dig your fork into those torch-shaped curls with crumbled merguez, chopped spinach, feta cheese, mint and sweet English peas in a spicy tomato-based broth. For dessert, a chocolate cake with cream cheese frosting is bested with a heavenly caramel sauce.

▓ 1580 Eastshore Rd. (off Hwy. 1), Bodega Bay
✆ (707) 875-2700 — **WEB:** www.terrapincreekcafe.com
▓ Dinner Thu – Mon

PRICE: $$$

THE FIG CAFÉ 🍴

Californian • *Neighborhood*

♿ ⚐

MAP: D3

Sondra Bernstein's Cal-Med café takes on a more modern look with communal tables, orange bar stools and geometric lighting. But pilgrims to this sleepy address shouldn't fret: Rhone-style wines (a house specialty) remain on the shelves and inviting horseshoe-shaped booths are still the best seats in the house. The nightly prix fixe—displayed on butcher paper—is as great a deal as ever, and approachable faves like fried olives and a burger are out in force. Start with a salad like grill-charred romaine Caesar with anchovy-spiked dressing; then segue to a seasonal entrée like trout with wild rice, caramelized onions and green beans.

For like-minded cuisine, visit the girl & the fig in Sonoma's main square.

▓ 13690 Arnold Dr. (at O'Donnell Ln.), Glen Ellen
✆ (707) 938-2130 — **WEB:** www.thefigcafe.com
▓ Lunch Sun Dinner nightly

PRICE: $$

VALETTE 🍴⊙
Californian • *Neighborhood*

⚙️ **MAP:** B1

Housed in the former Zin space, this contemporary darling is actually a full-circle comeback for Chef Dustin Valette and his brother/General Manager Aaron Garzini, whose grandfather owned the building in the 1940s. Its current look, however, is as cutting-edge as ever thanks to dandelion-like light fixtures, concrete walls and horseshoe-shaped banquettes. The bill of fare is modern American with a few French twists. Scallops arrive beneath squid ink puff pastry, into which a server pours caviar-flecked champagne-beurre blanc. Then, Peking-spiced duck breast set atop hearty forbidden rice is taken to the next level with a touch of tamarind sauce.

For an appetizing end, dig into the smooth block of chocolate mousse with a luscious salted caramel center.

🔲 344 Center St. (at North St.), Healdsburg
✆ (707) 473-0946 — **WEB:** www.valettehealdsburg.com
🔲 Dinner nightly
PRICE: $$$

YETI 🍴⊙
Nepali • *Elegant*

🛖 **MAP:** D3

Its sleepy location may be unusual, but with a creekside view and friendly service, Yeti makes for a pleasant getaway from the wine country grind. Inside the sunken dining room, soft folk music, Tibetan artwork and a blisteringly hot tandoor set an authentic scene.

Though this food may hail from the Himalayan frontier, most dishes are from both India's North (think grilled meats and biryanis) as well as her Southern coastal regions (fish curries and coconut sauces). Try the lamb chops coated with garam masala and served over a bed of charred onion and bell pepper. Vegetable momos (steamed dumplings stuffed with cabbage, carrots, beans and green onion) served with spicy sambal, cilantro and sweet tamarind dipping sauces are a party in your mouth.

🔲 14301 Arnold Dr., Ste. 19 (in Jack London Village), Glen Ellen
✆ (707) 996-9930 — **WEB:** www.yetirestaurant.com
🔲 Lunch & dinner daily
PRICE: $$

ZAZU KITCHEN + FARM 🍴

American · *Rustic*

♿ 🏕 🛋

A fun change from the rustic décor seen in much of wine country, this big and bright industrial space is practically translucent, thanks in large part to its garage-like doors and glossy cement floors. Natural wood tables and huge wildflower arrangements keep it from feeling chilly, as do surprisingly great acoustics—you won't struggle to be heard, even if the massive 20-seat family table is full.

Pork is the priority here, as evidenced by the sharp, spicy and addictive Cuban sandwich with house-made mortadella. Vegetarians will delight in the tart tomato soup with an oozing Carmody grilled cheese, or the black beans with baked eggs.

But the real key for carnivores is to bring home the bacon; it's a little bit pricey, but worth every penny.

▨ 6770 McKinley St., Ste. 150 (bet. Brown & Morris Sts.), Sebastopol

✆ (707) 523-4814 — **WEB:** www.zazukitchen.com

▨ Lunch Fri – Sun Dinner Wed – Mon

PRICE: $$

Look for the symbol 🍳 for a brilliant breakfast to start your day off right.

INDEXES

ALPHABETICAL LIST OF RESTAURANTS

C

T

U

V

RESTAURANTS BY CUISINE

AFGHAN

AMERICAN

ASIAN

CONTEMPORARY

ETHIOPIAN

FRENCH

FUSION

GASTROPUB

GREEK

HAWAIIAN

INDIAN

INTERNATIONAL

ITALIAN

JAPANESE

KOREAN

MEDITERRANEAN

MEXICAN

MIDDLE EASTERN

MOROCCAN

NEPALI

PERSIAN

PERUVIAN

PIZZA

Bar Bocce ⋔○	180
Cafe Reyes ⋔○	182
Casey's Pizza ⋔○	74
Del Popolo ⊕	42
Pazzo ⋔○	206
Pizzetta 211 ⋔○	123
Vesta ⊕	212
Zero Zero ⊕	146

PORTUGUESE

Adega ⋔○	224
Uma Casa ⋔○	32

PUERTO RICAN

Sol Food ⋔○	188

SEAFOOD

Anchor Oyster Bar ⊕	18
Bar Crudo ⋔○	19
Hog Island Oyster Co. ⋔○	43
New England Lobster Company ⋔○	204
Saltwater ⋔○	187
Shuckery (The) ⋔○	288

SOUTHERN

Bywater (The) ⊕	227
Elite Café ⋔○	58

SPANISH

Barvale ⋔○	20
Bellota ⋔○	132
Bravas ⊕	279
Coqueta ⊕	40
La Marcha ⋔○	166
Zuzu ⋔○	270

SRI LANKAN

1601 Bar & Kitchen ⊕	145

STEAKHOUSE

THAI

VEGAN

VEGETARIAN

VIETNAMESE

CUISINES BY NEIGHBORHOOD

MARIN _____

WINE COUNTRY

NAPA VALLEY

UNDER $25

STARRED
RESTAURANTS ✿

BIB GOURMAND 😀

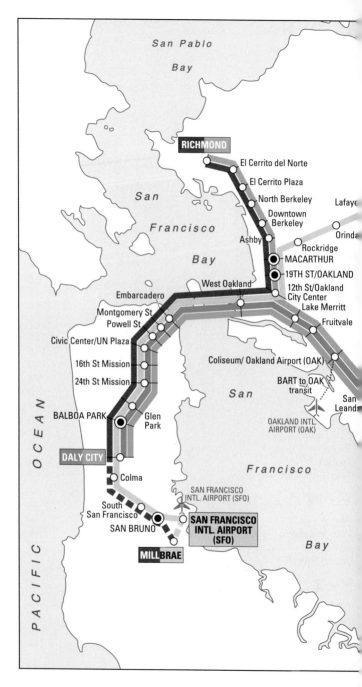

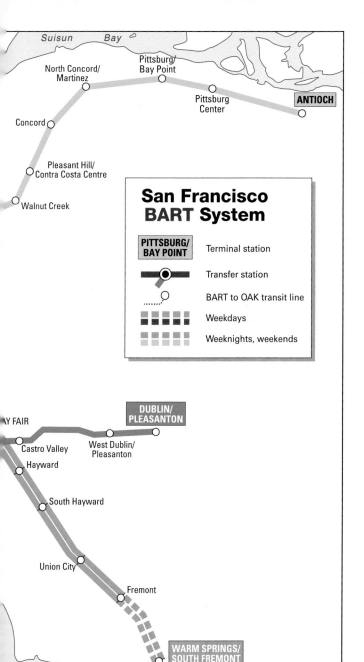

Suisun Bay

North Concord/
Martinez

Pittsburg/
Bay Point

Pittsburg
Center

ANTIOCH

Concord

Pleasant Hill/
Contra Costa Centre

Walnut Creek

San Francisco
BART System

**PITTSBURG/
BAY POINT** — Terminal station

Transfer station

BART to OAK transit line

Weekdays

Weeknights, weekends

Y FAIR

**DUBLIN/
PLEASANTON**

Castro Valley

West Dublin/
Pleasanton

Hayward

South Hayward

Union City

Fremont

**WARM SPRINGS/
SOUTH FREMONT**

MICHELIN TRAVEL PARTNER

Société par actions simplifiées au capital de 15 044 940 EUR
27 Cours de l'Ile Seguin - 92100 Boulogne Billancourt (France)
R.C.S. Nanterre 433 677 721

Printing and binding: Transcontinental (Canada)

Tell us what you think about our products.

Give us your opinion

satisfaction.michelin.com

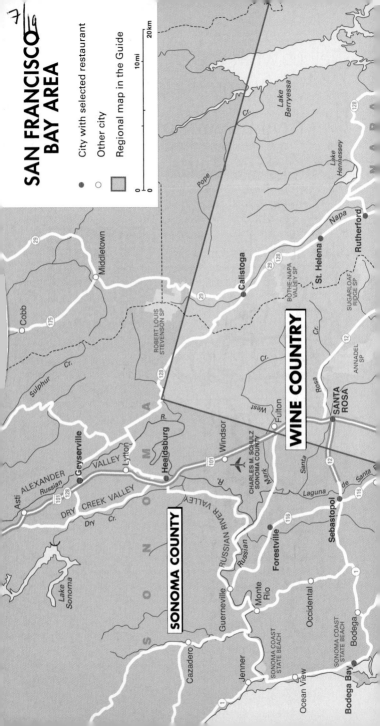

SAN FRANCISCO BAY AREA

- ● City with selected restaurant
- ○ Other city
- ▢ Regional map in the Guide

0 10mi
0 20km

WINE COUNTRY

SONOMA COUNTY

Middletown
Cobb
Calistoga
St. Helena
Rutherford
Napa
Lake Berryessa
Lake Hennessey
BOTHE-NAPA VALLEY SP
SUGARLOAF RIDGE SP
ANNADEL SP
ROBERT LOUIS STEVENSON SP
Sulphur Cr.
Pope Cr.
Rosa Cr.
West Cr.
Geyserville
Asti
ALEXANDER VALLEY
Lytton
Healdsburg
DRY CREEK VALLEY
Dry Cr.
Lake Sonoma
Windsor
Fulton
SANTA ROSA
RUSSIAN RIVER VALLEY
CHARLES M. SCHULZ SONOMA COUNTY
Russian R.
Mark West
Santa Rosa
Laguna de Santa Rosa
Sebastopol
Forestville
Guerneville
Monte Rio
Occidental
Cazadero
Jenner
Ocean View
Bodega
Bodega Bay
SONOMA COAST STATE BEACH
SONOMA COAST STATE BEACH